T0279644

RETURN TO
MY TREES

RETURN TO MY TREES

Notes from the Welsh Woodlands

Matthew Yeomans

2022

www.uwp.co.uk

British Library Cataloguing-in-Publication Data
A catalogue record for this book is available from the British Library.

ISBN: 978-1-91527-914-9

The right of Matthew Yeomans to be identified as author of this work has been asserted in accordance with sections 77 and 79 of the Copyright, Designs and Patents Act 1988.

The publisher gratefully acknowledges the funding support of the Books Council of Wales in publication of this book.

Typeset by Marie Doherty
Printed by CPI, United Kingdom

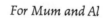

For Mum and Al

There is a phrase in the Welsh language, *dod yn ôl at fy nghoed* that means 'to return to a balanced state of mind'. Its literal translation is, rather beautifully, 'to return to my trees'.

Contents

Introduction   xi

PART ONE   The Fall of the Trees

CHAPTER 1   The Wisdom of the Druids   3

CHAPTER 2   The Story of the Saints   19

CHAPTER 3   The Attack on the Forests   31

CHAPTER 4   A New Forest Economy   41

CHAPTER 5   The Original Black Gold   51

CHAPTER 6   Stranded Assets   63

PART TWO   The Power of the Trees

CHAPTER 7   Reconnecting through Community   75

CHAPTER 8   The Science of the Trees   87

CHAPTER 9   In the Footsteps of the Welsh Robin Hood   101

CHAPTER 10   The Stuff of Legend   115

CHAPTER 11   Environmentalism's Romantic Past   127

PART THREE   The Rise of the Trees

CHAPTER 12   A National Forest is Born   145

CHAPTER 13   The Rights of Trees   159

CHAPTER 14   Forest Politics   171

CHAPTER 15   The Business of Nature   185

CHAPTER 16   Sheep and Trees   199

CHAPTER 17   Making Peace with Nature   217

A Note on Sourcing   233

Acknowledgements   239

Introduction

Here's when I first knew I had to write a book about trees. It was a warm, Friday afternoon in April 2020. I had walked five miles through the neighbourhoods of Cardiff in Wales and had reached the sprawling Pentrebane housing estate on the western fringe of the city. There, bizarrely, I discovered a public footpath that led into a large woodland.

I could see the path snaked up to a high ridge then disappeared in the trees. I had walked many parts of Cardiff but never seen this wooded route before. I was both exhilarated and a little scared at the prospect of entering this space. It would have been easy to turn back and walk the city streets I knew so well but I didn't. I stepped through the threshold and into the woods.

A few minutes before I had been walking in a busy housing estate. Now I was alone amongst the trees – hundreds of them standing side by side in a serene coexistence. Clumps of wild garlic grew on the sides of the ridge and shafts of sunlight bespeckled the ground where I walked. Right there and then in Pentrebane Woods, the power of trees and the natural world hit me. The beauty of this peaceful place and its sense of authority overwhelmed me – it seemed to hold a superiority over the messy city life I had left behind.

I walked back home almost in a trance, mesmerised by the sense of calm I'd felt in the woods. It was addictive and I knew I wanted more.

When lockdown started in late March 2020 daily life froze and my family, along with everyone else in the UK, were forced to stay at home for nearly three months – only allowed out to do essential food and medicine shopping and for one period of exercise each day.

We all adapted in our own ways. My wife hunkered down into her hobbies with an application I could only marvel at. First, she went on a crocheting binge. Huge, fluffy packages of wool would arrive by courier to be transformed within hours (or so it felt like) into blankets, sweaters and ponchos. Then she was introduced by a friend to sourdough baking. Before long we were feasting on sourdough bread, focaccia, pizza and even naan.

My 14-year-old daughter coped by binge watching Netflix and Amazon – who knew they'd even made 15 series of *Grey's Anatomy*? My 17-year-old son, meanwhile, did what he always did – playing video games online with friends. Aside from not going to school, his life seemed to carry on pretty much as normal!

I didn't take to lockdown as easily. I was the only one of the family who had worked from home before the pandemic hit. But now that I had to stay at home I was going stir-crazy. Worse still, the bouts of anxiety that I had been fighting for the past few years now came daily.

I distinctly remember when I first became aware that I was struggling with anxiety. It was a few years before in San Diego in a packed auditorium at a big corporate sustainability conference. I was due to run a workshop the next day for executives from some of the world's biggest brands. It should have been exciting – the perfect opportunity to build interest in a new online platform I had created. Except I felt like a fraud.

For the past 10 years I'd worked as a sustainability journalist and writer. I understood as well as anyone the issues that all these companies attending the conference needed to address. But, deep down, if I'm being honest, I didn't believe in myself enough as an entrepreneur to build and run the business I had started. I felt both like an outsider and an imposter.

As I sat in the audience, I felt myself tensing up, my breathing becoming laboured. I was overwhelmed with a sense of being trapped. I snuck out of the auditorium and headed straight back to my hotel room. Hours later, I realised that I had strained all my stomach muscles through stress.

Once I returned home, things seemed to return to normal – or so I thought. In hindsight, the periodic waves of worry, the underlying and persistent sense of dread about everything and yet nothing should have been a wake-up call. That came a few months later.

It was over really before it had begun – a random act of road rage over the right of way on my own street in Cardiff with an aggressive taxi driver who, after screaming at me from his cab, jumped out, ran at my car and tried to grab me by the throat through the driver window. It was farcical to be honest. With a few choice words I sent him cursing back to his taxi. But the damage was done. When I got home, I sat down and realised I was shaking uncontrollably. My ears were ringing, my heart was racing, and I felt frozen, locked in place by fear.

That's when I did something I'd been promising to do for months – I called my doctor. He called me in straight away. I was having a panic attack he told me. He suggested counselling and gave me prescription for beta blockers that would slow my heart rate and minimise anxiety.

Over the next six months, I took a couple of pills but, for me personally, I didn't really like the idea of being dependent on a drug – even one as benign as beta blockers. Instead, I turned to exercise, making my gym a second home and trusting the endorphin buzz of working out to counter my anxious feelings.

When Covid hit, my gym shut, and I had to find another option. Outside the weather was unseasonably warm and dry for early April so I decided to exercise and practise yoga in the garden. That would be just the peaceful, centring activity my body and brain required. But each time I settled onto my purple mat and tried to meditate my anxious thoughts away, noises from the neighbourhood, packed full of other families also confined to their gardens, ate into my brain. I tried playing music through my headphones but still I couldn't block out the laughing, barbecuing and general good-natured cacophony of people trying to the make the most of what was a very bad time.

The final straw happened one exceptionally warm afternoon when I was trying to work on my yogic breathing in the garden only to be soaked by next door's kids dive-bombing into their paddling pool. Outwardly, I laughed about it but deep down I felt desperate. There was only one solution. I had to escape.

So that's when I started walking – short distances at first around my neighbourhood and the local parks in Cardiff – but then longer meandering explorations of the city. Wherever I went – whether it be the hidden trails of Bute Park by Cardiff Castle, the tightly packed terraced streets of Cathays and Grangetown, the cycle route down to the Bay or the Taff Trail out to Castell Coch, the magical 19th-century Gothic Revival folly on the northern edge of the city – the same process would take place. I would start out anxious but, within 10 minutes of setting a steady pace, I would fall into a rhythm of walking, not thinking. As I did, I relaxed and my breathing (and the pounding in my chest that at home was so loud I could hear it as I tried to work) calmed. Soon I was walking seven or more miles every day and I was counting down the hours until I could start out on the next adventure.

I wasn't alone. It was remarkable just how many people had committed to walking on a daily basis. The parks were packed and even the local golf courses, normally reserved for the enjoyment of a privileged few, had been transformed into public spaces by families eager to embrace the outdoors. A national walking culture seemed to have sprung up out of nowhere.

Some days I had a plan for where I was headed. Other times I just put one foot in front of the other and went. Invariably I walked to music – specifically Spotify playlists compiled by myself and a group of old university friends. We would meet once a week on Zoom and talk music, select a genre or year to cover, then spend the next seven days building a playlist to meet the challenge. One day I'd be energised by the rhythms of Nigerian greats, Fela Kuti and William Onyeabor and the collective sound of Ethiopia's 1970s funk and soul scene. Another I'd feel nostalgic revisiting tracks from my university days like Joy Division's *She's Lost Control*, This Mortal Coil's *Song to the Siren* and *Temptation* by Heaven 17.

I revisited my love of New York Latin artists like Willie Colón and Héctor Lavoe. And I started to explore more of the new Welsh music scene – expanding beyond my comfort zone of Super Furry Animals, Manic Street Preachers, Cate Le Bon and Gwenno to take in artists like Alffa, Boy Azooga and 9Bach – all compiled for our 'Green, Green Grass' playlist.

On my walks I began to think more about the situation we all found ourselves in. Covid had come at us out of the blue, but the warning signs had been apparent for many years. Having charted the initial panic when the pandemic hit, the media was now turning its attentions to the root causes. Article after article highlighted how the pandemic was the result of a breakdown between nature and society – how decades of deforestation had forced the animal population closer to humans and how a disease that once might have remained hidden away deep in tropical forests had reached our cities and jumped from animals to humans.

Other commentators looked at the havoc this pandemic had caused and warned it was merely a taste of what climate change, caused by a breakdown in the relationship of humans to nature, would bring. 'Think This Pandemic Is Bad? We Have Another Crisis Coming' was the headline of one *New York Times* column that cried out for a new Green Deal to avert both climate change and future pandemics.

It felt like Covid, having brought our world to a screeching halt, had shocked people from many walks of life into realising that the old ways of doing things weren't working any more – whether commuting to work each day, burning fossil fuels to power our cars, homes and businesses or cutting down forests and treating nature like an afterthought just to satisfy our rampant consumer culture. The virus had exposed our greatest fallibilities but, at the same time, the vacuum of normal activity it had created was giving us the headspace to contemplate how we could live life better in the future.

With normal life and my business on hold, and with no real sense of when or even if it would ever come back, I also was on the threshold of a fundamental change. The pandemic had forced me to confront some harsh home truths. In the past I'd enjoyed (and had some success) being a writer and an author but my recent efforts to succeed as an entrepreneur had been a disaster. My heart just wasn't in it. Now, given time to walk and reflect, I could see how that experience had left me depressed and exhausted. I was stuck in what sociologists call a liminal state – I knew I needed to leave behind the work I'd been doing but I hadn't yet worked out a new way ahead.

Each day I contemplated how to move beyond this liminal state of mind. And as I did, it struck me that what I was experiencing on an individual level was a miniature version of the angst all of society was wrestling with – namely how do we move from the old existence that was dragging us down and transition into something new and better?

My dilemma felt inconsequential in comparison – what would my new work project look like? The world's dilemma was nothing less than existential – how to fundamentally make peace with nature to restore balance and limit the worst effects of climate change?

For many people, this imbalance had long been the most pressing issue facing global society, but the pandemic appeared to have put it at the top of the political and economic agenda. How could an industrialised world that, for centuries, had been so complacent, neglectful and wilfully destructive suddenly embrace nature as humanity's saviour instead of its dumping ground?

A United Nations global treaty wasn't going to help – a generation of climate change politics had proved that. Instead, all aspects of our modern world – including economic systems, political priorities, legal structures, financial markets, consumer and even popular culture – would have to embrace this change and act quickly. It was a huge undertaking even to contemplate, never mind put into action. But the pandemic had already shown us what the future looked like if we didn't.

After discovering Pentrebane Wood my outlook changed. Back home, once I'd come down from the euphoria of that brief escape into nature, I started researching the importance of trees to our future well-being.

I read about how trees, in one form or another, have been nurturing the atmosphere of our planet for nearly 400 million years.[*] Even our earliest ancestors only date back some two million years.[†] And ever since the majority of humans stopped hunting and gathering and began to form settled communities, they've cut down trees at an incredible rate. Two thousand years ago the earth was covered with more than six trillion trees. Today, just three trillion remain.[‡] At the current rate of deforestation, the world's great rainforests will likely disappear within 100 years.

I took in a raft of new reports published in the wake of the pandemic that raised the alarm about our long neglect of the forest and how it imperils our own survival. I read about how deforestation in the Amazon was surging even during the pandemic and how the wetland rainforests of the Pantanal on the border of Brazil and Paraguay were on fire for the first time in living memory.[§] Wildfires were consuming truly ancient Sequoias and Redwoods in northern California and, just a few months before, Australia's wildfires had destroyed entire species and ecosystems. I learned about global governmental pledges to plant millions of trees to combat climate change and mitigate the impact of destroying forests in the first place, and how some of these pledges had caused more environmental problems than they had solved.

I looked at the issue from a business point of view – how companies were starting to evaluate 'natural capital' – the term used in sustainability and accounting terms to describe the financial cost or value a company's interactions with nature has on its business. And I tried to get my head around new initiatives to provide forests and nature in general with the same level of legal protection afforded humans and companies. I learnt about Earth Overshoot Day: the date when humanity's demand for

---

[*] https://psmag.com/environment/the-tree-that-changed-the-world-11656
[†] https://en.wikipedia.org/wiki/Timeline_of_human_evolution
[‡] https://www.iflscience.com/environment/how-we-found-out-there-are-three-trillion-trees-earth/
[§] https://news.mongabay.com/2020/12/devastating-fires-engulf-brazilian-pantanal-wetlands-again/

ecological resources and services in a given year exceeds what Earth can regenerate in that year. I discovered that in 2020 we would reach that mark on 20 August.*

When my head hurt from all the economic, policy, technological, environmental and legal discussions I lost myself in legends, myths and folklore associated with forests – the mystical relationship that humans have with trees and why they so enchant and fascinate us.

I also started to explore just how intertwined our lives were with the well-being of the forests. This piece in the *Guardian* by Rob Penn captured it well:

> Trees give life. It's hard to overstate their benefit. They are fundamental to our rural and urban landscapes, our lives and the future of this planet. Trees reduce soil degradation on farms, provide vital habitat for wildlife, supply us with food, heat and medicine, safeguard water quality, give shade, build biodiversity and create spaces to walk lightly and breathe deeply in our cities. Trees diminish flood risk, improve air quality by absorbing pollution and yield a renewable resource in the form of timber. Most importantly, in the climate emergency, trees sequester carbon. They absorb carbon dioxide from the atmosphere, storing it in their trunks, branches and roots, before releasing oxygen back into the air. Trees mitigate climate change.[†]

Surely, if we could rediscover the importance of our relationship with trees and nature then we could move towards a way of life that restored the balance we desperately needed? I became convinced that I needed to throw myself into exploring how rebalancing our broken relationship with trees and nature could provide us with a sustainable way forward. But I felt I lacked the authority to make this my project. After all, there were plenty

---

* In 2021, Earth Overshoot Day occurred on 29 July.
† Robert Penn, https://www.theguardian.com/commentisfree/2019/nov/24/with-the-earth-in-peril-planting-a-tree-is-an-act-of-faith

of arborists, climate change experts, dendrologists, environmentalists, economists and cultural commentators who already knew far more about this topic than me. Maybe though, by pulling all these strands together, I could provide the big picture view of why our world had to change.

What I needed was a hook – an approach I could make my own. One morning, while going through news stories related to forests, I found it. Just a few weeks before, the Welsh government had announced plans to build a National Forest for Wales. The idea was to create a pathway of biodiversity through the country by linking existing woodlands and planting new trees along the way. Not only would the forest support different ecosystems, it would also help combat the climate emergency and provide spaces for leisure activities including walking and biking.

The launch statement was suitably vague – the government would spend the next year consulting with local communities to determine the exact route and make-up of the National Forest – but the intent was clear. The multi-decade project placed trees and forests at the very heart of a sustainable vision for Wales, building on the nation's already impressive credentials as the first country to enact a Well-being of Future Generations Act. The Act put the sustainable development of the economy and community at the heart of policymaking. Crucially, it required all public bodies to account for their impact on future generations who will have to live with the consequences, asking them to consider decisions not just from an economic growth point of view but also in terms of their impact on the environment and nature, and on the social well-being and health of communities.

The idea of a National Forest winding its way through Wales was very exciting. What might it look like? Where would it go? How would it get funded? What were the politics involved? Were there legal considerations? Would everyone buy into the idea? Most all, what could it teach us about how we live in harmony with nature and how our lives could be improved?

The potential lessons weren't just relevant to the people of Wales – these were universal considerations. However, Wales presented the perfect prototype for building this new relationship between people and nature.

Not only did it have sustainable development woven into law, but it was small, yet connected enough to build a nature-based culture and economy that could provide a scalable blueprint for the rest of the world.

And then it dawned on me. What if I mapped out a route for this proposed National Forest for Wales and explored it on foot? First off, it sounded great fun, would get me out of the house and could be a calming tonic for those anxious thoughts. At the same time, by walking through Wales, perhaps I could start to find answers to the crucial question – how can we make peace and restore balance with nature?

One Sunday morning, on a sunny day in early June 2020, I made myself a coffee, turned on the soothing sounds of BBC 6 Music and started to plan my woodland walking route through Wales.

At first glance the plan seemed straightforward. The Welsh government had already said its intention was to connect the ancient woodlands of east Wales – namely the enormous Wentwood Forest between Newport and Chepstow above the flood plains of the Gwent Levels, with a new woodland, Coed Brynau, being created outside Neath in south-west Wales. From there it wanted to link up with the coastal Celtic Rainforests of Parc Cenedlaethol Eryri (Snowdonia National Park) in north-west Wales then continue to woodlands in the north-east.

My route would start in Wentwood and take me west through the old industrial South Wales Valleys to the western edge of the Brecon Beacons and then into Carmarthenshire. From there I would walk north into the Cambrian Mountains of Ceredigion until I reached the seaside town of Borth, just north of Aberystwyth. Then I would head inland to the historic political centre of Wales, the town of Machynlleth, and into Snowdonia National Park. At that point, I would turn east and wind my way through the hills and forests until I reached Wales's north-east border with England at the town of Chirk. I would undertake the journey in different sections – some day hikes close to home and some longer (particularly in mid and north Wales that would involve more logistical planning). In total I estimated there was about 300 miles to cover – provided I didn't get lost on the way.

Initially I intended to create an entirely new trail but it soon became clear that Wales already had hundreds of public footpaths and long-distance walking trails. I decided my best approach (and the most useful for walkers who might follow my trail) would be to map a National Forest route that utilised and linked existing and proven trails. By studying online Ordnance Survey maps, I identified 27 official trails that I could walk along as part of my journey. They included famous routes like the Offa's Dyke Path and The Cambrian Way as well as some more off the beaten track, including St Illtyd's Walk and the Snowdonia Slate Trail.

I also realised that I wasn't just embarking on a nature and forest tour of Wales. I was going to be walking through the history of the nation – from the Iron Age to Roman rule to the Norman invasion to the Industrial Revolution and Wales's heyday as the King of Coal. I'd be stumbling through centuries of natural world folklore, myth and legend – every wood, village or nearby town I studied on the map seemed to have some wild and wonderful tale associated with it.

First though, I had to address three failings. The first was that I didn't know a lot about trees. Obviously, I knew one when I saw one in the park, and I had a rudimentary grasp of how they fed and grew – taking in carbon dioxide and water then harnessing sunlight to create sugars and oxygen through photosynthesis. But after that, not so much. I knew the names of most native trees – the ashes, oaks, beeches, birches, elms and so on – but was hard pressed to tell them apart. If I was going to write a travel book about wandering through woodlands and forests I needed a crash course in all things trees and nature. I couldn't go to the shops so, along with everyone else in lockdown, I turned to Amazon – splurging on tree books that might make me smarter.

Within days new books started to arrive at my doorstep. There was *The Wisdom of Trees* by Max Adams, *The Glorious Life of the Oak* by John Lewis-Stempel, *The Hidden Life of Trees* by Peter Wohlleben, *The Heritage Trees of Wales* by Archie Miles, *Around the World in 80 Trees* by Jonathan

Drori and *Welsh Woods and Forests – A History* by William Linnard. This last one would become my bible as I walked through Wales.

Soon, I was boring family and friends with facts: did you know the earth has 60,000 different tree species and over half of these are single species endemics, meaning they only grow in one country? That a large oak tree can consume 100 gallons of water in a day? And (a particular favourite) that trees can communicate to each other using an underground network of connected fungi known as the Wood Wide Web?

As more new books arrived, my wife subtly enquired whether my time (and our bank balance) wouldn't be better served by my getting out of the house and actually spending time in nature rather than reading about it. She was right. So I downloaded a tree identification app created by the Woodland Trust charity and made a mental note to consult it whenever I was wandering my local parks.

To get a better idea of the woods and forests that could be linked through a National Forest I also consulted the Woodland Trust's map of every established wood and forest in Wales. I quickly learned two things. First, despite the overall paucity of tree cover in Wales, there still existed pockets of woodland dotted all over the country. Second, the vast majority of the names of these woods were all in Welsh.

That exposed my second weakness. I don't speak Welsh.

I know, I know. How can I have been born and brought up in Wales and yet not speak its native language? The fact is, the majority of people in Wales don't speak Welsh because most live in the highly anglicised, English-speaking coastal corridor of the south and north – perhaps the most lasting legacy of Wales's industrialisation over the past two hundred years.

The decline in the Welsh language didn't start with the Industrial Revolution. Welsh speakers have been fighting to preserve their language ever since King Henry VIII decreed that English would be the official language spoken in Wales. But it was the UK government's 1847 *Reports of the Commissioners of Inquiry into the State of Education in Wales* – that really undermined the Welsh language. It blamed the poor state of literacy and education in Wales on the continued use of the Welsh language in rural areas as well as its people's preference for non-conformist Christian religions over the Anglican Church of Wales.

'The Welsh language is a vast drawback to Wales and a manifold barrier to the moral progress and commercial prosperity of the people,' the three English, Anglican commissioners wrote. 'It is not easy to over-estimate its evils effects,' they added: 'It dissevers the people from intercourse which would greatly advance their civilisation, and bars the access of improving knowledge to their minds.'

The reports (which later would be condemned as the 'Treachery of the Blue Books') also took aim at what the commissioners saw as the lax morals of Welsh women. Put bluntly, the reports were a character assassination on the Welsh people and their native language. For generations afterwards, the Welsh language would have been seen as a hindrance to success even though it was fiercely defended and continued to be the first language for large parts of rural Wales. Also in the 19th century, guaranteed work in the coal mines and iron works attracted large numbers of immigrants to the South Wales Valleys and some pockets of the north-east. They came from England, Ireland and continental Europe and were joined by increasing numbers of people from Welsh-speaking rural areas. As they assimilated into a what was becoming a dominant English-speaking environment, the Welsh language began to fade from use.

My own family is a mix of native-born Welsh and Irish, Swedish and English immigrants. My great grandfather, on my mother's side, had been born in mid-Wales in 1871 and was brought up a native Welsh speaker. He joined the army, became a sergeant-major in the Welsh Regiment and settled in Cardiff where his eight children, all born in the early 20th century, were brought up speaking English (though understanding bits of Welsh). By the time I started school in Cardiff in 1970 there was very little Welsh taught and even less spoken on the street.

I was part of a lost generation – I grew up identifying strongly as being Welsh but having only the slightest connection to its language. I was taught the basics in school but at age 13 I had to choose between learning

Welsh or French. It wasn't a hard decision at the time. From then on, the Welsh language barely touched my life. I moved away in 1984, first to Manchester for university and then to New York where I lived until 2004, not giving the language too much thought.

Imagine my shock then when, in the days after moving back to Cardiff from New York, I started hearing people talking Welsh on the streets of my neighbourhood. In the 20 years I had been away, a cultural rescue mission had taken place. In 1999 Wales had established its own devolved assembly separate to the UK's central government and it invested heavily in helping revive the national tongue with aims to achieve one million Welsh speakers by 2050. Welsh was encouraged in government, in the media and especially in schools. Today, it remains a minority language in Wales, but it is spoken by nearly 30 per cent of the population.* Both my son and daughter are fluent, having attended Welsh-language schools since they were three.

I hardly had time to get conversational in Welsh, never mind fluent, as I prepared for my trip but I would be walking through parts of Wales where Welsh was very much the first language and where all the villages, mountains, rivers and woodlands had Welsh names. I started taking a beginners' Welsh course online. I soon learned how to say *Bore da Draig* – Good Morning Dragon. However, even given Wales's rich tradition of legends, I wasn't convinced I'd be meeting that many dragons on my journey.

I decided to take a more practical approach. I bought a book – *The Place-Names of Wales* by Hywel Wyn Owen. Now, at least, I could decipher the origins of where I was headed. The beauty of Welsh place names is that they are descriptive of the place in relation to its landscape. My childhood home was in the city village of Llandaff. It meant the religious settlement (*Llan*) on the banks of the River Taff (mutated to daff). Coastal towns were also often named after the rivers that flowed through them.

---

* According to the Annual Population Survey, October 2020 to September 2021, conducted by the Welsh Government, https://gov.wales/welsh-language-data-annual-population-survey-october-2020-september-2021

Aberystwyth means mouth of the River Ystwyth. Aberdyfi – the mouth of the River Dyfi.

The third weakness was myself – or my body to be more exact. I tried to stay fairly fit but there was no denying that I was nearly 55 with a hip and knee that ached after exercise – especially after walking for three or four hours. How would my body hold up over 300 miles, often in the mountains? Was I taking on too much of a challenge? I guess I wouldn't know until I started.

Finally, I felt ready to start my adventure. By embarking on this journey, I could create my own blueprint for a National Forest for Wales Trail and I could explore humanity's relationship to trees, nature and biodiversity as I walked through the history of Welsh industrialisation, folklore and forests. Along the way I hoped to tell the stories of local people whose lives have been influenced by the woods and will be shaped by this national forest. This wasn't going to be any old walk in the woods – I was about to immerse myself in the very essence of what our ancestors understood to mean living as one with their environment.

In doing so I hoped to glimpse what the future could look like if we can rebalance human life with nature. And I hoped to rediscover something about myself – a reconnection with a part of me that I had lost.

Part One

The Fall of
the Trees

1

The Wisdom of the Druids

Exploring Wentwood to Caerleon

One warm, sunny July day, I drove east from my home in Cardiff along the M4 motorway, past Newport towards Wentwood Forest some 25 miles away. As I passed through the village of Langstone, dense, tall woodland rose up on the horizon to my left. The forest sat high on the hills overlooking the flood plain of the Afon Hafren (River Severn) – a dark, imposing silhouette in contrast to the bright green fields that sat below it.

I was meeting Andy, one of my oldest friends from our school days more than 40 years ago. Andy is one of those easy-going people you know you're going to have a good time with, chatting rubbish about sport, old stories of our growing up and other silly stuff. We've been doing it since the late 1970s so I knew he would be great company on a walk. Andy is also very level-headed and grounded in his thinking and decision making – a useful counterpoint to my occasional headstrong 'jump first, reflect later' approach to life. Better still, he already knew Wentwood as he now lived in Chepstow just a few miles away. A little local knowledge always helps.

Our plan, over the next two days, was to meander first to Caerleon – some eight miles away – and then continue to the village of Bassaleg a further eight miles to the west. It was hardly the most ambitious hike in the world but I was just getting started and needed to find my walking legs.

I'd chosen Wentwood because it was the biggest forest near the border with England and the Welsh government had earmarked it as a potential starting point for the new National Forest for Wales. With good reason. Wentwood Forest is part of the largest area of ancient woodland anywhere in Wales with a recorded history spanning over 1,000 years – though there have been woods covering the area for many thousands more. Its current parameters were one small part of a vast ancient forest that once covered the land between the rivers Usk and Gwy (Wye).

I had driven passed this forest many times before without venturing inside. It dominates the landscape around it, projecting a sense of other-worldliness and even foreboding. Back in the late 19th century the horror and supernatural fiction writer Arthur Machen, who grew up in nearby Caerleon, had fashioned many of his fantastical tales – notably *The Great God Pan*, later one of the inspirations for the film, *Pan's Labyrinth* – on Wentwood. As I approached it now, it was easy to see how the forest had fuelled Machen's sense of the macabre. The forest seemed to spread out as far as the eye could see. Dirt tracks disappeared into dark, dense rows of conifers. It seemed devoid of all life. It didn't take too much imagination to see how you could get lost very quickly in Wentwood.

We parked at the Foresters' Oaks car park on the eastern edge of the forest, pulled on our hiking boots and checked our water and snack supply. It was a warm but breezy summer's morning with not a cloud in sight. Perfect walking weather.

I had downloaded the walking route onto the OS map on my phone and was ready to head off when Andy suggested we walk up Gray Hill 'for a bit of a warm-up'.

Gray Hill was in a different direction to my route and I wasn't convinced we needed to add extra steps into what already looked like a decent day's walk. But Andy seemed keen and at least the elevation would give us some perspective about where we were heading in the forest.

At 270 metres, it wasn't the hardest climb by any stretch of the imagination but my heart was pumping by the time we reached the top – a pulmonary reminder that, after five months of lockdown, and despite a lot of city walking, maybe I wasn't quite as fit as I'd thought.

From the top of Gray Hill, we could see the expanse of the Gwent Levels – the reclaimed tidal plain that runs west from Chepstow all the way to Cardiff. To the east, we could clearly see the two road bridges connecting Wales with England over the Aber Hafren (Severn Estuary), both shining as the sun reflected off their high supporting beams. Below us sat the commuter towns of Caldicot and Magor. Further along the coast we could see Newport, its iconic Transporter Bridge towering above the town.

The Forests Are Born

At one point in Wales's history nearly all the pasture and urbanised land we could see from Gray Hill would have been dense ancient forest just like Wentwood had been. Some 12,000 years ago, as nature finally began to thaw out following the last Ice Age, vegetation once again began to flourish. To begin with, there was just sparse tundra – the carpet of herbs and subshrubs that we commonly associate with northern Scandinavia, Russia and other lands close to the Arctic Circle. However, as the climate continued to warm over the next few thousand years, trees began to take root. First, around 8,000 BC, came the birches – so-called pioneer species because of their fearless ability to put down roots in previously barren environments. Their light seeds could be dispersed by the wind and they spread rapidly. The birches were soon followed by Scots Pine. For the remainder of the Boreal period, which lasted 2,000 years until 6,000 BC, birch and pine continued to vie for dominance in these rapidly expanding forests. Over time though, birch declined as other broad-leafed species such as hazel, elm and oak gained a foothold.

Over the next six thousand years (during the Boreal, Atlantic and Sub-Boreal periods) oak would come to dominate the Welsh landscape. Two types in particular – pedunculate, or English, oak (*Quercus robur*), which is found mainly in the Welsh lowlands and borderlands with

England, and sessile oak (*Quercus petraea*), which dominates the uplands especially in the steep gorges and river valleys near its western coast.

During the Atlantic period (6,000 to 3,000 BC), the Welsh climate became warmer and wetter (as anyone who has visited Wales knows, it specialises in wet weather). Alder trees started proliferating at the expense of pine, while lime trees began to become part of large mixed oak forests. Together this combination of dominant oak, alder, hazel, birch, elm, lime and pine formed a dense green canopy across most of the landscape that lay below 615 metres (2,000 feet). A few ancient woodlands today, notably Ty Canol in west Wales, originate back to the Atlantic period.*

For the small communities of Mesolithic people who were living a nomadic existence in Wales at this time, the vast forests would have both provided a rich source of food but also posed significant obstacles to moving freely.

These first immigrants to Wales had walked from central Europe across the Doggerland land bridge that once connected the British Isles to mainland Europe via what is now the southern part of the North Sea around The Wash. They cleared forests where necessary using crude wooden tools but they were very much hunters and gatherers – mainly living amongst the forest rather than trying to tame it. By 6,000 BC, however, around the time rising sea levels flooded the land bridge and created the island we now know as Britain, the Neolithic descendants of their Mesolithic ancestors had become settled farmers.

Thanks to better metal tools and a more sophisticated understanding of how to harness fire, they set about clearing large tracts of woodland – a practice that continued throughout the Bronze and Iron ages.

And so began a few thousand years of cultivating while cohabitating with the rugged, mostly forested landscape of Wales. The woodland these early Celts cleared was planted and grazed – an army of sheep, domesticated pigs and cattle making sure that woodlands never had a chance to rewild. By 100 BC the British Celts were renowned through Europe for

---

* *Welsh Woods and Forests* – William Linnard, p. 5

their prodigious farming techniques including the use of a sophisticated iron plough that required up to eight oxen to drag it.

Yet, even as these early inhabitants of Wales sought to tame the woodlands, they also appeared to have revered them. At the heart of the Celts' relationship with their natural environment were the Druids.

The Druids' Connection to the Forest

Today, much of what we associate with Druids is the stuff of Celtic legends. We have grown accustomed to images of mystical high priests in flowing white robes and long white beards, chanting and casting powerful spells. In reality, that's all pretty much made up – the creative legacy of many generations of storytellers and antiquarians who reinvented the Druids to fit a particular narrative of Celtic and Welsh identity.

The main reason we know so little is the lack of a paper trail. The Druids didn't write down any of their philosophy, teachings or culture – not because they couldn't write but because they believed that learning through an oral tradition would both create the highest standards of knowledge and stop that knowledge falling into the hands of their enemies. Indeed scholars have speculated that it took between 12 and 20 years of study to attain the highest level of Druidic learning – much the way shamans today in the Amazon spend decades learning the ways of the forest so they can pass their knowledge down to the next generation.

Our most reliable knowledge of the Druids comes from contemporary Greek and Roman academics and scribes who, if they hadn't encountered them in person, would have heard stories of their power and influence from those who had.

In the early days of the Roman Republic and later Empire, the Celts were a true force to be reckoned with and held power over a large swathe of Europe and Asia Minor. There were dominant Celt communities in Galatia (now Turkey) and even in Egypt for a time. Indeed, it's fair to say that the Celts, at one time, scared the shit out of both the Greeks and the Romans – sacking Rome on multiple occasions.

The Druids held special power among the Celts. Rather than being religious high priests, British scholar, Peter Berresford Ellis, argues they were the parallel caste to the social group that developed in another Indo-European society – the Brahmins of the Hindu culture. He describes in his book, *The Druids*, how 'The caste not only consisted of those who had religious functions but also comprised philosophers, judges, teachers, historians, poets, musicians, physicians, astronomers, prophets and political advisers or counsellors. Druids could sometimes be kings or chieftains.'

From the earliest descriptions of these important people there emerges a very strong connection to nature, the forests and one species of tree in particular – the oak. Greek scholars in the 2nd century BC first mention them and, later, Roman writers including Pliny the Elder believed the name Druid was derived from the Greek word for oak – *drus*. Some Celtic etymologists have reasoned that Druid actually meant 'oak knowledge'.

Others think the oak connection in the name is over-emphasised and that Druid simply means 'immersed in knowledge'. Whatever the roots of the word, what we do know is that the Druid caste grew in importance when the ancient Celts would have been dependent on food gathering in the great oak forests of Europe. For these earliest hunter-gatherer Celts, acorns served as a plentiful and sacred supply of food. The Roman poet Ovid described how the acorn was the first food ever given to humans when they descended from the great tree of the sky god, Jupiter.

Pliny the Elder, landing on British shores in AD 49 to report on the Roman invasion, wrote how the Celts ground acorns to make flour and baked it into bread. He also described in his book, *Natural History*, how the Druids of Gaul put great faith in the healing powers of mistletoe, which grew on oak tree branches.

The Welsh Connection

Over time, as the Roman Empire expanded, the Celts retreated north and west until their last remaining strongholds were in Gaul – what we now know as north-western France – and what today we call the British Isles and Ireland.

In Wales, the Celts settled and divided into different tribes – the Deceangli in the north, the Ordovices in the west and middle of Wales and, here in south Wales, the Silures who Roman scribes described as fierce, wild, dark skinned and curly haired savages. That was a biased portrayal but we don't know a whole lot else about them. What does exist are the many burial mounds, cairns and standing stones dating back to the period when their Druid sect would have held sway over the Celtic communities.

That's exactly what we were staring at now on the top of Gray Hill – a jagged set of ancient and ruined standing stones that, according to antiquarians, could have been older than Stonehenge and potentially one of the most notable Druidic sites in Wales. Some reports say the stone circle was damaged by robbers in the 19th century. Despite their disrepair, the mere presence of the stones and their commanding position at what appeared to be the highest elevation in the forest have been interpreted by some Druidic afficionados as an indication that Wentwood could have been 'one of the most important Bronze Age landscapes in the whole of Monmouthshire', in the words of the *Journal of Antiquities*.

One such enthusiast was local writer, artist, historian and school-teacher, Fred Hando. From the 1920s until his death in 1970 Hando wrote more than 800 articles and several books about the history and folklore of this corner of Wales. He was fascinated by the stone circles, positing that the two stones inside the circle aligned with the spring solstice and claiming (completely without evidence of course): 'when the ancient observers saw their stones in line with these horizon sunrises and sunsets they were able to advise their agricultural tribesmen what the seasons were. Such knowledge was power!'

The standing stones were not the only relic of a potential Druidic past in Wentwood. Hando maintained that Gray Hill held many other Celtic secrets. Indeed, a mile or so north lay another Bronze Age treasure – a burial mound in the north of the woods that was estimated to be between 3,000 and 4,000 years old.

Andy and I made our way down from Gray Hill and started following the forestry paths through Wentwood. As we walked, I started to consider just how important and symbolic this area of woodland must have been thousands of years ago.

What did the Druids understand of the power of forests I wondered? What knowledge did they have that's been lost about living in harmony with nature? Whatever the Druids' relationship to ancient Wentwood, they'd have a hard time recognising it today.

The forest we encountered on the main track was a ragtag mix of neglected conifer plantations. Fallen trees lay stricken against one another as moss started to retake control of the bare forest floor now that sunlight could sneak in through gaps in the canopy. This part of the forest felt sad – bereft of life.

A thousand years ago, Wentwood would have been dominated mainly by oak trees. Over the centuries, though, successive generations of local dwellers reshaped this vast woodland as they used it for hunting, cultivated it for agriculture and managed it for timber.

By the late 13th century, Cistercian Monks from nearby Tintern Abbey were utilising Wentwood by buying all the available bark from felled oak trees in the forest for use in their tannery. Local people, meanwhile, depended on the woods to provide materials for repairing their homes, for fuel, for a place to graze livestock, to fatten up their pigs by letting them forage for acorns (known in those days as pannage), and a source for creating honey and wax from the wild bees that lived there: the woods were a B&Q of the medieval age.

By the 17th century, farmers were working the edges of the forest while other wealthy landowners harvested the old oaks through coppicing to produce charcoal for their ironwork ventures. (Coppicing is the woodland management technique whereby trees are felled at their base then allowed to regrow, so providing a sustainable supply of timber.)

In the 19th century, the then landowners, the Dukes of Beaufort, converted much of Wentwood to conifer plantation – the fast-growing trees quickly shading out many of the remaining oak and beech trees that had been coppiced through the ages. By the end of the First World War, most of the remaining native hardwood trees that were taken in order to support the war effort also were replaced by conifers. The monoculture undermined a woodland ecosystem that previously thrived in the mixed oak forest.

Over the past few decades, there has been a concerted effort to restore Wentwood's ancient heritage. In 2005, the Woodland Trust purchased half of the forest (some 430 acres) from the state-owned Forestry Commission after it raised £1.5 million thanks to the support of 250,000 members, local people, and celebrities such as author, Bill Bryson, and actor, Dame Judi Dench. Since then, the Trust has assumed control of the rest of the forest and has gained accreditation under the Queen's Commonwealth Canopy (QCC) initiative to create a sustainable conservation area. Being the starting point of a National Forest for Wales could only speed up Wentwood's rehabilitation.

As we walked Andy told me about how his grandfather used to work at Newport docks in the 1930s for a big timber company that imported telegraph poles from Sweden. 'He couldn't believe it when Wentwood started its own forestry and timber project. "Who needs Welsh wood when we're swamped with all this timber from Sweden?" he used to say.'

As we walked further west, the look and feel of the forest deteriorated further. The side of the path was littered with piles of household rubbish. An old fridge had been discarded and there was even a red car door that looked like it once belonged to a Ford Focus propped up against a tree. Clearly someone had reversed down the forest path to unload sacks of building debris. When I got home later in the day, I searched the news for any evidence of this forest vandalism and found a BBC story from a few days before: during lockdown, a tonne and a half of waste had been dumped in Wentwood.

Just as Andy and I were beginning to form a somewhat negative opinion of Wentwood it surprised us. We were on a wide straight track that cut directly through the forest from east to west – one of the logging roads built by the Forestry Commission – when we spotted a winding path that led down off the main track that cried out to be explored.

Within seconds, Wentwood transformed from a dusty, enslaved conifer landscape into a rich, cool and decidedly unkempt woodland – a mix of pine and ancient oak. The forest floor had come alive. Bright green moss sprung up everywhere and clusters of white fungi grew at the base of some of the trees. I cursed myself for not knowing what they were. I had so much to learn about the forest.

We stopped for a rest and drink of water in this peaceful spot and I tried to imagine how the Silures would have used this part of the forest. Could we be sitting on an ancient hunting ground? Or was this once a favoured Druid place for cutting mistletoe? Today, the trees that would know the Druids' secrets have long gone but in this part of Wentwood, at least, you got a sense that the spirit of the forest was still alive.

There was one tree in Wentwood Forest that I particularly wanted to find. It was Curley Oak, Wentwood's oldest tree – by some estimates over 900 years old. The OS map offered a general sense of where this Wentwood elder was located but this part of the forest was a jumbled mix of veteran deciduous trees and younger conifers spread out along numerous trails all heading in different directions. I studied the map carefully and determined what looked to my eyes as the correct path to follow. After a few minutes' walk I was no longer so sure but then we spotted the ancient tree, well camouflaged by thick moss and ferns but still recognisable by its obvious old age. At one time, Curley Oak might have dominated this part of the forest – at its peak, the tree's girth was said to be an impressive 6.35 metres. Nowadays the old timer was a shadow of its former self – more a robust skeleton than a full tree. Curley's trunk was split in two, though fresh branches and leaves continued to grow out of one flank. Even today, in its aged state, the gap between the two sections of the trunk was wide enough to stand in the middle. Which is exactly what Andy and I took turns in doing.

The Romans Are Coming!

The path from Curley Oak climbed back towards the main forest track. We could see daylight through the trees to our right – we were getting close to the edge of Wentwood Forest and Bertholau Graig – the ridge that drops down precipitously to the Usk Valley and the A449 road linking Wales and the Midlands of England. The forest was quiet but in the distance we could hear the faint hum of cars speeding up the road.

We reached a fork in the road where the main track veered off right in a series of switchbacks down the ridge while the route I had planned to follow lay straight ahead. But it was blocked by a big wooden sign that read: STOP – Forest Operations – Do Not Enter. It was early afternoon and, so far, we hadn't encountered a single other person since starting our walk through the forest. We certainly couldn't hear any sounds of sawing, chopping or any other forestry activity. My map said there was an ancient fort a mile ahead of us. That had to be worth seeing.

'It can't be any worse as when we were hiking in the Canadian Rockies and came across a sign that said, "Take Care – Grizzly Bears Spotted Feeding Nearby!"' Andy said cheerfully.

The track narrowed until we were shuffling through the undergrowth, ducking low-slung branches. Just as I thought my map reading had failed me, we came across a rusty red children's swing. Andy and I looked at it, both thinking the same thing. What is a swing doing in the middle of a forest?

Around the next bend in the path we got the answer. We'd stumbled on the garden of an old forester's cottage – a dilapidated house with ladders strapped to the roof and bits of old cars, including a Land Rover, scattered in the grounds. Next to the house was an even more dilapidated standing caravan – perhaps temporary accommodation for forest workers? 'I don't know,' said Andy. 'It's more like something out of the final scene of one of those Scandi-noir thrillers. You know, where the victim is strapped to the chair and slowly being tortured with pliers and a hammer.'

'It certainly does have a certain Deliverance feel about it,' I agreed as we picked up the pace and moved quickly away from the house.

The fort I'd spotted on the map was called Caer Licyn (*Caer* means fort in Welsh). It was marked as a Motte and Bailey (a style of fortification introduced by the Normans around the 11th century) but there was some disagreement about its validity. Some amateur historians speculated it was a folly built a few centuries ago. Others believe it pre-dated the Normans and perhaps was an Iron Age site. We could still make out the contours of a fortified structure situated on the top of the hill and surrounded by a neat cluster of trees. I couldn't help thinking back to the Silures who had built a similar fort a mile or so east at a similar elevation near the village of Llanmelin. Could this have been part of their defence against the Roman invaders who arrived in Wales around AD 48?

By the time the Romans came knocking, the Celts of Wales, Ireland and Scotland were the last holdouts against a military machine that had routed all of Europe and most of what we now know as England. In Wales, the Celts – many being refugees from Gaul – had settled in small agricultural hamlets amid a matrix of oak forests just like Wentwood.

A century before, General Julius Caesar had been repulsed by Celtic warriors. This time the Romans took no chances, arriving in Wales with an overwhelming force. Still, they hadn't factored in the ferocity of the Silures and their charismatic leader Caradog (known to the Romans as Caractacus). In a series of guerrilla attacks over a period of five or six years the Silures terrified the Roman forces by springing ambushes then retreating into their woodland hiding places.

In his book *The Annals XIV*, the Roman historian and politician Tacitus recounts the similar problems faced during earlier campaigns in Scotland, writing: 'When we used to plunge into the woods and thickets, all the hostile tribesmen charged straight at us.' Then after the initial skirmish, as the Romans chased the marauders back into the woods, 'they rallied and profited by their local knowledge to ambush the first rash pursuers.'

Ultimately, the Romans prevailed and Caradog was captured and taken in chains to Rome. Even then, he was able to win himself a pardon and his freedom because Emperor Claudius was impressed by his bravery. Surprisingly, Caradog chose to live out the rest of his days in sunny Rome rather than returning to the cold, wet forests of south Wales.

His countrymen and women back home didn't fare so well. Frustrated by the way the Celts could launch raids then disappear, and to break the Celtic spirit once and for all, they decided to annihilate the Druids.

In AD 61, the Roman general, Paulinus, drew up plans to attack the island of Mona – what we now call Ynys Mon (Anglesey in English) – the spiritual stronghold of the Druids. According to the Tacitus, Paulinus led his legions out of their stronghold in Chester and marched them towards Mona. The Roman army needed timber to build the flat-bottomed landing crafts it would use to cross the Menai Straits, the narrow channel of water that separated the Mona from the mainland. It also required timber to shore up the defences of the camps and forts it erected as it advanced. Furthermore, it needed straight, wide, military roads to effectively move the army around and, importantly, minimise the forest ambushes.

To address this need for timber, and to remove the threat of ambushes posed by the Celts, the Romans set about felling all the woodlands on their route to Mona. In doing so they ramped up their military and economic power over the local population. And, just as the carving of roads through forests continues to threaten indigenous communities all around the world today, the Roman roads hastened the demise of Celtic resistance.

They still had to conquer the island of Mona. When they reached the island, the Roman soldiers froze at the sight of the Druids. Tacitus recounted the scene this way:

> On the shore stood the opposing army with its dense array of armed warriors, while between the ranks dashed women, in

black attire like the Furies, with hair dishevelled, waving brands. All around, the Druids, lifting up their hands to heaven, and pouring forth dreadful imprecations, scared our soldiers by the unfamiliar sight, so that, as if their limbs were paralysed, they stood motionless, and exposed to wounds. Then urged by their general's appeals and mutual encouragements not to quail before a troop of frenzied women, they bore the standards onwards, smote down all resistance, and wrapped the foe in the flames of his own brands. A force was next set over the conquered, and their [oak] groves, devoted to inhuman superstitions, were destroyed. They deemed it indeed a duty to cover their altars with the blood of captives and to consult their deities through human entrails.

Clearly, something about the Druids really spooked the Romans. Both Tacitus and Pliny describe how the Druids indulged in human sacrifice and the latter suggested it was outrage at such practices that drove Rome to wipe them out. But some modern scholars believe that the real threat posed by the Druids was ideological. One, Jean Markle, has argued that the Druids, with their affinity to the natural world, 'represented an absolute threat to the Roman State' because their nature-based philosophy contradicted Roman materialism.

Perhaps, then, we should be considering the ancient Druids through a completely different prism. I liked the idea of them being the forefathers of the modern environmental movement – stewards and protectors of the forest against the myopic, materialist demands of the Roman Empire.

We had reached the Usk Valley Walk – one of a number of semi-official Long Distance Paths that snake their way through the United Kingdom. The Usk Valley Walk runs from Brecon to Caerleon and we were hopping on it for just a few miles.

The waymarker for the path took us off the paved land and down a precipitous descent through the wooded hillside of a part of the ridgeway known as Kemeys Graig. The walk down was tough on my middle-aged knees and must be deadly in winter – though it looked a favourite route for mountain bikers judging by the tyre tracks weaving their way through the wood. At the bottom of the path we came across one of the main forestry tracks used by logging vehicles. They had reduced the road to a sea of mud which we had to navigate with a large stick that we found in the forest – using it to prod the ground and feel for a crossing that wouldn't leave us up to our waists in the soupy mud.

Finally, we emerged from Wentwood into open fields and firm ground. Below us the River Usk took broad turns to make its way downstream – like a sedate skier making wide slaloms down a mountain.

By AD 90 the Romans had taken full control of the lands occupied by the Welsh Celts. The now vanquished Silurians were persuaded to live in a new Roman settlement just below Wentwood called Venta Silurum or Caerwent (from which the forest and indeed the entire region of Gwent) would get its name. As they did throughout the world the Romans shored up their military gains by building a network of armed garrisons throughout Wales connected by a series of stone roads. One of their most important forts was called Isca Silurum – we know it as Caerleon – on the banks of the River Usk. That's where we were headed.

The Story of the Saints

A journey from Caerleon to Bassaleg

The Romans were a dominant presence in south Wales for 300 years and Caerleon played a major role in their control of the west of Britain. Even after they left, Caerleon's aura and reputation was further enhanced by tales that it was King Arthur's seat of power where he gathered his knights at the fabled round table.

This was how one of Wales's earliest travel writers, Geoffrey of Monmouth, depicted Caerleon in his 12th-century book *Historia regum Britanniae* (History of the Kings of Britain).

> When the feast of Whitsuntide began to draw near, Arthur, who was quite overjoyed by his great success, made up his mind to hold a plenary court at that season and place the crown of the kingdom on his head. He explained to the members of his court what he was proposing to do and accepted their advice that he should carry out his plan in The City of the Legions. Situated as it is in Morgannwg (Glamorgan), on the River Usk, not far from the Severn Sea, in a most pleasant position, and being richer in material wealth than other townships, this city was eminently suitable for such a ceremony.

Little is known of Geoffrey, though some believe he was a Welsh monk whose education took him to Oxford University. Yet while his biography is lightweight, the influence his writing had was anything but.

Geoffrey's *Historia*, along with another book *Prophetie Merlini* (the Prophecies of Merlin) introduced what we now know as the Arthurian legends to people across Medieval Europe. In the books, Geoffrey outlined Arthur's true claim to the title, King of Britain, and he described how Merlin received the gift of prophecy after retreating to live with the animals of the forest.

They were great stories but probably an amalgam of historical sources, folklore and tales told and passed down by bards.*

Geoffrey's history appears to be one of the earliest examples of a recurring theme in Welsh history and literature: fact and fiction blending together until it's difficult to determine what is real and what is not.

Over the centuries King Arthur's importance grew as writers and antiquarians across the UK and France further burnished his legend, while his connections with Caerleon waned. But they were revived in the 19th century when the Victorian poet Alfred, Lord Tennyson travelled to the town to write his Arthurian poem *Idylls of the King*. He stayed at the Hanbury Arms pub and took long walks along the River Usk for inspiration.

The pub is still going and it's where Andy and I started today's walk. We left the car park and passed the grass-covered ruins of the old Roman amphitheatre. Young kids played tag amid the impressive stone remains while their parents chatted and drank coffee.

I could have used some more coffee, I thought to myself as we walked by. My family had been awoken at 4 a.m. by our two cats who'd dragged a poor, unsuspecting field mouse into the house and then let it loose so they could chase it up and down the hallway stairs. My wife had been due

---

* Bards were poets and storytellers who claimed direct links to the Druids of old. In the first centuries following the end of Roman occupation, Bards played an important role as storytellers, oral historians, song makers and praise poets. They were employed by noble families and royalty to celebrate their patron's activities and ancestral past. Indeed, such was their status in medieval Welsh society that the Laws of Hywel Dda (the Welsh Laws) classified a Bard as a member of a king's household with duties including the singing of the sovereignty of Britain.

in work a few hours later, so she suggested I deal with the problem. I'd had to lock the cats in one room then try and catch the mouse with a saucepan. It was small, brown with big eyes and was very scared. After five minutes 'mousing' I finally got it in the pan and released it outside the front door into the gloom of the pre-dawn. The cats looked at me in disgust.

Sleep-deprived, my head felt a bit groggy as we walked. The weather was cooler than the day before with a hint of rain in the air. I'd brought my rain jacket just in case, but it was still warm enough for shorts.

Today would be another eight-mile walk, following the River Usk into Newport before continuing along the old Monmouthshire canal to the suburb of High Cross where we would descend into the hamlet of Bassaleg.

It was, admittedly, a counter-intuitive route for a walking trail through the National Forest. We could have headed further north and visited Cwmcarn, a large conifer forest made popular by its extensive mountain bike trails. But part of my challenge was to imagine a walking route that might inspire people in Wales to reconnect with nature, and to understand that we can make that connection even when walking in urban environments. I'd decided to follow established walking trails as best as I could. Not only would it make a forest path more accessible to people but this way it could be achieved with minimal impact on the environment.

I'd also been inspired by a new grass roots walking initiative called Slow Ways. It hoped, through crowdsourced mapping, to create a network of accessible walking routes that connect all of Great Britain's towns and cities. Already, during the lockdown, some 700 volunteers had collaborated to add 7,500 public footpaths and rights of way that collectively stretched for over 68,000 miles. I thought some of my routes could be added to that map.

So I was keen to explore the relatively new cycle and walking trail linking Caerleon to Newport and to see how easy it would be to connect with the well-established network of canal walking paths that link up through east Wales.

Yesterday, we'd barely seen another soul but today was different. Local people were out walking their dogs and a small cohort of cyclists rode by, one ringing his bell with great urgency and importance as he sped by (though less so when he realised he was going the wrong way and had to turn around and pass by us for a second time).

Our conversation turned to the houses we walked past. They'd been built on the flood plain no more than 100 metres from the banks of the Usk. Earlier in the year the river had burst its banks during winter storms, flooding low-lying fields and prompting local authorities to lay down emergency flood barriers to protect residents. I wondered how these houses had fared during that storm surge and just how vulnerable this location would be in the future as climate change increases the chances of flooding. New projections from the environmental agency, Natural Resources Wales, suggested this whole area – along with large swathes of coastal Wales – could be underwater by 2050 because of climate change. When these houses went up it might have been considered a justifiable risk to build on a flood plain. Nowadays, it looked like foolhardiness on the part of the developers. I couldn't help thinking that, regardless of the best attempts of humanity to tame nature, it always has a way of restoring its own balance.

We were at the river now. It was high tide and the Usk looked picture postcard pretty as the sun broke through the clouds in streaks and reflected off the surface. Above us, a black cormorant performed aerial reconnaissance for its lunch.

This was the river in its best light. This far downstream, the Usk's waters begin to merge with the Aber Hafren and the river has a Jekyll and Hyde personality. At low tide it is reduced to a thin channel fighting its way through clogging, dirty grey mud that trap the little boats moored by its banks until the Hafren's surge frees them again.

Caerleon was well behind us at this point and we'd entered a sliver of countryside separating the town from Newport's industrial edges. Even so, it was a surprise to come across a sow and her litter of piglets sleeping on the dry mud at the side of the cycle path. Behind the pigs was a truly magnificent and very old tree growing at a precarious angle out of a steep hillside, its thick branches raised upwards as if to help it maintain balance.

'So what type of tree is that?' asked Andy with a hint of mischief.

'I've not quite reached that level of expertise,' I replied a little defensively, instead pulling out my handy Woodland Trust identification app. Five minutes later, Andy and I were still staring at the screen, comparing the shape and the colour of leaves in a futile attempt to identify this glorious tree, when an elderly couple walked round the corner. They introduced themselves – locals out for their daily constitutional down the river.

'The Usk looks beautiful today,' I said making polite conversation.

'That's only because you can't see the mud,' replied the husband with a laugh.

'We're trying to work out what type of tree this is,' I continued.

The couple looked at me as if I was a complete idiot. 'Well it's an oak tree. Obviously,' said the woman and they quickly walked on.

'Probably best not to tell too many people you're writing a book about trees just yet,' said Andy.

Car Trouble

We reached a bend in the river called Pill Mawr (which roughly translates into 'big tidal ditch'). Back in the 15th century it offered a natural dock where the Cistercian monks from nearby Llantarnam Abbey would load up wool and other goods for export to Bristol on the other side of the Aber Hafren.

Ahead of us we could hear the modern-day version of the River Usk transportation artery. The cycle path ran directly under the M4 motorway where it enters the notorious Brynglas tunnels – the daily bane for thousands of motorists trying to get from the English border to Cardiff and beyond. When the Brynglas (blue hill) tunnels were first proposed in 1959, the UK motorway system was still in its infancy (the first motorway, the M6, had only opened a year before). The tunnels were intended to reduce the time it took to travel across south Wales and avoid motorists having to drive through Newport. However, by the time the twin, two-lane tunnels finally opened in 1967, car culture had already firmly taken hold in the UK and the M4 was straining under the volume of traffic. Within a couple of years it became clear that the motorway needed to be widened to accommodate three lanes of traffic in each direction. The tunnels, unfortunately, had to remain two lanes wide.

The consequent monstrous traffic congestion just got worse over the years as the M4 became the central transportation artery for south Wales. The increased volume of traffic created environmental problems for the residential neighbourhoods on either side of the tunnel but finding a solution that would reduce congestion while not contributing to climate change has proven problematic to say the least.

For years developers and urban planners argued the need for a relief road to be built south of Newport but that new stretch of the M4 would have cut through miles of countryside and greatly increased the amount of road traffic and resulting CO_2 emissions. In 2019 the Welsh government declared the relief road project dead because it was incompatible with the Future Generations Act. The government argued that the new road would put future generations' well-being at risk by contributing to climate change and, instead, proposed a series of new metro rail connections to reduce the amount of traffic.

As we walked out from under the M4 the cycle route merged into the old industrial streets of Newport's Crindau neighbourhood. There we met another retired couple who were just finishing their first ride up and down the path on new electric bikes. They were in their 70s, tanned and trim-looking, and loading the bikes into a weathered Renault Romero white campervan.

'We've been doing loads of walks during lockdown. It's just great to get out and rediscover nature,' said the woman when I asked about their ride. 'But I just got this e-bike so we thought we'd give it a spin. And I only fell off once!'

The entrance to the Monmouthshire canal was directly opposite a gritty looking pub where locals were downing mid-morning pints. Spotting a gap in the traffic, we dashed across the main road, ducked down the paved access ramp and onto the canal towpath. Gone was the deafening roar of the traffic and the edginess of inner-city Newport. It was muffled by the calmness of water trickling through the canal; an abundance of reeds, bushes and moss growing on its sides and thick woodlands rising up above it.

We had stumbled on another threshold – this one being where the Crindau Pill (a tributary of the Usk) met the Monmouthshire and Brecon canals. One hundred years ago, this was a hub of industrial activity and as much of a transportation logjam as the Brynglas tunnels are today. This was where the Pontnewynydd and Crumlin arms of the canal came together and connected to Newport docks. Back then, the canal barges transported iron and coal – part of the great logistical machine that exported Welsh raw materials all around the world. This nexus of the canal industry would have been noisy, filthy and full of early city life. The canal system gradually fell into disrepair as it was replaced in importance first by the railways and later the roads. Today, despite the low hum of the M4 motorway passing through the tunnels above, the canal felt tranquil.

Above sat Allt-yr-yn (slope of the ash tree) Nature Reserve – a 32-acre expanse of mixed deciduous woodland. It provides an important natural buffer of biodiversity between the residential neighbourhood of the same name that sits on the hill above and the M4. Alongside the eponymous ash trees, the nature reserve is home to birch, cherry and oak as well as hazel and hawthorn growing beneath the canopies.

The reserve also has a five-acre ancient wildflower meadow and is home to 50 different bird species as well as grass snakes, frogs and newts. In summer, the spotted orchid and yellow rattle bring swathes of colour to the meadow.

Located close to the border with England and shaped by centuries of immigration, Newport is one of the most anglicised parts of Wales. Because of this, old Welsh place names like Allt-yr-yn have been reinterpreted and adapted to match the local dialect. The Welsh pronunciation sounds like 'Achht-ur-un' but the locals call it Oltereen – making it sound like something out of *Star Trek*.

Did the Druids Become Saints?

Newport's current generation of residents can be forgiven for their mangled interpretation of the Welsh language – it's been going on around there for at least a thousand years. Take Newport's own patron saint. His name was Gwynllyw Farfog. In English, however, he became known as Woolos the Warrior or Woolos the Bearded (a name that could have been lifted straight out of *Monty Python*). Today, Newport's Cathedral – once a monastery he's said to have built – is called St Woolos.

Gwynllyw ruled a chunk of south Wales at the end of the 5th century and is believed to have heralded from a storied Celtic lineage – he was supposedly descended from Macsen Wledig, King of the Britons (and possibly also a Roman Emperor), on his father's side and Cunedda, a revered Celtic ruler, on his mother's.

Gwynllyw was quite the rogue even by medieval standards. In one account, written around 1086, the king was described as 'given up to carnal allurements, and frequently instigated his guards to robbery and plunder, and lived altogether contrary to what is right and disgraced his life with crimes.'

Harsh words you might think. But consider his approach to wooing. At the height of his powers, Gwynllyw took a fancy to Gwladys, the daughter of King Brychan of Brycheiniog, the neighbouring kingdom to the north of his lands.

Gwladys was quite the beauty (King Arthur had a crush on her according to one story) and it would seem she also had a thing for bad boy Kings. Her father, Brychan, was none too impressed with Gwynllyw – you suspect his reputation went before him. Given the parental pushback, some suitors might have suggested meeting up for coffee or a nice brunch with their prospective father-in-law as a way of currying favour. Not Gwynllyw. He led a raiding party of 300 men into Brycheiniog to abduct Gwladys. This resulted in a pitched battle with Brychan's men that only ended when King Arthur turned up and sided with Gwynllyw.

Or so the story goes.

To be honest we don't really know the truth about Gwynllyw's courtship methods or anything else about him. We can't be certain that King Arthur was on hand to help out Gwynllyw or whether he even existed. The same is true for the whole of Welsh history during the period between when the Romans departed and the Normans arrived from France in the 11th century. As the famous Welsh historian Gwyn A. Williams described in *When Was Wales?*: 'From the fifth century the western regions of Britain drop out of history: they do not climb back in until the ninth century … These ages are dark ages because we cannot see anything clearly.'

The few contemporary histories detailing these five hundred years in Wales drew on a mix of ecclesiastic narratives, folklore and good old parochial bias. The 'history' was revised to reflect the sentiments, sentimentality and prejudices of those writing it.

Which brings us back to Gwynllyw and Gwladys. They might have lived out their days in complete Dark Ages obscurity if it hadn't been for their lone offspring – a son named Cadoc who was determined not to emulate his father's less-endearing tendencies.

The signs were there from the start. In the days leading up to Cadoc's birth around AD 497 strange lights shone in his parents' house and the cellars miraculously filled up with food. Then, an angel turned up to announce his birth and a holy well sprang up for his baptism. Even better, it then started spewing wine.

Cadoc clearly was destined to be an important holy man. Gwynllyw sent his son off to be tutored by the monks at Caerwent – the Dark Ages version of a Swiss finishing school. It was said that his piety inspired both Gwladys and, especially Gwynllyw, to embrace Christianity and even take vows of celibacy. However, so intense was their physical attraction to each other that Gwynllyw and Gwladys found it impossible to remain together. The only certain way to stay celibate was to become hermits. This is how St Woolos came about: Gwynllyw founded a monastery at Newport, which is now the Cathedral. Gwladys departed for the hills never to see her husband or son again.

Clearly, there's quite a lot of artistic licence when it comes to recounting the lives of early Welsh saints. Indeed, as one historian Madeleine

Gray wrote in an article in the local newspaper; 'like the stories of [King] Arthur and the Mabinogion,* their lives have been rewritten many times, to suit changing values and changing circumstances.'

Given how little we know about this period of history, I started to toy with some ambitious wishful thinking: maybe the Druids didn't disappear in the Roman purge after all. Instead, could they have morphed over the centuries into the early Celtic Christian saints? After all, this was an age when pagan and Christian traditions were celebrated together and sometimes merged into one. And many of the early saints were referred to as Druids. Illtyd, still one of the most important saints in Welsh Christianity, and a student of Cadoc's, was 'by descent a most wise Druid,' according to *A Life of Saint Samson of Dol*, the earliest known surviving biography of a British Celtic saint, written at about the end of the sixth century.

Wales's patron saint Dewi (David) also gained fame because of his supernatural abilities. Once, in mid-Wales, he commanded the ground beneath his feet to rise up so he could preach to a crowd. Dewi also possessed what you might call a true Druidic connection to nature. His emblem was a white dove and he extolled the monks in the abbey he founded to care for the natural world – even going so far as to ban them from using cattle to pull their ploughs. (He also made them take a vow of chastity prompting local rivals to parade naked young women in front of the abbey to tempt the monks ... but that's another story.)

Then there was Melangell. She was the daughter of an Irish king who renounced her status and headed across the Irish Sea to pursue a spiritual existence in Wales. In the year AD 604, she was praying devoutly when she encountered the hunting party of the Prince of Powys, which was chasing a hare. The poor creature hid inside the sleeves of Melangell's garment. When the Prince called to his hounds to catch the hare they recoiled in fear of her aura and ran away. The Prince was in awe of her holy power and granted Melangell all the lands where the hunt had taken place as a

---

* A famous compendium of Welsh legends, dating from the 12th and 13th centuries. They are the earliest British prose stories.

sanctuary. From then until her death 36 years later, no animal was killed on her land.

Of course, not all the Celtic saints had such a pure reputation. Even after his commitment to a hermit life, Gwynllyw's notoriety still endured. He was adopted as the patron saint of pirates because of his exploits terrorising ships in the Bristol Channel and was celebrated centuries later by the greatest Welsh buccaneer of them all, Sir Henry Morgan – himself a later inspiration for all sorts of popular culture homages ranging from a Donald Duck comic book to an Errol Flynn movie and a brand of spiced rum. So, the next time you find yourself 'partying with the Cap'n' as the advertising slogan goes, raise a glass to Gwynllyw. I think he would have approved.

That evening, I cooked a paella for my family and excitedly told them about my walks over the past two days. I spoke about the Druids and the Romans, the Arthurian legends and the mystical saints. Most of all though, I told them about the woodlands and walking paths I'd discovered and how, just possibly, my idea to plot a route throughout Wales might work.

My teenage son and daughter nodded and showed just enough interest to be polite but I could tell my middle-aged epiphany meant little to them. I hadn't shared with them just how anxious I'd felt when I was stuck at home without a project so, while they could see how upbeat I was about these new walks, they didn't really know just how important this was to me. My wife did. She knew just how difficult it was for me to 'relax' if I didn't have something creative or active to focus on. She also knew how I'd been sleeping better since I started walking around Cardiff and researching this project. Nevertheless, while she was interested in my stories, the idea of hiking through the hills of Wales was not really her thing. In fact, no one in the family was really putting their hand up to join my adventure.

That was okay. This was going to be my thing. Anyway, Andy was keen to keep exploring. And I had another candidate ready to join the adventure. Tomorrow would be his first day on the job.

3

The Attack on the Forests

A meander from Bassaleg to Caerphilly

A ndy was busy with work so my friend, Jeff, agreed to join me on the next stage of the walk – a 10-mile trek from St Basil's church in Bassaleg (dedicated to Gwladys) to the historic town of Caerphilly.

Jeff grew up in Brynmawr on the north-eastern fringe of the Valleys – home to some of the biggest steel and coal production in all of Wales. Jeff's dad had worked in the Ebbw Vale steelworks and that was where Jeff had gone straight after leaving school before realising that he was better suited to art college. We have been friends for 15 years. Our kids grew up together, we went to gigs and music festivals like Greenman and All Tomorrow's Parties and we played squash most Friday nights before heading to the pub with other friends to bet on the football pools (though we rarely won any money). Jeff was ideal walking company. He loved Welsh history, knew the Valleys well and always, and I mean always, had a story (and invariably an opinion) to share.

The day was warm and we were both dressed in shorts and sports tops – grey for me and orange for Jeff, it being his go-to colour of choice whether it be trainers, sweaters or even shorts. We headed towards Caerphilly following a collection of paths over the hills and ridgeways. The route looked manageable but I was slightly concerned about how Jeff would cope. Over the past couple of years he'd damaged the ligaments in both knees undertaking a series of what even he'd admit were ludicrous sporting endeavours for a man his age. One involved a heroic but frankly foolhardy attempt to slide into home base in a softball game. The second involved an overly ambitious, acrobatic move while playing squash. Unsurprisingly, he wore knee supports for our walk.

After a mile or so of tarmac-trudging we were clear of Bassaleg and heading into open country towards Park Wood. We could see a few farms dotted around and, in the distance, the wooded hills of Draethen and Rudry leading over to Caerphilly.

By the end of the 7th century, the Brythonic peoples living in the west of Britain found themselves cut off from their compatriots in the north of England on the Scottish borders. Wave upon wave of Saxon attacks had pacified most of England but the physical obstacles of the Welsh mountain ranges had kept the Saxons from overrunning what we now consider to be Wales.

Of course that didn't stop the local inhabitants living to west of the Saxon lands from launching guerrilla attacks and raiding parties before disappearing back into the highlands and woods. Sometime in the mid-8th century, Offa, the Saxon King of Mercia, decided he'd had enough of this western nuisance and walled off his land by building an imposing earthen dyke running some 150 miles from north to south.

This became the de facto eastern border of what we now know as Wales and, within this cut-off land, the modern Welsh people and language began to emerge. The territory was divided into a number of kingdoms – all vying for hegemony.

Apart from a few urban settlements along the coast, the majority of people in what was becoming the Wales we know today lived a rural existence based around simple farming and a dependence on the woodlands for hunting and foraging. What little we know about people's relationship to the land and nature at this time comes from the Welsh Laws, believed to have been laid down by King Hywel Dda (Hywel the Good) in the 10th century. Surviving manuscripts of the Welsh Laws suggest there was little institutional ownership of the woods at this time – people were largely free to use them for hunting and as a source of fuel and raw materials for building and utensils.

The laws made specific reference to *coed cadw* (preserved woodland) – a legal term for woodland that was protected for pannage and wood products. But there was also reference to *fforest y brenin* (the king's forest), a term used in relation to land that had been reserved for royal hunting.

We reached the entrance to Park Wood, one of those under-the-radar pieces of woodland that only local people really know about. It wasn't listed on the Woodland Trust map of woods in Wales but it's exactly the type of small, mixed woodland that could help piece together a navigable National Forest route through Wales. I couldn't find anything about its history but it felt like the sort of woodland that local folks in the age of Hywel Dda would have relied on. And it wouldn't have sat isolated like it does today – a lone island of woodland in a sea of farmland. The *Book of Llandaff*, a 12th-century account of all the land that the church's seat of power claimed to own, describes how much of this area was well-wooded – it provided numerous mentions of forests, woods and groves, and also described how species including alder, willow, yews and ash were used as boundary features, marker trees or woods.

Normally in summer, the route I'd chosen through the wood – The Graig Diamond Jubilee Path – would have been perfect for a walk. Today was not that day. Someone had ridden horses through here in the past few days and the track was now little more than a churned-up river of mud – so much so that we were forced to pick our way through the stinging nettles and bracken on the fringes of the path until we finally made it to open ground next to the Afon Rhymni (Rhymney River).

Here, the fields were alive with purple, yellow and white wildflowers. Orange and black butterflies – Painted Ladies perhaps – darted through the meadow. Our plan was to pick up another local path, the Rhymney River Circular Walk, that would take us into Draethen and then on to Rudry. We soon found a path running next to the river. It wasn't the most obvious of walking trails but it was headed in the right direction and we agreed it made sense to follow it. As a bonus, it ran by the side of a broad bean field. Jeff popped a few in his bag: 'These will make lovely frittata later,' he said.

In the distance we could see a lone walker heading towards us. He was a young man and exceptionally tall. 'It's a bit of a muddy adventure today,' I said to him by way of a greeting. 'Yeah, this trail has become very overgrown since I was last here six months ago,' he agreed.

What he didn't tell us was that the mud path was about to disappear into a cornfield. South Wales isn't particularly well known for prolific corn harvests but the hot weather we'd experienced at the height of lockdown in April had supercharged this particular crop. Some of the plants were well over eight-foot-tall and we were stuck in the middle of them.

Later, when reviewing exactly how an established walking path could disappear into a scene out of *Field of Dreams*, the enormity of my mistake became clear. In plotting the route using the online OS map, I'd confused the green dashed-line symbol of a bridleway with the grey dash symbol for a unitary authority (a form of local government). Apparently one of these boundaries ran along the Rhymney. To put it bluntly, the only way Jeff and I could have successfully completed this section of my planned route would have been if we were able to walk on water.

There was only one choice – to plough on and try and rejoin the trail near the river. For the next ten minutes we carefully navigated this maze of maize – walking down one row then moving laterally to another as if we were part of some giant game of Tetris – slowly inching our way west towards a footbridge over the river. The thick green corn leaves slapped our faces as we walked, stinging with each blow as if to scold us for my inability to read the map.

Finally, we emerged from the cornfield onto open land. Ahead of us we could see the river and could hear voices. Two people were walking on the other side. We'd found civilisation! What's more, they were on a real walking path.

The Normans Are Coming!

Just over a thousand years ago, all of the land in this part of south Wales would have been controlled by descendants of Welsh royalty. But change was coming from the east that would reshape Wales beyond recognition.

In 1066, William the Conqueror invaded the British Isles from Normandy, defeating the Saxon King Harold at the Battle of Hastings. And so the Norman Conquest of Britain began. William's French knights, lords and barons moved swiftly through England. However, making inroads into Wales proved a tougher proposition.

In the Welsh, the Normans encountered a populace who were used to living in the fluidity of constant domestic regime change, and could put up with the odd English incursion. The Normans, however, displayed a gratuitous cruelty that the Welsh wouldn't tolerate and so they started a 20-year campaign of guerrilla warfare – launching attacks from bases deep in the woods.

The Normans soon realised the threat posed by the woodland assaults. Over the next century they embarked on a military strategy not seen in Wales since Roman times – systematically felling forests to eliminate the threat of ambush. In 1277, during one particularly brutal act of arboricide, King Edward I advanced into north Wales from his border stronghold of Chester with a dual army – one made up of soldiers and another of woodsmen (including sawyers, woodcutters, carpenters and charcoal burners) who cut an invasion roadway some 230 metres wide, with another 60 metres of clearance on either side, through the dense forests for over 30 miles until they reached the town of Conwy.

The woodland historian, William Linnard, estimated that, to make way for this road, up to 2,000 acres of woodland were cut down in just four to five months. Another military tree attack took place not far from where we were walking right now. In 1287, a 600-strong force of woodsmen cut a path from Glamorgan to Brecon via the Taff Valley.

This process of taming the Welsh by felling the forests was repeated over and over until 1283 when Edward I took complete control of Wales by defeating Llywelyn the Last, King of Gwynedd. Ultimately, wrote Linnard,

'The axe and the flame were weapons just as important as the lance and bow.'

The threat posed to vulnerable communities by building roads through forests continues all over the world, though today's aggressors are often economic not military. Huge areas of tropical rainforest in Africa, Asia and South America have been opened up to agribusiness, oil and mining companies through the construction of exploration roads. Once built, settlers flood into the forest regions in search of land or work, clearing more of the forest and bringing with them diseases that local indigenous people can't fight (the common flu being particularly deadly) while transporting tropical viruses back to the cities.

Indeed, there is a growing body of scientific evidence that connects deforestation to the transmission of deadly pathogens such as the Nipah and Lassa viruses, and the spread of parasites that cause malaria and Lyme disease to people. One 2015 study of infectious diseases globally, conducted by US NGO, Ecohealth Alliance, found that nearly one in three outbreaks of new and emerging diseases were linked to deforestation and other drastic changes in land use.

Having fought our way out of the cornfield, we now reached Draethen, a pretty little village on the banks of the Rhymney, replete with rows of neatly painted white terraced stone cottages, a small grass playground and a rather enticing pub ... which was sadly closed. There was bunting up in the square and the locals were busying about their front gardens with an urgency that suggested they'd mistaken Jeff and I for the judges of the tidiest village in Wales award. Given how dishevelled we now looked following our cornfield adventure, that would be some case of mistaken identity.

My plan was to follow the public footpath that started by the red phone box opposite the pub and ran up the ridge into the Coed Cefn Pwll Du woods above the village. From there we'd follow the forestry track and then link up with a ridgeway walk to Caerphilly.

A man and his dog approached us as we reached the footpath stile.

'I wouldn't take that route if I was you,' he said. 'It's overgrown with brambles and stinging nettles.' The scrapes and blotches on his legs suggested he wasn't exaggerating. He pointed towards a country lane leading up around the woods and added, 'There's a much easier way to enter up there.'

So that's the detour we took. I was a little peeved to be pushed off the course I'd plotted – even more so when, after 15 minutes of walking, we still hadn't come across the supposed easier entrance. So, when I saw a break in the hedgerow and what looked like a walking path snaking its way into the woods, I impatiently persuaded Jeff to take my short cut. I reasoned that it was bound to link up with the main track we were looking for at some point.

Did I mention Jeff's two dodgy knees? Neither were suited for the type of scrambling climb I'd now got us into as we tried to reach the top of the woods. The tree trunks were thin and grew at contorted angles as if trying to keep their balance against steep angle of the ground. I crawled on my hands and knees up a particularly steep and slippery section. Jeff grabbed the branches of the thicker trees as leverage to haul himself up. One snapped in his hand and he slid back down the slope in a ski-less backward snowplough manoeuvre.

The forest floor was a tangle of undergrowth and the only reason we could even follow a path was because some fools had recently come down it on mountain bikes.

Actually, I also felt a bit of a fool. In my impetuousness to find a route through the woodland I really hadn't taken into account quite how either of us would handle the parts that would euphemistically be classed *off-piste*. No map had suggested this was the right way to go. I had assured Jeff that I knew what I was doing planning this walk. Clearly, that wasn't the case.

'It's not going to be easy getting the rescue helicopter to land around here,' I said to try and lighten the mood. I think Jeff laughed but it could well have been a curse.

Back on the main trail, we could see the off-piste triple black run of a climb I'd taken us on. Everywhere was pockmarked with large holes dug underground. These were the old lead and silver mines that had made this part of Glamorgan so important even before the Industrial Revolution took hold. It was a miracle we hadn't got ourselves stuck in one of them.

The Romans had exploited the mines when they were based in Caerleon and mining had continued at a pace throughout the proceeding centuries. Local industrialists worked and leased mines extensively in this woodland from the 17th century onwards – so much so that by the 19th century the land had been exhausted of its mineral wealth. So many mines had been dug that parts of the hillside woodlands from Draethen to Machen some four miles away resembled Swiss cheese.

Nowadays the forest had grown back with such vigour that many of the sunken holes had become camouflaged – so much so that the local council had cordoned them off, partly to stop idiots like me falling into them but also to prevent amateur spelunkers exploring and getting stuck.

The weather had stayed dry so far but now, as we walked through the heart of the wood, the heavens opened. We headed for cover under some large oaks, perching on two flat boulders for lunch. Jeff had made one of his favourite frittatas the previous evening. All I had was a disappointing, somewhat industrial-smelling, takeaway cheese and pickle sandwich.

A tall man in wet weather walking gear and Wellington boots walked by, flanked by two very large Dobermans. He had short grey hair and a ramrod straight military demeanour. The man stopped and the dogs stopped. He walked on ten feet – the dogs didn't move – until he dropped his hands either side of him in the form of a command. The dogs sunk forward slowly and joined him by his side. He looked down at them to make sure they knew he was in control and then they walked off together north, up a trail.

'Those are some very well-behaved dogs,' I said between bites of my sandwich. 'Yes, he's a man who looks like he knows his dogs,' said Jeff. 'Frankly I've always been scared stiff of Dobermans.'

I suddenly became aware of movement in my far left field of vision. As I turned my head, I caught a glimpse of a Doberman in full flight, hurtling towards me. The dog owner's cool, calm demeanour had disappeared, replaced with a mix of anger, frustration and a hint of resignation that suggested this wasn't the first time he'd been in this situation.

Within seconds, the dog was in front me, snout in my face, staring at my sandwich with an intensity that made me question just how much I really wanted it. To my left, Jeff was unusually quiet and stayed very, very still.

'What's in your sandwich, ham or cheese?' the owner called out to me.

'Cheese,' I replied meekly.

'Oh, that's his favourite. You're obviously downwind of him,' said the owner.

The man barked orders at the dog (I missed the name but it was something like mauler, destroyer or slayer). The hound took one more look at my lunch and then retreated.

'There, I told you that man knew his dogs well,' said Jeff when they'd gone.

We only had a few more miles to walk before we reached the town of Caerphilly. We were both quite fatigued. Not because the route itself was particularly arduous, but because my shortcuts had made it so. Yet despite the hiccups, today had been something of a revelation. We were only nine miles from home; I'd driven around this area many times. But I'd never explored – never mind got lost in – these woods and nature that were pretty much on my own doorstep. I felt like I was on a real adventure and it was exhilarating. What's more, I'd only just started.

A country lane led into the village of Rudry where we picked up a new footpath. It climbed through Coed Cefn-onn wood (the name in Welsh means hillside of ash trees) and emerged onto the ridgeway that separates Cardiff from Caerphilly and the threshold of the South Wales Valleys.

From this high vantage point, we could see the whole of Cardiff spread out below. The bronze-coloured dome of the Millennium Centre theatre shone bright, reflecting the late afternoon sun. The outsized exo-skeleton design of the Principality rugby stadium dominated the city centre – resembling an alien ship from *The War of the Worlds*. Off the coast, the islands of Steep Holm and Flat Holm sat like two giant stepping stones across the Bristol Channel.

Looking north one landmark dominated the surroundings: Caerphilly Castle. Its intimidating towers and moat overshadowed everything else around, as it had for nearly 1,000 years.

During the first two hundred years of occupation, the Norman lords built castles to protect themselves from wave after wave of Welsh rebellions– many feeding on the grievances of local people whose lands were being seized. Most Celtic castles had been erected using wood. The Normans put their faith in thick stone walls to repel their foes. In north Wales, King Edward I built what he termed a Ring of Iron – spending over £80,000 (about £58 million today) on fortifications. Here in south Wales, he constructed new castles or adapted old Welsh castles at Chepstow, Cardiff and Pembroke. But the biggest and most imposing of all was Caerphilly and it would play a dramatic role in reshaping the relationship of Welsh people to the woodlands they had long lived among and depended upon. It was also the starting point for our next walk.

4

~~~~~~

A New Forest Economy

Over the mountains from
Caerphilly to Pontypridd

By the early 14th century, the new English rulers had firmly stamped their authority on this part of Wales. Along with the lands in the south-west and most of the eastern border with England, it became part of Norman rule in Wales – known as the Marcher Wallia. The western part of mid-Wales along with north Wales remained independent. This was known as Pura Wallia.

Construction on Caerphilly Castle had started hurriedly in 1268 – the ruling lord of the area, Gilbert de Clare, was petrified of the threat posed by the new Welsh king, Llywelyn the Last, and so commissioned a formidable statement of defence and intent. It was the biggest castle in Wales and second only to Windsor in the whole of Britain. In total, the castle and its moat defences extended for more than 30 acres.

Caerphilly Castle was pretty much impenetrable and remained so for over 300 years until after the English Civil War when The Lord Protector, Oliver Cromwell, blew up one of its four stone turrets with gunpowder. Today, the damaged turret hangs off the rest of the castle by at least 10 degrees – that's a bigger lean than the Tower of Pisa. From across the moat, it looked like a giant had torn off a chunk of the castle with its bare hands.

The castle grounds were our starting point for today's walk. It was a beautiful morning and the water in the moat sparkled as the sunlight bounced off it. The torn tower was enjoying some extra support – someone had created a wooden sculpture of a man stood at the base of the ruin with his arms raised to help prop it up.

We were headed towards Pontypridd, an eight-mile trek based on the route I'd planned. ('Are you absolutely sure it's only eight miles?' asked Jeff, clearly a little sceptical about my route planning after our adventure in the woods above Draethen.)

Assuming everything went to plan, we would walk north up the Aber Valley towards the small village of Senghenydd before traversing Cefn Eglwysilan (the ridge of the church) and descending to where the Taff and Rhondda rivers meet.

We walked around the perimeter of the castle grounds, through a gaggle of geese and ducks looking to locate the Nant y Aber, one of three tributaries that flow into the Afon Rhymni. The route took us through a repetitive set of dull suburban housing complexes. 'This must have been beautiful before they made it a housing estate,' said Jeff. 'Like so much of the Valleys.'

Within a mile we had found what we were looking for – the Aber Cycleway, built on the site of the old Aber Valley branch railway line that transported thousands of tonnes of coal down from the Senghenydd and Windsor collieries to Cardiff docks.

Once an important part of the south Wales coal mining industry, the route was now used purely for leisure. This weekend morning, a small army of mountain bikers, dog walkers and families were out enjoying the elevated path. Dense thickets of rowan and hawthorn lined each side casting a mottled shade on the tarmac.

On the outskirts of Abertridwr, we came across a memorial to the old Windsor Colliery, where 155 miners lost their lives when it was in operation, from 1895 to 1986. It was an unusual-looking memorial. Its base was a 10-foot-high polygon. On top sat a sculpture of the old colliery perched on what looked like a silver flying saucer. On each side of the polygon were the names of the fallen miners.

Many of the local residents still remember the Windsor Colliery but I bet very few know just how significant this land was 800 years before.

There was no plaque, memorial or heritage marker to tell us but, at this moment, we were walking through the heart of what once was Caerphilly Castle's Norman deer park – one of the finest and largest in the whole of England and Wales. The park was enclosed by what was known as Senghenydd Dyke, a bank and ditch that ran for some nine miles round the current location of Senghenydd, and Abertridwr, enclosing 2,500 acres of upland woodlands in total. The dyke was constructed to face inward and would have been reinforced with up to 50,000 oak pales or stakes to prevent any deer escaping. Remnants of the ditch can still be seen on the outskirts of the two villages.

The Caerphilly deer park was one of some 3,000 created in Wales, England and Scotland between 1200 and 1350 partly to provide sport through hunting for the nobility but also to sustain the large volume of venison meat required for banquets and other high meals.

The Norman Marcher Lords who came to rule this part of south-east Wales, also established new 'forests' – a legally defined area of land (not necessarily woodlands) where Forest Law protected deer. Part of what we now consider Wentwood was one such 'forest'.

In his book, *Woodlands*, the ecological historian, Oliver Rackham, explains that: 'In South Wales, every petty marcher lord, seeking to be as good as the English king, declared the local mountain to be a Forest: there were more Forests than in all England, but hardly any were Royal.'*

People living near these new 'forests' found themselves at the mercy of a new three-layer system of legal bureaucracy set up to punish misuse of the land. It included new offences such as 'purpresture' (illegal enclosure of forest land), 'waste' (felling of trees), and 'assart' (the clearance of woodland to form arable land), along with illegal hunting and poaching.

The lower court was called the Woodmote. It referred cases up to the Swainmote, which tried the cases. The highest court of all was known as the Eyre of the Forest. The Forester's Court at Wentwood Forest, for example, was held twice a year in May and on Michaelmas

---

* *Woodlands* by Oliver Rackham, p. 120

Day (29 September). According to some accounts, punishments under Forest Law ranged from fines to blinding, castration and death.

However, the reality of how Forest Law was enforced suggests its draconian notoriety has been considerably inflated over the years. Rackham points out that Forest Law tended to issue monetary fines rather than blood-curdling punishments and even those fines were laxly enforced.

Nevertheless, the new laws still changed the relationship of Welsh people to the land. As Linnard writes in *Welsh Woods and Forests*, 'The establishment of special forest areas was new to Wales, and was resented by the people, because it involved the suspension of common law within a forest, and restrictions on or complete withdrawal of substantial areas of the common pasture. People dwelling in or near a forest were largely at the mercy of the forest officers in whom were vested arbitrary powers under the forest law, and who frequently abused these powers by petty tyranny and extortion.'*

The Cistercian Influence

On this warm afternoon, as we stood on the mountainside on the outskirts of Abertridwr, there were few signs of any homage to the Norman lords that once ruled the Aber Valley. In fact, the only nod to that bygone era was the local school, Ysgol Ifor Bach, located near the site of one of the deer park's main hunting lodges. It was named after the feisty Welsh lord who fought against the early Norman incursions into this part of Morgannwg before it was fully conquered.

Ifor ap Meurig aka Ifor Bach (Little Ivor) was Lord of Senghenydd and brother-in-law to Lord Rhys, the powerful ruler of Deheubarth in west Wales. In 1158, he launched a daring attack on Cardiff Castle, the seat of power of the Norman lord, William, Earl of Gloucester, who had laid claim to Ifor's lands. He scaled the castle walls with his bare hands, kidnapped William, his wife and daughter and brought them back here to the woods

---

* Linnard, p. 38

of the Aber Valley where he kept them hidden and held to ransom until William agreed to his demands. 'I bet local history lessons at this school are fun,' said Jeff as I described Ifor Bach's exploits.

The village of Abertridwr seemed to merge into neighbouring Senghenydd, as many of the old coal mining towns in the Valleys do. Often, the miner's houses were built just metres away from the entrance to the coal pit. As the town expanded, it would conjoin with neighbouring towns experiencing similar growth spurts. Only the sign for Senghenydd Rugby Club gave any indication that we'd left one village and entered another. Caught up in our chats while meandering around the memorial and school, we'd missed the walking trail and were now trekking up on the main road. We doubled back, walking around the rugby club until we found ourselves on the track leading directly to the old train station.

It was then that Jeff remembered he'd been to Senghenydd back in the 1980s when he and some other mutual friends were in a local band called Dada. 'This guy called Teto had seen us play down at the Poets Corner pub in Cardiff and invited us up,' he recalled. 'Said we were "proper good like" and booked us for the local pub. When we got up here to set up it was like the whole village had turned out – there were even old age pensioners skinning up joints in the corner of the bar.'

They weren't the only ones.

'When we asked where Teto was,' Jeff continued, 'his mates said he was in the nick down in Cardiff. Apparently, the police had busted the local pub a few days before and caught him disposing of evidence by eating a pound and a half of cannabis. They were waiting to question him, but he hadn't come down yet!'

The Aber Valley Cycleway ended at the old railway station in Senghenydd. We knew we'd arrived because the name of the town was painted in multihued graffiti across the hoardings of the iron bridge spanning the tracks. As we wandered through the streets of terraced houses, sardined together in rows running up the mountain, local people went about their business. One lady stood outside her front door, dressed in curlers and a pink dressing gown, chatting on a phone. A few doors down, a man wearing shorts and a white tank top stood waiting to greet his two children as they returned from Saturday morning rugby and dance lessons.

We pressed on to the top of the village, past the memorial to the Senghenydd mining disaster in 1913 when an explosion ripped through the local Universal Colliery, killing 439 miners. It was the worst coal mining disaster in British history. During that time of tragedy the eyes of the world were focused on Senghenydd. Today, the village feels forgotten; the memorial now the only reminder of the industry that made it famous – and infamous.

There was only one route out of the village up onto Eglwysilan Common – a winding, single-lane road – so we took our chances with the traffic. It was a steady climb and we had to jump into the hedgerow a few times as white vans and cars sped by. It felt like we'd stumbled onto a time-trial track for the local boy racers. We reached the top of the common just after midday, fatigued by climbing and in need of refreshment. This dice with the Valley's speed merchants didn't augur well for a national walking path so I doubled checked the map as we snacked on Cornish pasties. It turns out there was a real, actual public footpath we could have taken out of the village. Best keep this information to myself, I decided.

This was the northern tip of the ancient Senghenydd deer park where the ancient dyke fence looped away to the east. To the north we could see the mining towns of Nelson and Ystrad Mynach. In the distance, Pen y Fan, the highest peak in south Wales, rose up among the rest of the Brecon Beacons mountain range. We turned onto a dirt track that would lead us to towards Cefn Eglwysilan and the footpath down the mountain to Pontypridd. It was deserted apart from a few muddy long-tailed sheep.

This once was one of Wales's oldest pilgrimage routes, an ancient trail that the Cistercian monks from Llantarnam Abbey trod on their way to a holy shrine at Penrhys, 20 miles to the west. The Cistercians – a strict religious order hailing originally from the town of Cîteaux near Dijon in France – had been founded in 1098 as a breakaway from the Benedictine Order. Apparently, the Cistercian founders thought the Benedictines weren't austere enough. Dressed all in white, as opposed to the black garb of the Benedictines, the Cistercians pledged themselves to a life of hard manual labour and developing what today we would consider sizeable agribusinesses.

The Cistercians had arrived in Wales at the invitation of their fellow French Norman Lords. They quickly established important and influential monasteries at sites like Margam near Swansea, Ystrad Flur in mid-Wales, Cymmer in north Wales, Tintern on the border with England at the Afon Gwy (River Wye) and Llantarnam to the north of Newport. They brought with them an air of European sophistication – you might call it a Cistercian *je ne sais quoi* – to life in Wales, as well as a devotion to strict Christian doctrine that the Norman lords and knights were sorely lacking.

The Cistercians placed such importance on agriculture that very high-quality land standards had to be met before they agreed to establish a new monastery in an area. When a Marcher lord invited the Cistercians to establish an abbey, they first sent an advance team to assess the viability of the land before accepting.

This commitment to agriculture would have major ramifications for the woodlands that became part of the Cistercian estates. The monks felled large numbers of trees for assarting (clearing land for agriculture). According to one account by Gerald of Wales, the monks at one abbey on the Welsh/English border 'changed [one of the finest] oak wood[s] into a wheat field.' The monks also cut down forests on the order of local authorities in an attempt to stem crimes such as robberies and murders.

The biggest long-term impact of the monks' agricultural prowess came from their introduction of large-scale sheep farming. In 1291, the official *Taxatio Ecclesiastica* (a census of taxation on churches in England, Wales and Ireland) reported that just six monasteries in Wales were responsible for more than 18,000 sheep. The monks maintained these flocks by clearing large tracts of woodland for extensive open pasture enclosures and by letting sheep graze the surrounding woodlands that remained.

Over time the growing sheep population of Wales started to permanently reshape the Welsh landscape. As the sheep steadily grazed their way through the cleared uplands of Wales, they became a dominant barrier to any chances that natural woodlands could reforest – every time a new sapling started to grow, the sheep would devour it.

The Industrial Age Is Born

After 10 minutes on the track, we came across a truly bizarre sight. Fly-tippers had dumped an old sofa, an armchair and what looked like a dining room sideboard and a herd of cows had settled among the furniture. It looked like they were preparing for an evening in front of the television.

We had walked in a semicircle around the mountain. In the distance, we could see the twin hills of the Wenallt and the Garth that straddle the River Taff, standing like sentinels guarding the approach to Cardiff and the sea. At the foot of the Wenallt, just out of view, sat Castell Coch, the attention-grabbing Victorian Gothic Pennant sandstone fairytale castle.

Nowadays, Castell Coch is one of south Wales's top tourist attractions, partly because it seems so out of place compared to the rest of its surroundings. The castle looks like it belongs in the Austrian Tyrol, not the outskirts of Cardiff. It was built at the height of the industrial boom in south Wales – one that transformed this region from a rural backwater to an industrial giant – and is a reminder of just how much wealth was created from the mineral deposits of iron and coal discovered in this small part of the world.

Ironmaking had been practised in Wales on a small scale since the 16th century, mainly in rural areas using charcoal from coppiced woods as fuel for furnaces. By the mid-18th century, however, coal had replaced charcoal because it burned hotter and longer. So it made sense to locate the new ironworks near to known coal seams in the South Wales Valleys. By far the largest of these ironworks was Cyfarthfa in Merthyr, some 12 miles up the Taff Valley from where we were standing.

Cyfarthfa was started by the Homfray family of Cardiff but was taken over and revamped by a Yorkshire industrialist, Richard Crawshay, in 1786. He went on to create the world's most important ironworks (producing

29,000 tons of iron at its peak) by adapting and improving Henry Cort's pioneering puddling technique for making 'pig iron'. Known as the Welsh Method, Crawshay's approach provided a better way to turn the brittle pig iron into more robust and useful wrought iron, and it would soon be adopted all over the world – not least in the ironworks of Pennsylvania and Ohio in the United States.

The Cyfarthfa blast furnace was enormous and the working and living conditions for those employed there were incredibly hard. The Victorian travel writer, George Borrow, for one, was horrified when he visited Merthyr – as he described in his 1862 book, *Wild Wales*. On his approach to the town he was surprised to see a 'glowing mountain'. This was the red-hot dross from the Cyfarthfa iron works, lying discarded on the hillsides. Once in the town, his shock was compounded at the way industry had blighted the landscape and lives of the people. He wrote: 'There is the hall of the Iron, with its arches, from whence proceeds incessantly a thundering noise of hammers. Then there is an edifice at the foot of a mountain, halfway up the side of which is a blasted forest and on the top an enormous crag.' Merthyr, Borrow concluded, possessed 'a horrid Satanic character'.

The success of Cyfarthfa and other local ironworks was dependent on plentiful supplies of coal. Here in south Wales, industrialists stumbled on some of the richest deposits ever discovered. In the subsequent decades, the coal industry would eclipse the economic power of the ironworks it had initially meant to service.

The south Wales coalfields are what remains of an ancient wetland forest that extended over large areas of the tropics about 300 million years ago (known as the Late Carboniferous Period). They are known to geologists as the Coal Forests but were very different to the forests we know today. The main plants were tree-like lycophyte mosses – they could grow up to 50 m tall and their trunk consisted of a soft cork-like tissue that allowed the plants to grow to their full size in as little as 10 years. When they reached full size these lycophytes reproduced by producing cones and then died.

The rapid life and death cycle of these plants resulted in vast quantities of peat accumulating on the forest floor. Over time, the peat was consolidated and converted by the pressure of overlying layers into seams of coal.

One man, John Crichton-Stuart, the Second Marquess of Bute, understood the potential of south Wales coal before everyone else. He jump-started the mining industry that reshaped the economy and landscape of Wales and changed the world. Bute was not a geologist or even a particularly keen advocate of mining. His family were Scottish aristocrats and landowners. But, at the turn of the 19th century, some of the land his family owned in northern England had proved quite lucrative because of the coal seams sitting below it. The Bute family also owned thousands of acres of rural land in the Glamorgan valleys – the landscape we were looking down on now – and also laid claim to many thousands of acres more of common land through ancient feudal titles.

In the early years of the 19th century, geological surveys had identified potential rich veins of coal under these lands. Bute moved quickly to consolidate his holdings – buying new parcels of land close to potential coal seams so that he would own the mineral rights. It was a risky strategy because, while the Butes were land rich, they were cash poor. However, it paid off. The Butes' land prospecting in the Taff, Cynon and Rhondda valleys would form the foundation of the biggest coal mining industry in the world. Crichton-Stuart also realised that if Welsh iron and coal was to truly prosper it would need to be exported by sea. And that would entail crossing his land. So he set about building rail and canal transportation links across the new industrial heartlands in the valleys and developing the port in Cardiff. Within half a century, the Bute family had established itself, arguably, as the most influential in all of south Wales. So much so that they even acquired a derelict castle in the woods overlooking Cardiff and rebuilt it: its name was Castell Coch.

5

The Original Black Gold

A walk from the outskirts of Pontypridd to the Bwlch Mountain

The next weekend's walk began in the car park of Rhondda Heritage Park – a museum devoted to south Wales's coal mining past – a few miles outside of Pontypridd town centre. The plan was to walk up to the Cistercian pilgrimage site of Penrhys and then climb Bwlch y Clawdd, a small mountain 439 metres high, some 12 miles north-west of where we currently stood.

Both Andy and Jeff had agreed to tag along for another day's walk and I'd also invited another mutual friend, Tim, to join us. Tim and Jeff had been friends for nearly 50 years, having grown up together; Tim had been the lead singer in the band with Jeff and now worked in event management. I'd done many walks and mountain hikes with him over the years, so I knew he'd be up for a bit of modern tramping.

Our starting point was well-suited for a walk through the history of the industrial valleys. From the mining museum we traversed the back streets of Porth, passing through row upon row of terraced houses – homes built in the 19th century to accommodate the mine workers.

We cut through the busy car park of the local Morrisons supermarket. 'This is quite the forest walk you're taking us on,' said Tim. 'You're new to this, you have to suspend your disbelief and go along with his madcap routes. It's all liminal apparently,' Jeff reassured him.

This wasn't exactly the ringing endorsement of my journey planning that I'd been hoping for but at least I had a good reason for bringing us here. One hundred and seventy years before this had been the site of Cymmer Colliery, one of the most important and most notorious mines in the history of the Welsh coal industry. It was owned by the Insole family, who pioneered and made a killing (literally) off the mining and export of coal.

The Insoles hailed from Worcester in England but settled in south Wales at the turn of the 19th century. Using the wealth from their coal business, the Insoles first bought and then developed a grand double-gabled mid-Victorian mansion named Ely Court in Llandaff, on the sleepy outskirts of Cardiff.

Both Andy and I grew up in the shadows of the mansion, now known as Insole Court. The semi-detached home I lived in backed onto the mansion's gardens which, when I was a child, provided a vast playground for all the kids in our neighbourhood. I remember sitting on the stone lion sculptures at the top of the main lawn and playing hide-and-seek in the 'fairy garden' at the bottom of the grounds when I was very young. By the time Andy and I had reached our early teens we were using the lower paddock of Insole Court as our cricket pitch, sturdy trees forming wickets.

George Insole arrived in Cardiff as a young entrepreneur in 1827 when coal was just a minor player in the industry of south Wales. At the time there were only two collieries in the lower Rhondda Valley – mainly providing coke fuel for the booming ironworks industry. Cardiff, though already established as the shipping port for the local iron industry, handled very little coal and was still a fairly small market town. Insole saw an opportunity to export coal by ship first to England and later Ireland – a career move that would turn his family into one of the most influential forces in the history of coal.

For nearly 25 years, George Insole ran a steady if unexceptional business shipping coking coal. However, to gain more market share and fend off a competitor (the wonderfully named Walter Coffin), Insole speculated by buying mineral rights and then building collieries.

In 1844, Insole and his son, James, secured a 70-year lease for the mineral rights below 375 acres of land owned by Evan Morgan of Tyn-Y-Cymmer Farm, 20 miles north of Cardiff. A local artist, John Petherick, painted the rural hamlet at the time. His work now sits in the National Museum of Wales in Cardiff. It depicts a few houses and farms along with one Independent Chapel nestled amid rolling hills and thick deciduous woodlands.

Needing to attract miners, the Insoles built 50 cottages in Cymmer. They also established another new settlement across the river in Porth that became known as America Fach (little America) because it attracted so many expatriates who had left Wales for a better life in the US but were lured back by the coal boom. America Fach even had a local pub called The New York Hotel, which still stands today.

It wasn't just Welsh expats who came to the Valleys to work the mines. People flocked there from England, Scotland, Ireland and all across Europe. Many families from southern Italy escaped the poverty of their homeland, establishing cafés called bracchis to serve the workers.

By 1847, the Insoles had the Cymmer Old Pit up and running, sending over 5,000 tonnes of bituminous coal to Cardiff via a new branch of the increasingly influential Taff Vale Railway. This type of coal was instrumental in powering the new Victorian advances in street lighting and heating. Such was the demand that mining operations at Cymmer were extended. Soon new coal speculators were flocking to the Rhondda Fawr valley.

George Insole suffered a stroke Christmas Day, 1850 and died one week later. James, just 29 years old at the time, now took over the full running of the business. Headstrong and eager to build on his father's legacy, James rapidly increased production at Cymmer, sinking a second pit, the New Cymmer, partly to meet the increased demand for coal due to the outbreak of the Crimean War in 1854. The younger Insole doubled the workforce to 160 men and boys and further expanded the underground reach of the mines. But he did so without increasing the number of ventilation shafts needed to keep air flowing underground and minimise the build-up of flammable gases – notably methane, which was known in the industry as firedamp.

There was scant attention paid to the safety of mine workers at the time, and government regulation of this new industry was woeful. On the morning of Tuesday 15 July 1856 disaster struck at the Old Pit. At six in the morning, just as 160 men and boys descended the shaft to begin their shift, a huge explosion ripped through the mine killing 114, some as young as 10 years old.

Later, the government Mine Inspector's report would call the Cymmer disaster 'a sacrifice of human life unparalleled in the history of Britain at that time.' It shattered the communities of Cymmer and Porth. At the inquest, convened at the Butcher's Arms pub in nearby Pontypridd, it became all too clear that the safety precautions at the colliery were minimal, and even those had been ignored. Survivors testified that pockets of gas were an everyday feature of life below ground, and that it was commonplace for the workers to carry naked flames down into the mines.

In short, Cymmer was a disaster waiting to happen but James Insole, who was the first witness to testify at the inquest, denied all responsibility for the management of the colliery. Instead he laid the blame on the colliery manager Jabez Thomas and his team. A year later, Thomas and four senior officials at the mine were found guilty of manslaughter, though this verdict was later overturned.

Just seven months after the disaster, James Insole and his family moved into the mansion and would spend the next decades transforming it into one of Cardiff's finest private estates. Standing in front of the Cymmer memorial, it was hard to reconcile the happy memories I had playing in Insole Court with the knowledge that the house had been built on the sacrifice of those men and boys who perished below our feet.

On the Pilgrimage Path

We left the legacy of the Cymmer disaster behind us and headed towards the far side of Porth, crossing the garish concrete and steel bridge that straddled the confluence of the Rhondda Fawr and Fach (big and small) rivers as it became one, flowing downstream towards Pontypridd where it joined the River Taff. Porth means gate in Welsh and the town gets its name from being the gateway to the two river valleys.

Today, the Rhondda River was clear but just 40 years ago it would have been black as soot, polluted by mine water industrial tailings that were pumped directly into the river. When the mines had been at their peak a century before, domestic sewage from the towns also flowed into the river.

As kids growing up in Cardiff in the early 1970s, we were always warned to stay away from the River Taff because it was so polluted. I remember it being a murky black colour as it flowed out to sea. It wasn't until the 1990s, with the coal industry in mortal decline, that fish, birds and other wildlife started to populate the river once again.

Our route today aimed to bisect the Rhondda Fawr and Fach valleys by climbing up over Mynydd Troed-y-Rhiw (which confusingly translates as the mountain at the foot of the hill) by way of a bridleway and public footpath.

The path began at the driveway of a set of farm buildings situated at the very top of a very steep street. Rusting, stripped-down cars lay discarded around the yard and what once had probably been the main farmhouse now appeared to be mainly inhabited by chickens.

The path rose above the local cemetery. We followed it until we reached the outer perimeter of Rhondda Golf Club. The morning chill had burned off and we took the opportunity to shed a layer while we waited for one group of golfers to tee-off before we walked through. The course was packed this Sunday morning with groups of middle-aged men splaying golf balls all over the shop. You could tell they considered the four of us quite a curious spectacle.

'Nice day for a walk,' said one of the men as we passed by. 'Where are you going?'

'Penrhys,' I said. His face was a picture of astonishment as he replied. 'Penrhys? Why?'

His reaction was understandable. Sitting ahead of us in the distance, isolated on top of a mountain, was one of Wales's most misguided urban experiments – a 1960s public housing project intended to provide support for the mining community but which quickly became a symbol of neglect and decline.

The Penrhys estate had been unveiled, inauspiciously it would turn out, on Friday 13 September 1968. It sat high on a hill above its immediate neighbours, the villages of Llwynypia to the south-west and Tylorstown to the east. Its design was distinctly modern – a maze of concrete pods that was the very opposite of the compact terraced houses that hugged the sides of the valleys down below. It had been built to provide affordable housing for coal miners and their families but, with the coal industry in steep decline, most of its first residents were unemployed and had been forced to relocate there by the local town councils. As one local wrote in a letter to the *Rhondda Leader* newspaper, 'It's a ghost town before it starts.'

Whether it was warranted or not, the estate quickly gained a reputation for being a dysfunctional dumping ground for families who had fallen through the cracks. By the 1980s, unemployment on the estate stood at 93 per cent and arson and street violence were rife. In the 1990s nearly two-thirds of the estate was demolished with the remaining houses given a facelift. Today, just 800 people live in Penrhys. However, they enjoy some of the best views in south Wales.

So you can see how, over the past 50 years, Penrhys had developed a reputation as a place to avoid. Back in medieval times, however, this was *the* place to visit – perhaps the most important destination in all of Wales for the pious and wealthy as they embraced pilgrimage – one of the earliest forms of tourism. The modern Penrhys was even built on the site of a manor house and hostel affiliated to the great Cistercian Abbey at Llantarnam.

The central attraction for medieval pilgrims was the Shrine of the Virgin Mary located next to a holy well, Ffynnon Fair (St Mary's well). According to local legend, a beautiful statue of the Virgin Mary had first appeared in the branches of an oak tree near the well. People tried to take the statue from the oak but even the combined efforts of eight oxen could not release it. Only when the monks of Llantarnam built a chapel to celebrate the shrine was the statue set free by the oak.

As the story spread, the monks had to build a hostel to accommodate all the pilgrims who came to see the miracle. By the 15th century, Penrhys's reputation as a holy site was known far and wide. Gwilym Tew, a famous Welsh bard of the time, described Penrhys as, 'an island at the forest's edge … with consecrated bread and holy water.'

Such was the importance of Penrhys to the Catholic church in Wales that, when King Henry VIII set about the dissolution of the monasteries in 1536, his consigliere Thomas Cromwell dispatched local officials to destroy the shrine and seize the statue. In 1538, it was taken to London where it was publicly burned with other sacred Catholic artefacts.

However, the holy well survived the attack and Penrhys's reputation only increased. Folk tales recount how travellers, lost in the mountain mist, would be guided to safety by a tall female figure carrying a light.

Today, you can still visit the holy well. It lies very much off the beaten and muddy track – secluded some 200 feet below a replacement modern stone shrine to Mary that was erected at the top of the hill in 1953. We had to slide down the path to get to the well. It's not much to look at nowadays – the spring is protected by a nondescript stone cradle and has none of the tourism information you might expect explaining a place of such historical and spiritual importance.

To be fair, some effort had been made to make Ffynnon Fair more accessible. In recent years a set of concrete steps had been laid down near the entrance. But it was a token effort and even the workers who laid the steps were unimpressed We could clearly read a message scrawled into the concrete: 'The boss is shit.'

Full Steam Ahead

It was time to move on. We climbed back up the grass hill to the new stone shrine. We navigated our way around the Penrhys estate towards Mynydd Ty'n-Tyle and the tightly planted conifers of Penrhys wood that sprouted up above it. From a distance, the mountain looked like it had a Mohican haircut.

A wide forestry track led out onto the heart of the mountain. The weather was fresh but clear. It felt invigorating to be exploring a part of south Wales I didn't even know existed a few weeks before. What's more, this track led straight down the mountain without any further need for map reading. Just as I was congratulating myself on my navigation prowess, we arrived at the entrance of a large windfarm. The access road was blocked by a steel gate and a large sign told us to keep out – this was private land. I was sure this was a public footpath when I'd mapped out the route earlier in the week, I explained. Jeff gave the others a knowing glance, our recent misadventures in a corn field and in Machen woods still fresh in his mind.

Clearly, I'd have to find a new route for my National Forest walking path that avoided the windfarm – perhaps by heading a bit further north through the large Llanwynno Forest on the other side of the Rhondda Fach. But, right now, we needed to reach the top of the Bwlch Mountain by the time the daylight faded and we were still two hours' walk away. So, just for today, we agreed to ignore the sign, hop the fence and keep on moving.

The wind turbines were majestic and mostly quiet, despite spinning with considerable speed. Walking through this new generation of Rhondda industry, it felt like the energy equation truly had been turned on its head. Once, local people dug deep underground for the fuel to power their homes and businesses. Today that energy was being harnessed from the skies above. The wind energy revolution was cleaner and healthier for everyone, though it employed a fraction of the workers who once made a decent living from coal.

High above the Rhondda Fawr Valley, we could see how the towns of Tonypandy, Llwynypia, Ystrad, Gelli, Ton Pentre and Treorchy all butted up against together and snaked their way up the valley on either side of the river. Just over a century ago, this was the epicentre of the Rhondda Valley coal boom.

Back in 1851, less than a thousand people lived in Rhondda Fawr. By 1911, the population had jumped to 150,000. The catalyst was coal, but not the coking variety James Insole first exploited in Cymmer. No, what made this part of Wales so important to the global economy was a new seam of coal found much deeper underground – anthracite or steam coal as it was known.

The steam engine revolution (powered by steam coal) had been slowly transforming industrial output across the United Kingdom for nearly 50 years. However, in 1851, a report by the British Admiralty dramatically changed the fortunes of the coal mines of south Wales. It concluded that, for the British Navy to command hegemony across the high seas, it would require a constant supply of Welsh steam coal because it burned cleaner and longer than other veins of coal. That meant the Navy ships would be harder to spot at sea and they would need to carry less of it.

Soon, Welsh steam coal was in demand throughout the world. Steam engine technology also had allowed mine owners to drill deeper pits so new collieries sprung up throughout south Wales in rapid succession. The Insole family had been trading steam coal since the 1830s but now their wealth, along with other coal merchants, soared as new concessions opened throughout the Valleys.

Building and maintaining those new mines required large amounts of pitwood. So, once more, forests and woodland were 'harvested' for industry. That didn't mean these new industrial giants destroyed the woodlands. Much of the pitwood they needed was sourced from local oak woodlands that were coppiced to allow regrowth. As Oliver Rackham explained in his book, *Woodlands*: 'The thesis that woods were destroyed by heavy industries cannot be sustained. On the contrary, wherever there remained a big concentration of woodland, there is an industrial or urban use to account for its preservation.'

However, due to the high demand for timber, many landowners started to convert ancient oak woods into new plantations consisting of fast-growing soft wood such as larch and conifers. Some of the biggest mines had direct connections to these forestry estates but even that supply wasn't enough. Soon the mine owners were buying vast amounts of timber from all over Wales. By the late 19th century, Wales was importing large quantities of pitwood from Europe – 226,000 tonnes arrived in Cardiff alone in 1882 according to local records. No wonder Andy's grand-father had been so nonplussed by plans to plant new trees in Wentwood Forest.

We had come down off the mountain, exiting through hillside farm-ing fields into the terraced streets of Ystrad before walking up William Street to the town of Ton Pentre. Here, we crossed over the Rhondda Fawr River and climbed up to the streets that led towards Bwlch Mountain. We paused for a few minutes, admiring the view back down the valley and quietly preparing ourselves for what we could see was going to be a challenging final climb at the end of an already long day.

You wouldn't know it today but, 150 years ago, Ton Pentre was the most important steam coal centre in the world – a boom and bust tale that rivals the great oil discoveries at Oil City in Pennsylvania or Spindletop in Texas.

In 1864, David Davies, a successful railway owner from Llandinam in mid-Wales, took out a mining lease on land just above the current town of Ton Pentre. For nearly 15 months Davies's men searched for a workable seam of coal with no luck. The cost of prospecting exhausted Davies's funds so, one morning, he gathered the men together to pay them their final wages. To demonstrate how he'd run out of money, Davies put his hand into his pocket, took out his last half-crown and held it aloft. 'There you are. That's all I've got,' he said. Someone in the crowd shouted, 'Well we'll have that as well!'

Davies, possibly out of disgust or maybe just resigned to his fate, threw that last coin into the crowd. The workers were so impressed by the gesture that they voted then and there to dig for one more week without pay. On the very last day, they hit upon a thick seam of steam coal – one of the biggest strikes ever in south Wales. David Davies's business was saved and the Rhondda Fawr Valley would never be the same.

A muddy single-track winding path led out of Ton Pentre up onto the Bwlch. We were weary after a long day so our ascent was not much more than a measured plod past yet another old Iron Age fort (I was getting a little blasé about ancient history at this point) and the imposing Llwynypia Forest that towered above us to our left.

'I bloody well hope we're not climbing up through there,' said Jeff, vocalising all our concerns.

Halfway up, we stopped to catch our breath and to marvel that some-one had installed a park bench high up on one side of the ridge. When I checked Google maps later, I saw the location had been tagged as 'Percy's tiny bench'.

The car park at the top of the Bwlch was now in sight and it was busy with sightseers on what had turned into a warm and sunny afternoon. The views from the mountain were stunning. We could see the elaborate hairpin bends in the road leading over the mountain and, at the bottom of the valley, the site of the former Parc Colliery at Cwmparc. Behind it, in distance, we could just make out the top of Pen y Fan.

As we got closer to the car park however it was clear not everyone had respect for the beauty surrounding them. The slopes directly below were littered with discarded beer cans, soft drink bottles and crisp packets. Far down the valley, stuck in a ravine, was a car's rusting chassis. Three teen-agers picked their way down the mountain to take selfies next to it. Right now, at this inspiring summit, it was clear just how disconnected so much of society had become from nature.

6

Stranded Assets

*A frustrating attempt to walk
from the Bwlch to Maesteg*

The next day, Andy, Jeff and I returned to the top of the Bwlch to continue our trek across the Valleys – Tim had gone back to work. Our goal was to reach the town of Neath just north of Swansea by going via Maesteg and the Spirit of Llynfi woodlands – a designated part of the proposed National Forest. We would follow one of the ancient Celtic walking trails over the mountains, which once helped people avoid walking through the thick oak forest that once dominated the valleys below.

The weather was damp and extremely foggy – we couldn't see more than 10 metres ahead of us, never mind the bottom of the valley. This was a little worrying given that the route I'd chosen involved traversing the Craig Ogwr ridgeway with a 200-metre sheer drop on its south side.

Nevertheless, we pressed on, following a dirt-and-stone public footpath that led off over the ridge from the car park. The previous day, we'd seen a group of some 20 dirt bikers gathered up here, revving their engines hard and making tracks through the hillside. Now we witnessed the full extent of the damage they'd caused. The top of the ridge should have been a carpet of soft, mossy deep green grass. Instead, it had been carved, slashed and churned apart by hundreds of tyre tracks as the bikers scaled a steep gradient of the ridgeway. Deep puddles of dirty water had formed in tracks on even ground making our attempts to walk the ridgeway even more precarious.

It was such a depressing sight. The bikers were most likely locals (we'd seen people washing down their muddy bikes at a petrol station when we'd walked through Ton Pentre). How could they have such little regard for the natural beauty right on their doorstep?

Unfortunately, this was a recurring theme wherever I'd walked so far in south Wales. Incredible woodlands, mountains and valleys were taken for granted by people – often licensed, but barely regulated, contractors – who used them for dumping rubbish and thought nothing of destroying the habitat and the history connected to it. On the one hand, I really felt that this landscape would be better off without this environmental wrecking crew. On the other, I felt sorry for them; how they couldn't appreciate being around nature without damaging it.

What did it say about the damaged psyche of a society that could rip up places of such obvious beauty without any concern? Was this the ultimate legacy of our modern, industrialised world – to have lost that fundamental connection to nature at exactly the time when we needed it most of all?

An Industry Lost

As with so many other parts of the Agrarian and Industrial Revolutions, Wales's coal boom fundamentally altered people's relationship to the countryside. Just as the Welsh language was undermined by the move from rural areas to the new towns that grew up around the coal mines, so was people's connection to the land. Many of the new town dwellers who came from all over Britain had been forced into urban living after the common land they depended on for subsidence farming and grazing had been awarded to private landowners through Acts of Enclosure – a legal process that intensified across England and Wales in the late 18th and early 19th centuries in the pursuit of more intensive and productive agriculture. They were no longer reliant on growing their own food or tending their own livestock – their provisions came from the local shops serving the mining communities and their daily lives were divorced from the rhythms and cycles of nature (though that's not trying to sugarcoat the many challenges of poor rural living during this time).

The immigrants who settled in the South Wales Valleys during this coal rush came looking for, and expecting, a better life than the one they had left behind, whether it had been in rural mid-Wales, the English Midlands, Ireland or beyond. Huge fortunes were made but the real wealth was generated and remained in Cardiff, Barry, Newport and Swansea, where the coal was sold and exported. Very little, if any, of that vast wealth flowed back up the valleys to the mining towns we were looking down on now.

The early morning mist had cleared and below us on either side of the mountain we could spot stranded ex-coal villages – strange mini-pockets of humanity jammed in among the steep sided valleys. On our left was Nant-y-Moel – once home to the Wyndham/Western Colliery until it closed down in 1984. To our right we could just make out the fringes of Abergwynfi and Blaengwynfi, two sister mining communities on either side of the Afan River.

Perhaps the most sobering thing about the south Wales coal boom was how short it was. More than 57 million tons of coal was produced in 1913, by 232,000 men working in 620 mines in a thin corridor of valleys. By 1920 the industry employed 271,000 men across south Wales but in the following years demand for Welsh coal began to wane. Top-grade Welsh steam coal now faced new competition from mining operations in Germany and the United States, and from an existential threat – an oil industry that was fast replacing the old steam age.

Nearly 250 mines closed across south Wales between 1921 and 1926. That year, a Royal Commission concluded that the coal industry had to be reshaped and that miners needed to accept lower wages. The private mine owners jumped at the opportunity and demanded large cuts. The miners' union refused and, on 30th April, workers were locked out. Coalfields in south Wales and across the UK came to a halt.

For nine days, the UK economy was paralysed as most of the workforce went on strike to support the miners. However, on 12 May, other unions returned to work after agreeing terms with the Government. The miners carried on until the end of the year when starvation forced them back to work.

Many no longer had a job however. To stave off mass unemployment, the UK government put some miners to work on large-scale infrastructure projects including the Bwlch Mountain bypass (part of the larger Glamorgan Inter-Valley Road project), which was completed in 1928 and which we were walking above right now. Before the road was built, the mining towns had no way of accessing neighbouring valleys unless they undertook the type of hike we were on, following the ancient paths up and over the mountains.

The Bwlch bypass wasn't just a public works project to ease the unemployed miners' unrest – politicians in London also thought it could provide communities with a way to access nature and escape the often dark, dank existence at the foot of the valleys. For this reason, the road (with so many switchbacks it felt like navigating an alpine pass) was built to accommodate both motor vehicles and pedestrians. Over the decades, generation after generation of local sightseers hiked to the top of the mountain. The Bwlch became so popular that one enterprising Italian immigrant family set up an ice cream van in the car park at the summit. Their reputation grew to such an extent that the mountain is now known as Ice Cream Slope by the many hang-gliders who head up there to float on the thermals formed as warm air from the coast hits the cold air at the top of the mountain.

The other major project that the UK government put Welsh miners to work on after the First World War was planting vast forests of conifer trees. All across Wales, the Forestry Commission set up camps for miners – primarily to 'rehabilitate' and 'recondition' the men so that they were ready, once again, for tough manual labour. Here in the Ogmore and abutting Afan Valley, major new forest projects were launched. As we wandered now through a sprawling windfarm on our way to Maesteg we could see the results to the north of us – a wide carpet of connected coni-fer forest starting at Coed Bwlch and running across the horizon to Rheola Forest (where some 13,000 acres was planted over a 20-year period) near the town of Neath. This monocultured expanse would become known as Coed Morgannwg (Glamorgan Wood) and nowadays, Afan Argoed Forest Park.

Coal still employed 140,000 people in 1936 but south Wales had lost 241 mines since the end of the First World War. At the end of the Second World War, the UK government nationalised the coal industry, invested in new machinery and raised safety standards. However, the rise of the oil industry left coal unable to compete financially. More than 50 collieries closed between 1957 and 1967.

Even as the coal mines closed, their environmental legacy remained. Everywhere we walked in mining country, it was startling to see just how bare the hillsides above the towns and villages were. That's because much of the waste material from the mines had been dumped here. A few days before, as we'd walked through the windfarm above Penrhys, we'd seen for ourselves the problems this practice had caused.

Below us we'd looked down on Stanleytown and Tylorstown, once thriving coal villages named after English engineers who came to speculate for coal. Today, both villages sat stranded and forgotten in the steep, glacial valley of the Rhondda Fach.

Tylorstown, however, had been in the news just recently but not for good reasons. In February 2020, what used to be called 'unprecedented' heavy rainfall caused a 60,000-tonne landslide at the site of an old coal tip above the town. We could see it from our position on the mountain – a wide black scar on the hillside across from us.

Looking down at Tylorstown, it was hard not to think about another village just a few miles north-east: Aberfan. On 21 October 1966, at around 9.15 a.m., a coal tip that had been piled on a mountain slope above the town gave way, sending an avalanche of slurry pouring down upon Pantglas Junior School where the young students had just started their lessons. The entire school was engulfed in the avalanche and local people were forced to dig with their hands in a desperate and ultimately futile attempt to save the children. One hundred and nine pupils and five teachers died that morning.

The Aberfan disaster shocked the entire United Kingdom, reminding a nation of the brutal reality of its heavy industrial legacy. That shock turned to anger as it became clear the accident could have been prevented – reports revealed that the coal waste had been dumped over a natural spring and that the government-run National Coal Board had been aware that the tip was unstable. The tribunal convened to investigate the disaster laid the blame squarely on the Coal Board – writing that the 'Aberfan disaster could and should have been prevented.'

Today, there seems a very real danger that another Aberfan-style disaster might occur in the future. According to a recent report commissioned by the Welsh government, the Tylorstown tip was just one of nearly 300 old dumping grounds across the South Wales Valleys that are at significant risk of slippage – a threat that geologists warn is exacerbated by climate change.

Now, as we walked across the spine of mid-Glamorgan coal country, we began to play a new, dark, game: spot the disused coalmine. Often, it was easy – you just looked down the valley for the last row of houses and next to it would be a thin chunk of grassland where the pithead and colliery buildings would have been. Other times you could see how the land was shaped somewhat differently (often from where discarded coal tailings or slags had been dumped) or how the grass had a different hue to the rest of the ground around it.

We were deep in one of these conversations, walking on a public footpath through the windfarms north of Mynydd Llangeinwyr, when I decided to check the map. Once again we had ventured off track. At some point the footpath had split off from the windfarm utility road but none of us could remember seeing any alternative route. We could stay on this gravel track but it would take us miles away from what I thought had been a carefully planned route. My OS map showed that the track rejoined the elusive footpath about half a mile up the road so we carried on. When we got there, our route was blocked by a freshly constructed barbed wire fence. We were frustrated and we weren't the only ones – someone had cut the barbed wire next to a large wooden supporting post. We embraced their largesse and hopped over the defenceless fence.

Now we were headed due west, climbing over Mynydd Caerau, another of the seemingly endless mini-mountains in this area at the top of Ogmore Vale. We had another two miles until we reached the town of Maesteg and the weather on this exposed elevation was starting to worsen. A misty, chilly rain danced around our faces as we stopped for coffee. In front of us were two conifer plantations – Caerau and Garw forests. I checked the map and our route bisected them. After that it all looked easy-going and Maesteg would be squarely in our sights.

Map Mayhem in Maesteg

The south Wales coal industry limped on through the 1970s even as more pit closures and job losses ate away at the local communities. Then in 1984, Margaret Thatcher's government decided to push through a wave of new colliery closures that would deprive entire towns and communities of their *raison d'être*. In response, the National Union of Mineworkers (NUM) called a national strike that lasted for nearly a year. Striking miners were supported financially by fundraising efforts in the local community and beyond but, as the months went by and the Thatcher government grew more determined not just to win the strike but to destroy the NUM, it became increasingly hard for the mining towns to survive. When the strike collapsed, the south Wales mining industry was finished, its communities shell-shocked and abandoned.

For the Thatcher government, the decision to call time on mass coal production in Wales made economic sense. But business expediency can't excuse the brutal and cynical way they treated the people of south Wales. What stung most back then was the knowledge that there were still great quantities of coal that could have been produced if the government had wanted to support the industry. Instead, it wanted to break the unions so an entire industry was shut down without any plan for how the local communities that were completely dependent on coal would survive and rebuild.

In the aftermath, the entire South Wales Valleys region descended into a spiral of economic and social depression, the effects of which continue to this day. Unemployment became chronic and crime rates soared, as did substance abuse, alcoholism and social unrest. Thirty years later, when Thatcher died at the age of 87 in 2013, many a pint was raised in the pubs throughout the valleys accompanied by a toast: 'Ding Dong … The Witch is Dead.'

The way the UK government destroyed the south Wales coal industry – and the fallout and stagnation that followed – should be a cautionary tale as global society plans its post-fossil fuel future. Today, governments all over the world are fast-tracking policies to wean industry and the public off coal and oil, a shift given fresh urgency as politicians start to grasp that the economic devastation brought by the Covid-19 pandemic is just a minor dress rehearsal for what climate change will bring.

We now know that the world must limit global warming to well below 2°C, preferably 1.5°C, compared to pre-industrial levels if we are to avoid the worst impacts of climate change. That means not just the end of all coal production but, ultimately, also oil exploration. Effectively, all the coal and most of the oil sitting under the earth has to be considered what economists call 'stranded assets' – natural resources that exist but can never be used.

When Welsh coal mining shut down, a generation of people lost their jobs, their pensions and their investments. Today most people's pensions are invested in some way in the oil industry and millions of people around the world are directly dependent on producing fossil fuels.*

The pandemic might have opened our eyes to the need to transition to a post-fossil fuel economy but unless we have a very clear roadmap

---

* To give one example, according to a 2021 Friends of the Earth Survey, UK pension funds have an estimated £128 billion invested in fossil fuels, equivalent to nearly £2,000 for every person in the country.

of how to proceed, and why it's important to do so, progress will be too slow, many will suffer and the much-needed energy transition's chances of success will rapidly diminish.

At the moment, people around the world feel just as lost, confused and depressed as the people in south Wales did when their world turned on its head. Collectively, we are trapped in that liminal state – we are looking for a better way of moving forward but we still have one foot stuck in the past. The world needs a new map – one that shows us how to appreciate, value and navigate our world without destroying it. And we need to find it fast.

Which, in a more literal way, was exactly how I felt at that moment. We had made it up onto Mynydd Pwll-yr-lwrch, the hill that overlooked Maesteg (one of the many towns left devastated when coal died), which spread out across the Llynfi Valley. It was much wider than the neighbouring Ogmore and Garw valleys we had walked above today and we could make out some of the course of the Llynfi River as it meandered down towards Bridgend and the sea. What we couldn't see was where the footpath was meant to be – the one oh-so-clearly marked in green on my OS map.

To make things worse, we were lost on a steep bit of hill. In front of us was thick bracken, boggy ground and big rocks but no discernible path. 'We have to find another route,' I said, deflated. On the OS map I could see there was a second footpath leading from the nearby Bryn Rhug farm a few hundred metres below us but reaching it meant scrambling over stone walls and through boggy terrain. The new path could provide us a clear route into the Spirit of Llynfi Woodland but committing to it meant surrendering the high ground we currently held. What if I sent us down the hill only to have to climb it again if the route didn't work out?

We briefly debated our options and agreed it was better to find the clearer route rather than plough on up the hill. So we picked our way down through thick, brown bracken and green, spiky tussocks growing out of the bog. We scrambled over derelict stone boundary walls and sloshed through soggy farmers' fields until we found a new, reliable, solid track that led into the Spirit of Llynfi.

This was a wake-up call. When I started planning my route through Wales I had assumed that, if the OS maps documented a footpath, it meant there was one. The reality was quite different. Footpaths are only as good as how often they are used. By trying to map an original walking route (albeit one that utilised existing paths) I was heading up and down routes that maybe hadn't been regularly walked in a long time. As we'd just discovered, sometimes those paths simply dissolved into overgrown landscape. At present, the route I was mapping was not fit for general public use. But I guess that's always the case when you're trying to create something original.

Part Two

The Power
of the Trees

7

Reconnecting through Community

A long hike from Maesteg to Upper Brynamman

The 75-acre Spirit of Llynfi Woodland sat just above Maesteg, on the site of the old Coegnant Colliery and Maesteg Washery that closed down in the 1980s. The land was elevated but not really a hill – in Welsh it was called Twmpath Mawr (the big hump). It had been established in 2015 as part of a 10-year regeneration project to reintroduce local people to the wealth of green space close by, to promote biodiversity and alleviate the likelihood of flooding. The Welsh government also hoped to promote the physical and mental health benefits of embracing nature and woodlands to a community with high levels of chronic illness and depression.

Five years later, over 60,000 trees had already been planted by the community and new walking and cycle paths had been constructed. The project was being funded through a Welsh government grant and also, partly, by the Ford Motor Company as many of the workers at its nearby Bridgend plant lived in the area.

'That's very corporate citizen of them,' said Andy as we walked towards the woodland's centre point – a 15-foot-tall carved oak statue of a miner known as the Keeper of the Colliery. 'But who is sponsoring the cows?'

In front of us, a herd of black cows surrounded the wooden miner. Some were munching on the grass. Others snacked on the plants and bushes lining the walking paths that spread out through the woodland. The animals stopped eating and stared at us in unison.

'I don't think those are cows,' said Jeff. 'Those are young Welsh black bullocks and I'm not sure we want to walk through them.'

I couldn't tell one cow from another but I do have a healthy sense of self-preservation. Jeff was right. Hastily, we retreated towards Maesteg. 'They weren't kidding when they said this park was all about reconnecting with nature,' said Andy.

We sought a new route through the woodland, backtracking until we reached a cycle path that ran on its southern perimeter just above the local high school. There we met a man walking in our direction, his dog running a little ahead. We gave him a heads-up about the bulls he was about to encounter.

'Oh bloody hell, not them again,' he said. 'They're becoming a right menace.'

As we walked north through the new woodland park we theorised about how big a menace this herd could be. I'd heard stories about people exploring the countryside during lockdown being sadly trampled by cows but fortunately the problem had hardly reached epidemic proportions.

'Perhaps they've organised into rival cow gangs,' suggested Jeff.

'Personally, I like the idea of Maesteg becoming the new Pamplona,' said Andy. 'It would certainly help boost tourism.'

The Spirit of Llynfi Woodland bordered the communities of Maesteg, Nantyffyllon and Caerau. I'd read about the latter village recently because it was part of Project Skyline, another new initiative aimed at helping local communities build stronger connections to the woodlands on their doorstep.

Central to Project Skyline was the belief that people become more engaged and invested with nature when they have a sense of 'ownership' of the land. Sometimes that involves communities actually buying some, but it can also mean managing and being stewards of publicly owned land.

In Scotland, community land ownership is reshaping a country where much rural real estate had been cordoned off by private estates. In 1997, the Isle of Eigg in the Inner Hebrides was the first major piece of land to be transferred from a private landowner into the stewardship of the local community. Since then, over 400 community land transfers have taken place – that's around 250,000 hectares or three per cent of Scotland.

Project Skyline aimed to bring that model to the South Wales Valleys and had chosen Caerau, along with two other old mining towns, Treherbert and Ynysowen, as test cases. In all three towns the local community would decide on the types of woodland relationship it wanted. Some might be commercial while other parts could be for recreation and greater community well-being. In some ways, the idea harked back to the relationship people might have had with woodlands back in the time of the medieval Welsh Laws. The big question people today were asked to consider was: what might a community choose to do with the land if it could plan not for the three years, but for three generations?

Whether the Skyline project ever becomes a reality is unclear but its vision – 'imagining a future where land is managed sustainably to meet the needs of the people who live there in a way that doesn't compromise the ability of future generations to meet their own needs' –sounds like a blueprint we need for all of society.

The Making of an Evolutionary

Castell-Nedd (perhaps better known in these parts by its English name, Neath) was once a strategically important Roman fort and, later, an industrial hub for coal mining and iron works taking place in the surrounding hills and valleys. Today those former glories have faded but local people still enjoy exploring Gnoll Country Park, once home to the Mackworth industrialist family. Next to the park sits Coed Brynau, a new woodland that was a pilot planting project for the new National Forest.

We'd arrived in Neath first by following St Illtyd's Walk, one of the long distance walking trails that help hikers traverse Wales. It took a northerly zigzag through Afan Argoed Forest Park, one of Wales's largest woodlands. It's also one of the UK's best mountain biking and trail walking destinations. *Mountain Bike Magazine* named the 48-acre site one of the top 10 places in the world to 'ride before you die'. Bikers come here from all over the world to tackle perilously technical trails with names like the Blade and the Wall, while walkers can explore many miles of paths through the conifers planted by ex-miners a century ago.

We veered off St Illtyd's Walk to wander on a new walking path that started in Pontrhydyfen, and built in honour of the actor Richard Burton who was born in the village. It followed the Afon Pelenna north-west towards Coed Brynau (Brynau Wood). Burton might be one of Wales's most famous sons, but I was more interested in walking in the footsteps of another local area resident. His name was Alfred Russel Wallace and today he is acknowledged as one of the most important thinkers on nature that ever lived.

Wallace was born in 1823 in the town of Usk, a few miles from where I had started walking a couple of weeks before. He was brought up in England but in 1841, he joined his brother in Neath to pursue a career as a land surveyor. Wallace fully embraced the return to his homeland, learning Welsh and lodging with Welsh-speaking families.

One of the projects Wallace worked on was the construction of a new railway line in the upper Neath Valley. Being there opened his eyes to the beauty of the surrounding countryside and he would spend his free time walking the hills and valleys.

I enjoyed myself immensely. [The work] took me up the south east side of the valley along pleasant lanes and paths, through woods and by stream and up one of the wildest and most picturesque little glens I have ever explored. Here we had to climb over huge rocks as big as houses, ascend cascades, and take cross levels up steep banks and precipices all densely wooded.

Wallace's experience in the Neath Valley convinced him that his true calling was studying nature, and zoology in particular. In 1848, Wallace travelled to South America where he spent the next four years studying the palm trees of the Amazon and embarking on scientific expeditions with other leading naturalists of the day. In 1852 Wallace moved from South America to the Malay Archipelago. There he collected more than 125,000 specimens, including more than 83,000 beetles, several thousand of which were completely new to Western science. It was during this trip that Wallace developed a historic scientific breakthrough: a theory of evolution by natural selection that proved to be identical to one being developed at the same time back in England by an already highly regarded naturalist called Charles Darwin.

Somewhat in the thrall of Darwin's reputation, Wallace wrote a letter to him, excitedly explaining his theory. Darwin was less than thrilled to receive the letter. He quickly contacted two powerful friends in the London scientific community and they arranged for both his and Wallace's evolutionary theories to be presented as a joint paper at a meeting of the Linnean Society on July 1, 1858, even though Darwin only had an abstract to share while Wallace had written a short but fully fleshed out paper. In doing so, Darwin's reputation was bolstered by Wallace's work and the following year the more established scientist would publish *On the Origin of Species* – the book that captured the imagination of the Victorian world. Over time it would be Darwin who gained the credit for developing the theory of evolution.

The Roman Road

Jeff's journey along my trail had ended and he'd returned to Cardiff to work. Andy, however, had agreed to accompany me on one further long trek before I headed north into Carmarthenshire and mid-Wales. Today, we were going to follow in Wallace's footsteps – tracing a route from Aberdulais Falls, on the outskirts of Neath, to the village of Crynant where Wallace had stayed in what he described as a 'small beer shop' (possibly what became the Red Lion pub) while working as a land surveyor.

79

The first part of the route would follow Sarn Helen – the ancient stone road built by the Romans to connect their fortifications in the north and south of Wales. The route is believed to be named after Saint Elen of Caernarfon, one of the early Celtic saints, and according to legend, the wife of the early Welsh king Macsen Wledig. As the story goes, Elen instructed her husband to build roads across her country so that the soldiers could more easily defend it from attackers.

We'd been climbing steadily as we followed the ancient, rutted dirt-and-stone track that led into the hills. Around us flocks of sheep steadily munched their way across the hillside, ignoring the thick brown bracken, focussing instead on the tufted grass and any other green vegetation on offer. Below us we could see the Gower Peninsula and, in the far distance, across the Bristol Channel, England's Devon coast. We hadn't seen a single person since leaving Neath an hour before but now we came across a man using a blowtorch to repair a buckled metal farm gate. It looked like it had been hit by a battering ram.

'It's those bloody 4×4 drivers. They don't have any respect for farmland,' he told us.

The man was a local artisan, probably in his late 50s, his face weathered by a life working outdoors. He was surprised to meet anyone walking the hills this far out of Neath. Where were we headed?

'We're following Sarn Helen up to St Illtyd's Walk and then onto Crynant,' I explained.

The man smiled.

'It's a common mistake but the real Sarn Helen is over there.' He pointed west to the other side of the hill. 'All the maps place it right here but when you see the other old straight stone track you can tell it's the original.'

'I don't see any need to tell anyone we're on the wrong Sarn Helen if you don't,' said Andy.

We wished the man luck with his task and continued up 'our' Sarn Helen until we joined St Illtyd's Walk for the second time in a couple of days and headed towards Crynant.

This part of the pilgrim's path undulated through the pine forest – in some parts it was more like a stream with water flowing down over the stones. I could only imagine how hard it would be to navigate in winter and spring.

After some 30 minutes carefully negotiating the semi-flooded trail we reached a gap in the forest at the top of a hill. Below us in the valley sat the village of Crynant surrounded by thick larch woods on either side and, in the distance, the silhouette of the Black Mountain stretching high across the valley. I could see why this part of Wales is often described as 'Little Switzerland'.

Descending through the forest, we came across a small clearing offering a view of the valley. A wooden bench bookended by two wooden sculptures – one of an acorn and another a pine cone – had been placed in the gap. Further along we found another bench, inscribed with the words, Crynant Community Forest.

Volunteers built this little refuge to help make the woodlands above the village more accessible and attractive to the local community. Much of the woodland around the village had traditionally been reserved for commercial timber growth. However, after a large number of the larch trees had to be felled due to a killer fungus, *Phytophthora ramorum*, a group of local people jumped at the opportunity to rebuild a connection to the woods and nature that surrounded them.

In the course of just 20 miles I'd now come across three local communities, Maesteg, Caerau and here in Crynant, who all were looking to reconnect with nature as a way of relieving the stress of their daily urban lives. And though they may not have realised it, their initiatives mirrored a trend that was beginning to resonate throughout the world.

There have been numerous scientific studies conducted in recent years demonstrating the benefits of nature on mental health. One, by King's College in London, found that exposure to trees and birdsong in cities improved mental well-being and the benefits were still evident hours after being outdoors. Another, described by Shane O'Mara in his book *In Praise of Walking*, showed how students at Carleton University in Ottawa,

Canada who took a 17-minute winter walk outdoors among trees were nearly a third more likely to report being in a better mood afterwards than those who took the same walk indoors.

In Japan, a study of 585 people found that 'urban living is associated with increased risk of health problems', including anxiety, depression and psychosis and recommended walking through forests and nature as 'a simple, accessible and cost-effective method to improve the quality of life and health of urban residents.'

This isn't surprising given Japan's embrace of Shinrin-Yoku – literally, forest bathing. Shinrin-Yoku was developed in 1982, after scientific studies showed that spending time outside with trees could reduce blood pressure, lower cortisol levels and improve concentration and memory. Scientists were able to identify that one chemical released by trees and plants – phytoncide – offered a significant boost to our immune systems. The practice was also embraced by Japan's Agency of Agriculture, Forestry and Fisheries to help protect forests. It reasoned that if people visited forests for their health, they would be more likely to want to look after them. Before long the Japanese government had incorporated Shinrin-Yoku into its national health programme.

In his book *Into the Forest – How Trees Can Help You Find Health and Happiness*, Dr Qing Li explains forest bathing as taking in the forest through our senses:

> This is not exercise, or hiking, or jogging. It is simply being in nature, connecting with it through our sense of sight, hearing, taste, smell and touch. Indoors, we tend to use only two senses, our eyes and our ears. Outside is where we can smell the flowers, taste the fresh air, look at the changing colours of the trees, hear the bird singing and feel the breeze on our skin. And when we open up our senses, we begin to connect to the natural world.

There is another, spiritual, reason for tree bathing being taken so seriously in Japan. As Li explains, 'Both of Japan's official religions – Shinto and

Buddhism – believe that the forest is the realm of the divine. For Zen Buddhists, scripture is written in the landscape. The natural world is the whole book of God. In Shinto, the spirits are not separate from nature, they are in it.'

Before I started this journey, I was pretty dismissive of concepts like tree bathing. Not anymore. I'd only been walking in the woods and forests for a few weeks but I'd already experienced the calming, restorative effects that tree bathing can bring. When I was out in the woods there were no waves of anxiety. My mind didn't race and I didn't worry about mundane things. I felt at peace and content. And when I wasn't out walking, I found myself craving that sense of calm that comes from putting one foot in front of each other in nature.

A Walk Up the Big Gutter

We'd been walking over the hills for nearly two hours so, when we got to Crynant, we stopped for a rest by the local chapel. Across the street was a corner shop called Segadelli's –part of the long-established Welsh-Italian valleys heritage. The red sign above the shop promised 'Confectionery – Ices – Drinks – Tobacconist'.

'Maybe I can get us a coffee here,' I said to Andy. 'What would you like?'

'A latte would be nice if they have one,' he replied.

I entered the shop and was met by a petite, elderly lady – dressed in a check-patterned blue and white housecoat. Later, I would discover her name was Stella and she'd been running Segadelli's ever since her father died in 1961. The shop had been in business for nearly 100 years; her father used to sell home-made ice cream from the back of a pony and trap to the families of the mine workers. Today, the shop was packed with large supplies of chocolate bars, bottles of cola and bags of crisps.

'Do you serve coffee?' I asked.

'Yes,' she said. I took this as a positive sign.

'What type do you have?' I asked, while scanning the shop for the old-school hand-pulled espresso machine I imagined a storied Italian café establishment like this must have.

'Coffee,' she replied matter-of-factly. 'White or black.'

As Stella added hot water to the instant coffee granules she asked what brought us to the village. I told her I was on a 300-mile walk through Wales exploring the forests and the importance of nature.

'Oh, there's lovely,' she said in that way people in Wales do when they really can't figure out what to make of you or consider you 'out of your tree'.

We rejoined St Illtyd's Walk on the other side of the village, following it for another few miles as it snaked up the other side of the valley. There were warning signs along the way cautioning us to keep to the path. 'Crynant Forest is riddled with rock faces and steep drops from former mining and quarry activity. Many drops are hidden in the trees,' one read.

From the top of Mynydd Marchywel we could see the town of Ystalyfera and the River Tawe as it eased its way down towards the sea at Swansea (*Abertawe* in Welsh, *aber* meaning mouth of the river). Six miles hiking to the north-west of us, the Black Mountain loomed large, dominating the skyline. And just below its western tip I thought I could just make out the old mining town of Upper Brynamman. That's where we were headed so Andy could attend to a bit of unfinished family business before leaving me as I headed north alone.

Back in the mid-19th century, George Borrow walked through Brynamman on his own journey through 'Wild Wales'. Back then the village was known as Gwter Fawr (the big gutter) and it consisted of 'one street, extending for some little way long the Swansea road, the [iron] foundry and a number of huts and houses scattered here and there. The population is composed almost entirely of miners, the workers of the foundry, and their families.'

Borrow stayed the night in the local tavern and was not in the least bit impressed (though he had kind words for the 'couple of buxom wenches' who were the daughters of the unfriendly landlady). Today, the old pub is still serving locals and the tourists who pass through on their way to the Brecon Beacons National Park. There also remain some opencast coal mining operations south of Brynamman – the last gasp of the industry in Wales.

In general though, Borrow would have found the lands surrounding Upper Brynamman unrecognisable – the scars of heavy industry expunged as nature had taken control once again.

At the Black Mountain Centre in the centre of town, small groups of visitors stopped by to get coffees and bacon sandwiches – some hiking, others having cycled over the Black Mountain on a Brecon Beacons loop. I had come to Upper Brynamman because it provided a natural gateway out of the Valleys into the western Brecon Beacons (we'd reached the town by following an old disused railway line that had been transformed into a walking and biking path). Andy had wanted to join me because Upper Brynamman was where his maternal great grandparents came from. They had died many years ago but he was keen to find out more about where they'd lived.

Andy knew the name of the part of the village where their house once stood – Pentir – so while we were in the Mountain Centre we asked some of the locals if they knew where it was. One young mother sipped a cup of tea as she tried to keep her toddler amused. 'I've heard of it on Facebook,' she said. 'But couldn't tell you where it was.'

'How about the Gibea Chapel?' asked Andy. 'That's where they are buried.'

At a table just behind the young mother, an old lady looked up from her newspaper. 'The chapel is just across the street,' she said. 'But when did they die, because the graveyards have been moved in recent years?'

Andy said it would have been about 1940 and the old lady nodded and pointed in the direction of the hill leading up to the Black Mountain. 'Head to the old cemetery. That's where you'll find them,' she said.

We walked up Quarry Road towards the foot of the mountain until we reached the cemetery. It was a sunny day but there was a cool wind blowing down off the mountain across the cemetery where hundreds of graves sat in neat rows.

'What was the surname of your great grandparents?' I asked Andy. 'Thomas,' he replied.

We chose a row of graves each and started searching. It didn't take long for us to realise just how difficult this task was going to be.

'I know Thomas is a popular Welsh name but this is ridiculous. It looks like everyone in this graveyard is called Thomas!' I said.

Andy nodded in agreement. 'What was your grandfather's first name? That might help us locate it quicker,' I added.

'Thomas,' Andy said. 'Thomas Thomas.'

I looked at the multitude of headstones facing us. 'This could take a very long time.'

8

The Science of the Trees

A walk from Upper Brynamman to Myddfai

The route over Mynydd Ddu (Black Mountain) from Upper Brynamman followed an old drover's road down into the wide and verdant Tywi Valley. In the 19th century this was a corpse road, where the bodies of local men who had perished working the coal pits of Brynamman were carried back to be buried in their home village of Llanddeusant, nestled in the valley below. Brynamman men would start the journey and meet their counterparts from Llanddeusant at a Bronze Age cairn situated on the mountain.

Thousands of years ago, much of the more sheltered parts of this mountain would have been covered by woodland. You can still see tiny remnants in the stream-carved ravines that run down its flanks, left alone by the local sheep (I presumed these few morsels were probably too much effort for them). The rest of the mountain, however, was bare.

The name 'The Black Mountain' is a little misleading – it's neither black (though it can appear so when the storm clouds sit above it) nor a singular peak. Instead, it's a series of ridges that stretch some 20 miles from Ammanford to Sennybridge and form a foreboding natural border between the South Wales Valleys and rural Carmarthenshire – the gateway to mid-Wales. The Black Mountain (like much of the Brecon Beacons) is made up predominantly of Devonian Old Red Sandstone though its southern edge also features Carboniferous Limestone, and Millstone Grit. Its highest point, the minor summit of Fan Brycheiniog, sits at 802 metres.

The walk over the mountain this cool, sunny morning marked a transition in landscape and nature – I was leaving behind the legacy of the fossil fuel industry and entering a land shaped by folklore and legend. Where Merlin myths abound. Where faeries were said to protect the entrances to the underworld. And where the fabled Lady of the Lake was said to reside.

I stopped for a snack at a remote car park and vantage point at Brest Cwm Llwyd on the Tywi side of the mountain and took a seat on the soft, thick mountain grass. Below me the river valley spread out wide. There must have been at least five miles between myself and the hills on the other side – a geological acknowledgement that I was looking at the longest river that runs solely through Wales (the Hafren and the Gwy both split their allegiances with England).

The Tywi (known as Towy in English) is 75 miles long. It starts high in the Elenydd range of the Cambrian Mountains before flowing south, first helping mark the border between the mid-Wales counties of Powys and Ceredigion, before then connecting the market towns of Llandovery and Llandeilo. Further south, the Tywi flows through the town of Carmarthen and from there it heads to the coast.

To my left, about a mile or so away, the ruins of Castell Carreg Cennen sat proud but battered on top of a sheer limestone cliff face. Castell Carreg Cennen means 'castle on the rock above the River Cennen' and the geological fault is of such significance that it even has its own term: The Carreg Cennen Disturbance. The castle once was a key stronghold of Rhys ap Gruffydd –The Lord Rhys as he became known – the Welsh ruler of Deheubarth, who, through keen diplomacy and not a little military muscle, carved a niche of power for himself in a land that was being swallowed up by Norman rule.

Many people through the centuries have marvelled at Carreg Cennen's dark beauty, with its ruined battlements shadowed by the Black Mountain. In 1798, it was sketched by the artist J. M. W. Turner, creating a dramatic and dark Sublime homage. Today, that painting hangs in the Tate Gallery in London.

In the valley below the castle I could see a thick patch of woodland so pronounced that if this flank of Carreg Cennen had been a face the trees would have been its thick bushy beard. Coed Castell, as the wood is called, has a split personality. Because of the geological fault upon which the castle sits, two different seams of rock are exposed. One, limestone, is perfect for ash trees while the other, sandstone, better suits sessile oaks. They face off on two sides of the fault, mirroring how I imagine Lord Rhys and the Normans put up with each other – through mutual respect while maintaining a cautious distance.

It was time to press on north. I kept the Tywi River to my left as I headed towards Llandovery, about 10 miles away. This was the first time I'd been walking solo since I started in Wentwood Forest and at first it felt strange not to have the conversation and company of my friends. I also felt slightly nervous. All along I'd been making the decisions about routes, directions and conditions but I'd had the comfort of knowing there were other people supportive enough (and foolish perhaps) to trek with me. If I screwed up now, I'd be on my own and that added an element of stress to this morning's walk.

Yet there was something quite liberating about being completely alone. I noticed things I might have missed when walking and chatting with my friends – the complex, rich red and brown of the bracken on the hills; the hidden limestone shake holes that made this part of the mountain appear to have a bad case of acne; the pair of red kites swooping and dive-bombing each other as they fought for the chance to lunch on some unsuspecting creature.

I also had time to take stock of the journey I'd made so far and what I might learn going forward. I'd started out hoping to answer the question of how we might reconnect with nature and better understand the importance of trees and the role they play in protecting the Earth – nature's gladiators, as I'd heard them referred to a few times. Now that I was a quarter of the way through my journey, having walked some 75 miles, I was confident that I knew plenty about how humanity had made a mess of things but I'd only just started scratching the surface of how we restored the balance.

My previous walks had shown how, by coming together to nurture woodlands, communities could both help their own well-being and also the environment around them. Surely, for the next stage in our rehabilitation, we had to start understanding the trees themselves – what made them tick and what ticked them off.

What Do Trees Dream of?

I'd become captivated by the science of trees almost a year earlier, after stumbling across a TED Talk titled 'How Trees Talk to Each Other'. It was delivered by Dr Suzanne Simard, an unassuming, almost folksy, 56-year-old Canadian professor of forest ecology. The talk had already been viewed more than four million times when I found it – clearly I was not alone in my fascination.

Dr Simard had grown up in the forests of British Columbia and her grandfather had been a logger. From a young age she'd been fascinated by trees and, in particular, their roots and the soil around them. At university she studied forestry. As part of her post-doctorate work in 1997, Simard was keen to understand the mysteries of what was happening underground in the foundations of the forest. The answer, she believed, lay in mycorrhizas – the biological term for the relationship between tree roots and mycelium (the vegetative part of fungus that manifests itself as white threads that spread throughout the soil and connect with other roots). Mycelium can be enormous and can connect thousands of trees in a forest – even different species. In 1998 US forest scientists discovered one humongous fungus in Oregon's Blue Mountains that stretched for nearly four square miles.

Scientists already knew that mycelium help tree roots extract water and nutrients like phosphorus and nitrogen from the soil and, in exchange, the roots share (or the mycelium demand) carbon-rich sugars that the trees produce through photosynthesis. Recent laboratory experiments had demonstrated that pine seedling roots could transmit carbon to other pine seedling roots via mycelium connectivity. Could this be evidence of greater communication?

Simard set about an 'in the forest' experiment – having to fend off overly curious grizzly bears and biting bugs as she worked. She planted a group of young paper birch trees and Douglas fir in separate forest plots and covered the trees with plastic bags. Then she injected the birch bags with radioactive carbon dioxide and the Douglas fir bags with a stable carbon isotope. Simard waited an hour – enough time for the trees to photosynthesise and send the carbon heavy sugars to their roots. Then she checked the birch trees using a Geiger counter. It went off the scale. So far so good. Next, she checked the fir trees. To her joy and excitement they also set off the Geiger counter. However they had been exposed to the radioactive carbon, it hadn't been through the air. It had to have taken place through the mycorrhiza.

'I had found something big. Something that would change how we look at how trees interact in forests. From not just competitors but co-operators. And I'd found solid evidence of this massive underground communications network – the otherworld,' Simard explained in her talk.

Since Simard's talk there's been a groundswell of mainstream, non-scientific interest in the concept of the Wood Wide Web (as the mycelium connection has been dubbed), and this has prompted much debate around the intelligence of trees. Simard's thesis has been widely acknowledged by the scientific community and her work has become a case study at universities around the world. She even experienced literary fame with her memoir, *Finding the Mother Tree*, and as an inspiration for the character Patricia Westerford in Richard Powers's 2019 Pulitzer Prize-winning novel, *The Overstory*.

The intelligence of trees and what that means for our own relationship to nature was given even greater exposure in 2018 with the publication of *The Hidden Life of Trees* by German forester, Peter Wohlleben. He expanded on Simard's conclusions documenting a range of eye-opening and startling activity including how acacia trees in Africa deter giraffes from eating them by releasing a chemical into the air in the form of ethylene gas that signals to other trees that a threat is at hand. Upon detecting the gas, the neighbouring acacias pump tannins into their leaves which can sicken or even kill large herbivores. (This being evolutionary nature, of course, the giraffes have learned to move ahead about 100 yards to acacias that haven't yet received the warning.)

Wohlleben also shed light on the duelling battles between species – how the fast-growing beech will bully its way through the crowns of slower growing oaks to hoard the sunlight and so stunt their development.

Both Wohlleben and Simard had previously worked in commercial forestry operations and had come to abhor industrial logging practices that they could see were doing long-term damage to the sustainability of forests. Their work and advocacy demonstrating how trees nurture, support, feed and protect each other – even when one tree has been felled or is dying – raised even more uncomfortable questions. Not least, could trees be sentient beings?

Take the research done by Edward Farmer at the University of Lausanne in Switzerland. He has studied electrical pulses sent out by trees and identified a voltage-based signalling system that appears strikingly similar to animal nervous systems. More contentious still, Monica Gagliano, a scientist at the University of Western Australia, believes some trees may communicate using a crackling noise in their roots that resonates at 220 hertz – a frequency inaudible to humans.

Gagliano is also perhaps the most outspoken scientific booster of plant intelligence. In one 2014 experiment, she dropped potted Mimosa plants from a short distance. At first, they curled up their leaves in self-defence. However, after repeating the experiment a number of times the plants 'relaxed' and stopped protecting themselves. Gagliano surmised it was because they quickly learned no harm would come to them.

Gagliano's conclusion was that, while plants don't have a central nervous system or a brain, they behave like intelligent beings. If plants can summon knowledge gleaned from a repeated experience then might they be able to remember and learn from that experience?

The notion that trees could be sentient is not a new scientific theory. In the 19th century the German psychologist and philosopher Gustav Fechner was a leading advocate of panpsychism – the philosophy that all things (including trees and plants) have a mind or a mind-like quality. Even Charles Darwin, from his evolutionary perspective, was loathe to dismiss the concept of matter having a consciousness.

Wrote Wohlleben, 'Sometimes I suspect we would pay more attention to trees and other vegetation if we could establish beyond a doubt just how similar they are in many ways to animals.'

It's worth dwelling on that thought for a moment in the context of how differently society views animals as food today than it did just 40 years ago. Back then vegetarianism and veganism were fringe movements and only its most committed advocates considered the effect of eating meat on the environment. Today those movements are mainstream. Dairy consumption is in freefall and consumption of plant-based food products and reduced meat intake diets like flexitarianism are rapidly on the rise.* This is partly due to increased food allergies and intolerances. It is also partly due to our increased understanding of animals' intelligence and a growing awareness that eating meat and dairy is directly contributing to climate change.

If society has so dramatically changed its perception of consuming meat and dairy products, how would our relationship to trees change if we understood more about how they grow, act, perhaps think and maybe even feel? Would we still be so inclined to fell millions of trees for timber and to clear space for agriculture? Would we even consider burning trees in our homes for fuel?

Could we be witnessing the birth of a tree-protection movement with as much influence as today's animal rights movement? This may well sound far-fetched. But if you'd told me 40 years ago that I'd be putting

---

* According to one market survey, in 2020, 36 per cent of US consumers identified themselves as flexitarian, consuming meat or poultry as well as vegan or vegetarian meals, according to one market survey.

oat milk in my coffee and eating burgers made out of pea protein I'd have considered that pretty far-fetched as well.

Not surprisingly, many mainstream scientists treat Simard, Wohlleben and Gagliano's analysis with extreme scepticism (others are less gracious). Some question the notion of whether trees are actively working together or if the underground signals we are seeing are just a confused jumble of individual self-preservation. Others complain that science is being embellished with human emotion and that the intelligent/sentient tree narrative that appeals to a growing audience is simply not borne out by the facts.

What can't be questioned is the fact that we are just starting to understand the complex relationship of trees, forests and biodiversity in general. In the future, science may prove trees don't communicate or feel in the way Simard and her fellow scientists have so far demonstrated. But right now, their findings and their writing have awoken a sensibility and sensitivity towards trees that might just provide the foundation for the healthy relationship with nature we need.

The Physicians of Myddfai

Science may only now be starting to explore and understand the true nature of trees and the connections of forests but people have appreciated the medicinal and healing power of trees and plants for many hundreds of years.

No more so than in the place where I was right now in the shadow of the Black Mountain, walking on the Beacons Way towards the village of Llanddeusant. It was here that one of the greatest medical dynasties began – a family of physicians born of other-worldly heritage whose knowledge would be passed down through successive generations of doctors over the next 700 years. These were the Physicians of Myddfai and their nature-based remedies and philosophy, however folkloric it might be, continues to resonate today.

As with so much Welsh history, the origins of this medical dynasty is cloaked in folklore and legend. Back in the mid-19th century, a local vicar,

William Rees (and later publisher) is said to have written down the story that local people had long told about the Physicians and their connection to a 'gwraig annwn' – the fairy who lived in a lake.

According to the story, a remote farm called Blaensawdde (just up the lane from where I was standing right now) was once home to a widow and her only son. The area around the farm was so heavily wooded that the only clear grazing land for their cows was on the moorlands of the Black Mountain, by a lake called Llyn y Fan Fach (Lake of the Small Peak).

One morning, as the son walked with the cattle, he saw the most beautiful woman rise from the lake. She was looking at her reflection in the water when, suddenly, she set eyes on the young man and was smitten. He offered her some of his bread and cheese but she refused, saying the bread was too hard. When he tried to take her hand, she disappeared back into the lake. The next day he returned and tried to tempt her again with unbaked bread. Once again she appeared and smiled at him but said, 'O! thou of the unbaked bread, I will not have thee!' and disappeared once more. Undeterred he returned the third day with bakestone bread (perhaps what we know today as Welsh cakes) that his mother had made. This time, she accepted the bread and agreed to marry him.

But on one condition. Should he ever strike her with iron she would return forever to the lake. The young man agreed – how could he ever strike someone who he loved so much?

The couple lived happily for years at Esgair Llaethdy on the outskirts of Myddfai and they had three very handsome sons. Then, one day, tragedy struck. The man was trying to catch some ponies so he and his wife could go riding. In doing so he threw the bridle at the pony but missed and the iron struck his wife. Without hesitation she walked away, disappearing back into the waters of Llyn y Fan Fach. (In other variations of this folk tale, and there are many given how it was passed down orally through the generations, the husband struck his fairy wife three times and on the final blow she, understandably, returned to the lake.)

What became of the man, no one knows. But the three sons often walked up to the lake to visit their mother. One day, as she rose from the lake, she told them that their mission in the world would be to heal sick people. Then she walked with them into a deep wooded dell nearby and taught them about the medicinal plants and herbs of the forest.

At the heart of the Lady of the Lake legend lies the belief by local folk that she was one of 'Y Tylwyth Teg' (the Fair Folk). In Welsh folklore the fairies were believed to be the souls of the Druids – existing in a liminal state because, as pagans, they couldn't be afforded passage to heaven but were too virtuous to be cast into hell. For this reason, they existed in a realm known as Y Annwn (the underworld or otherworld). They were said to be immortal and could make themselves invisible – a handy trait for all mythical creatures.

While their origin story is open to some serious folkloric debate, the Physicians of Myddfai do appear to have been real people. The *Red Book of Hergest*, one of two medieval Welsh-language tomes handwritten on vellum in the 14th century, recounted how a father, named Rhiwallon the Doctor, and his three sons, Cadwgan, Gruffydd and Einion, were physicians at the court of Rhys Gryg, the son of the Lord Rhys. Rhiwallon was said to be the eldest son of the Lady of the Lake.

The *Red Book* included some 500 herbal remedies prescribed by the Physicians, including everyday medieval ailments like how to treat a snake bite (drink juice made from fennel, radish and wormwood), how to reduce swelling and pain in the thighs (a mix of rue, honey and salt applied topically) and how to stop a nosebleed (betony powder and salt applied inside the nostrils).

The book also included what might be considered more optimistic remedies for curing vomiting ('immerse the scrotum in vinegar'). And then there's the remedy for expelling reptiles in the stomach ('mix wild chamomile powder in wine until it is thickened. If he drinks this, it will relieve him of the reptiles.').*

The manuscript also offered up general observations on the virtue of various plants and trees. They include the oak and mistletoe – the two

---

* *The Physicians of Myddfai* by Terry Breverton, p. 95

species that were said to be considered the most sacred by the Druids. Of mistletoe (now known to be poisonous) the book advised: 'Its property is to strengthen the body more than any other plant.' Oak was recommended for all diseases proceeding from weakness in the nerves, spinal marrow and brain while its inner bark was considered an 'excellent tonic' that could be boiled in ale or the milk of cows or goats. The book particularly recommended eating ripe acorns, which we know to be particularly rich in fat and oils – hence breeders in Spain and Portugal fatten their prize pigs on them. And it drew on ancient Celtic traditions of baking bread with acorn flour to provide 'an excellent diet' for 'all weak persons'.

Academics have questioned whether the remedies that appear in the *Red Book of Hergest* can really be tied to Rhiwallon and his sons. They note that many of the remedies were well known in medieval times. However, by the 18th century, Welsh antiquarian intellectuals (including a rakish poet named Iolo Morganwg – more on him soon) had embraced, adapted and, in some cases, embellished the Physicians of Myddfai story and remedies in an attempt to trace a modern Welsh national identity back to the ancient Druidic heritage. The Physicians' connection to the trees and nature, and their expertise in herbal medicine, also matched the values of the Romantic age that shaped these ideas.

Clearly, when it comes to making sense of the Physicians of Myddfai, it is hard to separate fact from the fiction. Were they really the offspring of the Lady of the Lake? Unlikely. Did they provide counsel to the Rhys dynasty and did they continue their tradition of herbal medicine for centuries? I like to think that part's true. Certainly, even in the late 19th century there were still doctors in Wales who claimed direct lineage to the Physicians of Myddfai.

Whatever the veracity of the original story, the Physicians' understanding of nature to help cure disease still resonates. Just ask the pharmaceutical companies who invest millions each year into ethnobotany to discover and monetise plant-based medicines.

Medicinal plants contribute to pharmacological treatments for cancer, HIV/AIDS, malaria (arteether), Alzheimer's (galantamine), asthma (tiotropium) and, of course, many types of painkillers (aspirin was derived from a similar substance, salicin, that is found in willow bark) while morphine comes from the opium plant.

The philosophy espoused by the Myddfai clan continues among communities all around the world. The World Health Organisation estimates some 20,000 medicinal plants are used to treat ailments and promote health worldwide. In Sarawak, Malaysia, 1,220 species are employed in traditional remedies while in South Africa, an estimated 80 per cent of the population embrace them. In some Amazon communities of South America, shamans embrace the psychedelic properties of plants such as the liana vine to provide wisdom and guidance to their communities.

Back in Wales, I could have done with some shamanic wisdom about how to navigate rainforest-worthy rain. Torrents of water poured down the steep, narrow country lane that led down off the Black Mountain. I'd been pretty lucky so far with the weather but now the elements were testing the limits of my rain jacket. I was still in shorts, now ringing wet, and the water was starting to trickle down into my socks until I could hear and feel my feet squelching in my low-cut hiking boots.

So it was with great relief that I finally arrived in Myddfai, surely a candidate for sleepiest village of the year. The only thing open was the Community Hall and Visitor Centre. It had a simple café, gift shop and exhibition celebrating the Physicians. I ordered a cheese toastie, Welsh cakes and a pot of tea from the lady running the café. I perused the Physicians of Myddfai exhibit as I waited, learning how one of their descendants was buried in the local graveyard.

Just as I finished the lady came by carrying my lunch. Her name was Mair and she told me that she lived in a house once owned by a famous local historian. 'He wrote a book all about Myddfai. Now why can't I remember his name,' she said, frustrated.* I asked if she'd been busy during

---

* I later found out it would have been David B. James, author of *Myddfai, Its Land and Peoples*.

lockdown. 'Been rushed off my feet all summer,' she replied. 'There's not much else around here so we get lots of tourists stopping by.'

She asked how I'd found Myddfai and I told her I was on a walking trip through Wales. 'How far you going?' Mair asked. 'About 300 miles in total,' I replied.

Just like the old lady at Segadelli's in Crynant, Mair had a very simple response. 'Well, there's lovely,' she said.

9

~~~

In the Footsteps of the Welsh Robin Hood

A challenging walk from Rhandirmwyn to Tregaron (sort of)

The next part of the journey was going to be tricky.

When I first started planning a walking route connecting the woodlands and forests of Wales one issue kept leaping out at me from the map. How was I going to get across the Elenydd, the sparse and barely populated upland region that lay between the two market towns of Llandovery and Tregaron?

Most of it sat above 400 metres and was sliced by a series of steep valleys through which upland tributaries feed into the River Tywi. On the OS map, the part of the Elenydd I needed to cross was an intimidating squash of orange lines signifying a very significant hike.

Unable to come up with a satisfactory route myself I started researching long distance walking paths across. That's how I stumbled upon The Cambrian Way, a challenging 288-mile hike across the major mountains of Wales, running from Cardiff in the south to Conwy in the north. It was the creation of Tony Drake, a former department store owner who sold the family business so that he could pursue his true calling – walking. In 1968 Drake convinced both the Ramblers' Association and the Youth Hostels Association to back the creation of The Cambrian Way so that it would be clearly marked on OS maps and have official markers positioned along the trail to guide hikers adventurous and hardy enough to undertake it.

One section of the route connected the village of Rhandirmwyn with the ancient Cistercian abbey of Strata Florida near the village of Pontrhydfendigaid. The town of Tregaron was five miles south of here – surely there was a way to follow the Cambrian Way and then peel off to my destination?

My Cambrian Way guidebook and OS map suggested that if I started near Rhandirmwyn, I could follow the Cambrian Way up the Doethie Valley until I reached a remote hostel called Ty'n Cornel. I could spend the night there and then continue following the Cambrian Way until I reached what the guide described as Nantymaen Junction, a red public phone box situated near Esgair Gelli ('grove' or 'copse ridge' in English). From there, I plotted a walking route down into Tregaron. In total it looked to be about 20 miles which, given the amount of climbing involved, seemed a little ambitious for one day but a pleasant walk if split over two.

At this point Covid got in the way. Because of the pandemic both the Ty'n Cornel hostel and the pub in Rhandirmwyn where I'd planned to stay were shut. My only option was to wild camp. This wasn't a proposition that filled me with joy but one I convinced myself I was ready to undertake – all in the spirit of adventure. However, before I committed to that I decided it would make sense to do some reconnaissance of what, exactly, I was letting myself in for.

So, on a stunningly clear and sunny late summer morning, I drove out of Llandovery, where I'd stayed the night before, past Rhandirmwyn, over a wooden pontoon bridge spanning the Tywy River, and wound my way up an access road, braking sharply as what looked to me like a pine marten scurried across the lane, until I reached Troed Rhiw Ruddwen farm, where the owner, Huw, had kindly said I could leave my car.

My plan was to scout this part of the Cambrian Way in three circular walks. The first would be a six-hour round trip up the Doethie Valley starting just past Huw's sheep farm.

Ben was a youthful-looking man with short blonde hair and the solid build of someone used to working the land. He had been grazing 900 sheep on this remote upland outpost for the past 20 years, but the farm had been in family for generations. As I pulled on my hiking boots and checked my snack supply, he was preparing to bring the sheep down off the hills so that heather could regrow through the autumn and winter – part of a regeneration scheme coordinated with the local environmental agency, Natural Resources Wales, to balance the benefits of sheep farming with the impact the animals have on the environment.

'It makes good sense,' said Huw when I asked about the scheme. 'It's just that sometimes, they're telling you to do something that we've been doing since long before my grandfather!'

I started off down the track. Huw called out after me. 'Keep an eye out for the Skyliners, they're bringing down the ash trees.'

I wasn't quite sure what he meant but I waved before turning and heading out through the farm gate. About 200 metres down the track that led to another farm I saw the Cambrian Way trail logo. It featured a black traditional *Y Het Gymreig* (The Welsh Hat) – a type of top hat worn by rural Welsh women in the 19th century. The sign pointed towards a single grass track leading up at an angle onto the hill to my right. I walked through a flock of Huw's sheep until I reached the crest of the hill and looked down the Doethie Valley in front of me. It was still quite early in the morning and the mist that had settled overnight at the foot of valley hadn't yet evaporated. It felt like I was hiking into the clouds.

Above the mist, the sides of the valley were covered with thick brownish-red bracken, heather and a mix of rowan, birch and willow trees. This was the ffridd (the upland fringe, also known as coedcae) of mountainous hinterland that lies above often enclosed lower pastureland and below the bare mountain top, a bit like the tastiest layer in a cake. It's some of the most valuable land in terms of biodiversity, providing a place to perch for birds such as willow warblers, tree pipits and whinchats. It was incredibly rugged territory but breathtakingly beautiful.

It was a dry, sunny morning so I'd worn light, breathable trousers for the walk. Normally I'd have been in shorts but the reputation of the

Cambrian Way suggested I'd be picking my way through brambles and who knows what else along the way. I'd only been walking for 30 minutes but I was soaked – my distinctly un-waterproof trousers being in constant contact with the dew-laden bracken that reached up to my waist.

But what a sight lay before me. Ahead lay miles of meandering river valley walled in by steep ffridd-dominated hillsides – a patchwork blanket of red, brown and green flora – and it was topped off by the bare, exposed ridge on either side. In the distance I could see the tall Sitka spruce trees of the Tywi Forest plantation standing to attention like a military guard.

To my left the Allt Rhyd y Groes nature reserve stretched up from the valley floor to the very top of the ridge, a reminder of what this land-scape must have looked like before man, sheep and other livestock gained control. The wood was a dense, almost impenetrable jungle of temperate rainforest, its characteristic sessile oaks grew out of the mountainside at seemingly impossible angles.

Allt Rhyd y Groes is one of Wales's least known but most important woodlands. In the 1980s it provided the last refuge for the endangered red kite. Kites were highly valued in the Middle Ages – they kept the streets clean from rodents and waste and killing one could result in capital pun-ishment. Attitudes started changing in the 16th century as more people began to keep domestic and game birds. Over time, kites were seen to be a predatory threat and they were an easy target because they didn't fear people. The red kite became extinct in England in 1871 and Scotland just eight years later.

In Wales, however, the species survived – but barely. The last remain-ing few pairs of red kites nested in Allt Rhyd y Groes so, in the late 1980s, conservation teams set about a plan to protect the birds and try to reha-bilitate them. The British Army even got involved, dispatching teams of Nepalese Gurkha soldiers to patrol the nature reserve and ward off poach-ers looking to steal the red kites' eggs. ('They also scared all the bloody sheep away!' Huw had told me earlier.)

The red kite revival is one of the great conservation stories of the UK over the last 100 years and a testament to what can be restored when a community works together to protect nature. Today, red kites can be found all through Wales and as far east as the outskirts of London.

In the Footsteps of Twm Siôn Cati

I was walking deeper into the valley trail through a dense section of mixed woodland when I came across a warning sign.

It read: 'Rhybudd/Danger – Gwaith Coedwigaeth/Forestry Work'

In front of me the woodland on the valley hillside had been completely cleared. Two hundred metres above on either side of the valley (and at least half a mile apart from each other) were two enormous cranes – the Skyliners Huw had mentioned. Forestry workers stood high above on the hillside using walkie-talkies to send instructions to the crane operators. They expertly guided a winch across the valley and then vertically down until it connected to felled diseased ash trunks, which then were lifted out of the forest before they could infect other trees.

For the last 30 years 'dieback', a fungus originating in Asia, has been destroying ash trees all across Europe. The fungus doesn't do much harm to Asian native trees like Manchurian ash and Chinese ash but the European ash appears to have no natural defence against it. Once woodland becomes infected foresters usually opt to remove the trees to restrict the disease's spread. The Woodland Trust believes that the UK will lose up to 80 per cent of all its ash trees to the disease.

The forestry clearing work only reached for a few hundred metres (even though it extended high up the valley) and soon I was back navigating through tall bracken and picking my way over cascading little streams (or *nants* in Welsh) that ran down the hillsides and cut through the path.

In the 16th century, this was the playground of Twm Siôn Cati – a local gentlemen outlaw who became known through multiple folkloric writings and layers of embellishment as the Welsh Robin Hood. Born as Thomas Jones in Tregaron around 1530, Twm was said to have descended from noble blood and have been a poet and bard of some renown – some say he won the chair at the Llandaff Eisteddfod in 1561. His reputation as an outlaw is based more on mischievous trickery than any thuggery though – he had an art of outwitting and outfoxing his victims. In one story, Twm visited an ironmonger to buy a porridge pot. The ironmonger brought out several pans and declared their quality was fit for a king's kitchen. Twm picked up one of the pots and said he could see a hole in it. Incredulous, the ironmonger took the pot and held it up to the light. Twm quickly forced the pot over the ironmonger's head and joked: if there was no hole then how could such a large, stupid head get caught inside?

What does seem true is that Twm Siôn Cati got on the wrong side of the Sheriff of Carmarthen and so spent a good deal of time on the run. Earlier in the day I had passed the dense Gwenffrwd-Dinas nature reserve, another of the few remaining Celtic rainforests where, according to folklore, Twm would hide from the sheriff in a cave high on the hillside.

I stopped to watch two birds dart between a fallen tree that spanned the Doethie – knocked down in a storm judging by its shape. I retrieved my breakfast – a bacon sandwich that I'd picked up a few hours before in Llandovery – took a seat on a patch of dry ground and took a few minutes to appreciate just how isolated this part of Wales was.

I imagined how easily Twm Siôn Cati could have avoided detection by travelling up the Doethie Valley to his home in Tregaron. Looking at the mountains around me and the severity of the terrain outside of the valley, the chances of the local magistrates ever laying hands on Twm would have been slim at best – especially given his knowledge of the land and his ability to travel in the pitch black of night.

I'd been to lots of desolate places around the world in my career as a travel writer but rarely had I felt quite as alone as I did at that moment. I knew that it was highly unlikely I'd meet any other walkers in the Doethie Valley – it was that far off the beaten track and no mountain bikers were going to attempt this route when their only refuge for the night, Ty'n Cornel, was closed. Suddenly I was overcome with a feeling both of exhilaration and trepidation at being out here alone.

Part of me was really excited to be here all alone in this wilderness.

For one thing, I really loved the quiet. So much of the anxiety I had been suffering in recent times had been exacerbated by noise. Seemingly mundane sounds – the pitch and tone of someone's voice for example or the noise of a car engine – would penetrate my head, raising my stress levels and playing havoc with my sense of perspective. I felt myself fighting this sonic overload on a daily basis. Innocuous noises would put me on edge, each additional sound escalating the tension in my body until I felt like I had to scream.

Up here, in the heart of the Doethie Valley, on this day, I had escaped everyone. I loved that feeling. Of pushing the boundaries of where I could wander. Even of flirting with danger a little.

Almost instantly that sense of excitement disappeared. It was replaced by an overwhelming sense of failure as I realised that I had to turn back and return to my car at the farm, when what I really wanted to do right now was keep walking, exploring up the valley. I had told myself beforehand that I needed to do reconnaissance for this particular route but maybe that was just an excuse I'd made because I was scared of undertaking this long stretch of walk alone.

It's not like I lacked the equipment to do it. I'd even bought a one-man tent, but right now it was sitting at home. When the tent arrived my wife, who knows me better than I know myself, had gently questioned why I needed it.

'So it's just going to gather dust in the attic with all the other tents that we don't use,' she said in a way that I gently pointed out wasn't very constructive.

She was right though. The fact was, I had lost my confidence. Twenty-five years ago I had backpacked across South America. I had travelled for days by open canoe in the Amazon Rainforest and had camped with indigenous communities. I'd even done hallucinogenic drugs with an 80-year-old shaman in a Kichwan village hundreds of miles from the nearest hospital. Taking risks had never been a problem. Or perhaps I'd just not considered them. So what had changed now?

It wasn't about being scared. I'd always been a little nervous before heading off on adventures around the world. I think everyone who takes on a big challenge has to be – it's what gets you going, keeps you alert and alive.

However, at some point over the past few years the fear factor that once propelled me forward had become an obstacle. As I became more afraid of failure, in business and life, the greater that sense of fear and anxiety became.

As I sat there, halfway up the Doethie Valley, I had to confront a feeling that I think I had been burying for a long time. What if this loss of confidence – this fear that I'd failed in life – was permanent? I had felt so euphoric and now I felt crushed. I'd made it miles up the valley but had to turn around. As I trudged back to the farm and my car, my feelings of self-pity were replaced with anger. I was mad at myself for failing and accepting failure. If I was going to finish this walk, I would have to be bolder and start to believe in myself once again.

Of Sheep, Farmers and Religion

I got back in the car, wished Huw well, and drove out of the Doethie, back past Twm Siôn Cati's cave and joined the winding mountain road that led around the giant Llyn Brianne reservoir towards the 19th century, isolated Calvinist-Methodist chapel, Soar y Mynydd. It sat on the banks of Afan Camddwr, just a couple of miles from where I'd abandoned my trek in the Doethie Valley, yet it took me nearly an hour's driving to get there. You can imagine how annoyed I felt.

Soar was built in 1822 to offer the residents of the remote sheep farms in the Elenydd a place of worship. With no other buildings for miles around, it's regularly referred to as the most remote chapel in all of Wales and by 1968 there were just two regular worshippers. Today its iconic, remote status draws worshippers from across Wales who travel to the occasional services in summer.

When I arrived a family – a mother, father and three grown-up children – was walking around the chapel's exterior and posing for photos

(Covid restrictions meant we couldn't go inside). They had driven up for the day from west Wales specifically to visit the chapel.

'I haven't been here since I was a kid,' said the mother. 'My dad worked for the Forestry Commission and we used to visit him on weekends. Then they flooded the forest to create the Llyn Brianne reservoir. This is the first time I've been back up here since.'

I left them to admire the old white stone chapel and walked up the gravel track that led off over the hill. This was the old road once used by the drovers of west Wales to move their livestock over the Elenydd wilderness to the village of Abergwesyn some 15 miles away before heading east through mid-Wales to the markets in England.

The road had an ancient, other-worldly feel to it – a sense you were walking where generations of men had toiled in the past. The landscape was desolate and almost devoid of vegetation, a noticeable difference to the ffridd I'd walked through a few hundred metres below in the Doethie Valley. This was blanket bog country.

Generally blanket bog is found in upland habitat (it could be anywhere on land at an elevation of 1,000 m down to sea level), and where peat has accumulated to a depth of at least 0.5 m. It's not a natural phenomenon in Wales but rather a product of thousands of years' deforestation. Very few plants can survive the acidic, infertile conditions but bog mosses, heathers and cotton grasses thrive. The Elenydd is one of the foremost examples of blanket bog in the UK and comprises the largest example of it in the central Wales uplands. It tends to be found on acidic bedrock in places where the volume of rainfall exceeds the loss of water through evaporation and plant transpiration – i.e., the sodden landscape of mid-Wales. Nowadays, considerable areas of the blanket bog are showing signs of degradation, with mountain grasses such as Molinia dominating the dwarf shrubs and widespread bog mosses that once were prevalent. One reason for this is the expansion in sheep grazing that took place during the 19th and early 20th centuries. Sheep generally love blanket bog mosses, but find Molina unpalatable. As a result, it has proliferated at the expense of the moss.

I walked on the stone track through this so-called Desert of Wales until I could see the Doethie Valley once again. In the distance I could just make out the roof of the Ty'n Cornel hostel. I forded a small stream and carried on up a stone lane to the gate of the hostel and let myself through.

It was deserted and locked apart from the storage barn the owners maintain to let hikers and mountain bikers hole up for the night if there is no room at the inn. Outside the hostel's front door was a plaque dedicated to Tony Drake, creator of The Cambrian Way 'He worked tirelessly in Wales and England for the RA (Ramblers' Association) for 60 years but his greatest love was always the wild beauty of his creation, The Cambrian Way.'

I continued up the track away from Ty'n Cornel towards the mountain road leading to the village of Llanddewi Brefi. A right turn took me up a mud track situated just in front of the barbed wire fence around the perimeter of the Cwm Berwyn Forest plantation, which extended to the west as far as I could see. According to The Cambrian Way guide I was still on the official track, but there were no markers and, ominously, given how unreliable well-marked OS map footpaths tended to be, there was no sign of one of those either.

Still, I carried on climbing up this track and headed due north. After about 20 minutes I met an older couple walking down the hill. The man wore a green cap, had a thick grey beard and was aided by two large wooden walking sticks. His wife had short white hair and was dressed in blue boots and a matching rain jacket. Their names were John and Mary Morgan and they lived down the valley in Llanddewi Brefi.

'We grew up around here,' said Mary. 'John lived on one side of the hill and I lived on the other. We come up here from time to time just to revisit memories.'

'Where are you headed?' asked John. I told him I was following The Cambrian Way over to the old red phone box on the top of the hill high above Tregaron. He seemed sceptical.

'There's no real path across so you'll have to pick your way through. Look out for the one lone fir tree in the bog and make sure you stay above it. You know why they call this the Desert of Wales? Because the horizon looks a mirage. Everything is further away than it seems.'

We said goodbye and I watched the couple carefully make their way down the rutted and sodden path.

After about fifty yards Mary turned back, 'You take care of yourself out there walking alone,' she shouted, with a hint of concern in her voice.

For the next half hour I followed two tyre tracks made by an off-road vehicle that headed in the direction I wanted and, importantly, stayed on high ground. Nevertheless, the going wasn't easy and even on the hills the ground would suddenly give way into soft bog.

The Cwm Berwyn Forest was a constant companion on my left while to my right the Elenydd appeared vast and endless – a green, yellow and brown blanket bog of daunting beauty. There was no way you would want to get stuck out in the middle of it. In the distance I thought I could make out a red phone box but, as John had said, I could just have been willing myself to see it. Either way my 'path' was now blocked by a high barbed wire boundary fence. The only way around was to drop down off the hill into the bog below or double back.

Even if this was the official Cambrian Way route I didn't fancy what it was suggesting. So I turned back and prepared to approach the route from the phone box instead.

I'm a Celebrity? Get Out of Here...

The red phone box on the Tregaron to Abergwesyn mountain road is one of the best-known landmarks in the whole of the Elenydd. Coming across it in the middle of nowhere feels other-worldly. Like running into a red Tardis.

In 2015 it almost disappeared – not by whirring itself off into space but because the telecoms company wanted to decommission and remove it. Local tourism and walking groups successfully petitioned to keep the box, though the phone was removed.

It's also an important navigational marker for The Cambrian Way.

When you reach the phone box you know you have successfully made it through the bog and can carry on up the hill, over Nant y Maen stream, past Blaendoethie farm and over the mountains towards the old Cistercian abbey at Strata Florida.

The phone box was just over three miles away from Capel Soar y Mynydd, a short drive along the mountain road. As I approached, something was not right. If this was the most remote phone box in Wales, why were there so many cars, vans and people?

I parked my car behind what looked like a telecoms utility van and was about to get out when an officious young man in a high-vis jacket and with an earpiece and a walkie-talkie shouted at me. 'You with the crew? Move that car now.'

'I'm just here to go for a walk.'

The man looked taken aback – he obviously hadn't expected anyone else to be turning up at the remote location either.

'Um, well we're doing some filming and your car is going to be in the shot.'

At that point a heavyset security guy came over and pointed up the hillside track. 'Stick the car up there, *butt*.* By the first aid van. It will be fine there.'

Thrown off by all this activity, I rushed to tie my hiking boots and grab my backpack.

The security guy was from Rhandirmwyn and had been hired by the film crew to help run logistics as he knew the area. He couldn't tell me what was being shot but said I'd work it out soon enough.

'Just out of interest, where are you going?' he asked.

'I'm trying to find the path of The Cambrian Way,' I said, adding: 'Do you know if I can walk over from here to Ty'n Cornel?'

'You can go anywhere you want my friend. This is the Cambrian Mountains.'

---

* Butt is short for butty – a slang phrase used mainly in south Wales instead of mate or friend.

That wasn't quite the response I'd been looking for, but I liked his enthusiasm and it buoyed me for my final bit of reconnaissance. I strode down the hill, smiling at the film crew as it continued its set-up, and confidently ventured off over the stream and into the hills.

I knew I had to stay on higher ground so I pulled out my phone to activate the OS map app where I'd planned the route based on *The Cambrian Way* guide. That's when the problems started. In my hurry to get started, and flummoxed by the film crew, I'd forgotten to download the map. Making matters worse, I had no phone signal. I had the hard copy of *The Cambrian Way* guide but it had already proved problematic, shall we say, on the previous section of the walk.

At least the sun was still shining. Even though I didn't have a map to rely on, I figured there wasn't any harm climbing up towards the first big ridge on the horizon called Esgair Hir. Standing some 480 metres high, it should have provided me with the relief I needed from the boggy ground all around me. However, the further I walked the wetter and more treacherous conditions became underfoot. I must have gone too far into the blanket bog before heading towards higher ground because soon my ankles were buckling and twisting with every step as my feet sunk deep into the boggy ground that surrounded the knee-high tussocks I was trying to get around or over.

Before long I was completely off track and found myself closer to the boundary fence of the forestry plantation than the ridge I had set off to reach. At least the forest ground was higher and looked drier so I decided my best bet would be to hop the fence and carry on through the forest.

Another bad choice: the fence gave way under the wet ground and I snagged my bare legs and my hand on the barbed wire. Now I was wet, my ankle felt twisted, my hands and legs bloodied and I still had no phone signal or accurate map to guide me. I'd made every bad decision I told myself to avoid when standing on the ridge on the other side of the bog just a couple of hours before.

I felt like an idiot. A very exposed idiot. It was nearly 5 p.m., the sun was starting to fade, and I was, if not stuck, certainly faced with a very big challenge to extricate myself from the bog without breaking my ankle, twisting my knee or picking up some other injury. The only reassuring thing in my mind at that point was that at least the film crew had seen me wandering off into the wilderness – surely they would raise the alarm if I didn't return.

Slowly (frankly, there was no other speed available) I retraced my steps – standing on felled logs and dry-looking tufts of grass in the hope that I didn't sink up to my thighs in water. Once more I had to jump the barbed wire fence and once more I cut myself on the wire. Above me I could see the mountain road running next to Cwm Berwyn plantation. I decided to cut my losses and climb up to it. It was a big detour but at least I'd be walking on solid ground. So, I pushed on through the bog, sometimes falling into standing water waist deep until, finally I reached the road.

Wearily, I walked back down to my car. My legs were bleeding, I was pretty sure I'd sprained my ankle and I was absolutely shattered both from the physical effort to walk out of the bog but also the fear about getting stuck in the first place. The film crew was shooting as I approached but called 'cut' as I came into view and let me through. As I walked past the red phone box I looked inside. Staring back at me with a bemused expression were Ant and Dec, arguably the UK's most famous TV personalities and hosts of *I'm a Celebrity, Get Me Out of Here*. They were filming a promo for the new series that, because of Covid, was being filmed in Gwrych Castle in north Wales rather than the Australian jungle. They were dressed in safari gear complete with khaki pith helmets. I nodded to them in a nonchalant way that suggested I walk past costumed major celebrities in the Welsh mountains every single day. Ant smiled in a way that said, 'who the hell is this?' and, almost without realising, I gave a little wave back.

10

The Stuff of Legend

A short pilgrimage from Tregaron to Ystrad Flur

The western portal of Ystrad Flur (Strata Florida) is the most significant reminder of just how powerful and culturally important this ruined abbey once was: a grand stone Romanesque arch some seven and a half metres tall, which marks the main entrance to the monastery's church.

Today, much of Ystrad Flur is just a memory save for this Norman stone facade, the foundation outline of the abbey, some ornate medieval tile work and the graves of 11 Welsh princes. Yet, when you stand in the grounds of the abbey and cast your eye around the valley that envelops it, you can imagine just how influential this place once was.

Sitting in the foothills of the Elenydd, backdropped by the soaring Tywi Forest, the abbey took its name, Strata Florida, from a Latinisation of the Welsh name, Ystrad Flur, which means Vale of the Flowers in English. The idea to build an abbey came from the Marcher knight, Robert FitzStephen, who, following the Norman invasion, had established himself at Cardigan Castle on the west Wales coast. However, within a year, he had been supplanted by the Lord Rhys of Deheubarth who ruled from his stronghold at Dinefwr Castle outside of Llandeilo.

In 1184, Rhys granted the Cistercian order more than 80,000 acres of land and became their official benefactor and patron. Over the next two centuries, Strata Florida would grow in importance as a spiritual centre.

Strata Florida was considered so important to Deheubarth power that, after Lord Rhys died and his sons began a bloody internecine struggle, the English King John (the deceitful brother of Richard the Lionheart in the Robin Hood legends) ordered the abbey be destroyed. It survived the attack but the monks had to pay £800 to John's henchmen. In a later altercation with English royalty, the monks were commanded to chop down large amounts of woodland as part of the military strategy to quell local rebellions.

My original plan had been to reach Strata Florida by way of The Cambrian Way, walking directly from Ant and Dec's phone box (as I now thought of it) all the way over Esgair Llyn-du (the ridge over the black lake) through the Tywi Forest and down into the valley to the abbey. However, after my misadventure on the previous walk, I decided to rest my ankle and attempt a less challenging route. So, this morning, I set off from the market town of Tregaron and followed a tarmacked walking and bike path that had been built on a stretch of the abandoned Manchester and Milford Railway line that once ran through the heart of Wales. It would lead me towards the village of Pontrhydfendigaid (known locally as Bont) and Strata Florida.

The path took me through Cors Caron National Nature Reserve, a large expanse of wetland on the floodplain of the River Teifi that is home to 44 different species of animals, birds, insects and fauna. They include the peregrine falcon, merlin, hen harrier and even, on occasion, the lesser spotted Montagu's harrier. Wild fowl like the water rail and teal flourish here as do red grouse and tree pipits.

Cors Caron features three significant raised bogs and so plays an important environmental role trapping and absorbing carbon dioxide. Peat bogs like this one are the most efficient carbon sinks on the planet – even better than trees.

The bog started forming some 12,000 years ago when retreating ice from a glacial age left a hollow. Water from the hillsides soon rushed in and, over the centuries, the lake became marsh and then fen. As it did so, the standing water turned acidic and plant deposits from rivers and streams feeding into the fen created peat. The trees that grew in the bog also died and became peat. Their remains have helped scientists, using carbon dating techniques, surmise that, 5,000 years ago, the bog would have been surrounded by dense deciduous forest.

Luckily for me this path was paved, well marked and stayed well clear of the bogs – I'd had more than enough of those up in the Elenydd. A young woman jogged past me as I admired the calmness of the nature reserve; less relaxing was the young family out for a bike ride, the child in tears while the father cajoled him to keep pedalling.

Eight hundred years ago the monks of Ystrad Flur worked this area of Cors Caron, cutting peat for fuel; part of an agricultural enterprise that made full and efficient use of the land they had been given to manage. The monks diverted rivers to provide drinking water, power machinery and reclaim arable land. They used the fresh water to fill their fishponds and they cultivated willow, reeds and the meadowsweet herb. But it was upland of the river valley where they applied most of their agricultural expertise.

The Cistercians quickly established themselves as one of the largest sheep farming communities in Wales. An estimated 15,000 sheep and other livestock were introduced by the monks, radically reshaping the landscape and establishing an upland farming tradition that continues to this day. The monastery was so well-respected that in 1212, Ystrad Flur became one of the earliest monasteries granted permission by the Normans to export its wool internationally.

I left the old railway line near Brynhope farm and followed the footpath through the fields to the village of Pontrhydfendigaid and on to Ystrad Flur. Along the way I passed Coed y Bont, a community enterprise set up to care for two interconnected woodlands, one previously coniferous and the other an ancient wood full of hazel and oaks with birch and alder in its marshier parts. From there it was just a short stroll to the abbey.

Looking around the wide, green and flat Teifi Valley, with Tregaron to the south and rich hillside pastureland all around, it was easy to see just how influential Ystrad Flur would have been. The business of the monks, and the abbey's strategic importance to, and support from, the heirs of Lord Rhys, would have shaped every part of life for miles around. It certainly attracted the ire of successive English rulers whose periodic attacks and raids took a toll on the physical structure of the abbey.

Ultimately, though, it was Ystrad Flur's cultural influence that would prove its most enduring legacy. It was here that the monks recorded on velum and with ornate penmanship folklores and legends that continue to intrigue and inspire readers and writers all over the world.

The Legends of the Mabinogi

Sometime around 1330, the scribes of Strata Florida created one of Wales's most important historical works. It was called *Brut y Tywysogion* and provided a year-by-year account of the history of Wales beginning in 682 and concluding in 1282 with the death of Llywelyn ap Gruffudd (Llywelyn the Last).

Some 20 years later, the monks received a new commission from a wealthy local man named Rhydderch ab Ieuan Llwyd. He was said to come from a family of bards and, based on the work the monks went on to produce, it appears he wanted to create a physical record of the Welsh legends and folklore stories that had been passed down by fellow bards, going back perhaps as far as the 6th century.

The stories were recorded in what became known as *The White Book of Rhydderch* (because of its white cover). They conjure up a magical post-Roman age where mythical kings, noblemen, magicians, witches and giants come together in a land that is unmistakeably Wales.

The main content in *The White Book* was comprised of four connected stories, known as *The Four Branches of the Mabinogi*. They are tales of love, of war, of betrayal and revenge – allegories and themes that would have been all too familiar to the noble men and women who were entertained by these romantic stories in the 12th and 13th centuries.

As with so much (or little) that we know of Welsh history, the stories inhabit that space between fact and legend, reinforcing the ancient connections between Welsh people and nature first documented with the Druids and continued through the feats of the early Celtic saints.

In the first branch of the Mabinogi, Pwyll, Prince of Dyfed, swaps places with Arawn, king of Annwn (the underworld in Welsh mythology) and both rule each other's kingdoms for a year. Pwyll is married to Rhiannon (the inspiration for Stevie Nicks's Fleetwood Mac song of the same name). She has special powers connected to horses – perhaps because, as medieval scholars have suggested, she was modelled on Epona the Celtic horse goddess.

Their son, Pryderi, is the only character who appears in all four branches of the Mabinogi though ultimately he is killed in a fight with a sorcerer and trickster known as Gwydion.

The meaning of the name Gwydion has long been a source of debate but many scholars believe it is derived from the middle Welsh word for tree and so means 'Born of Trees.' Certainly his magical connections to, and command of, nature are strong (and not dissimilar to the talents of that other legendary Welsh magician, Merlin). In one Mabinogi tale, Gwydion helps his nephew, Lleu, break a curse that prevents him from ever marrying a human female by combining the 'flowers of the oak, and the flowers of the broom, and the flowers of the meadowsweet, and from those … conjured up the fairest and most beautiful maiden anyone had ever seen.' Her name was Blodeuedd, which means 'of the flowers'.

Quite what the austere, devout Cistercian monks of Strata Florida thought of the fantastical stories they were commissioned to write down is anyone's guess. What we do know is that the stories weren't the creation of the monks themselves because many of the same tales also were recorded in the *Red Book of Hergest* (where we first learned about the Physicians of Myddfai).

Today, just a single copy of each book still exists. The *White Book of Rhydderch* is kept at the National Library of Wales in Aberystwyth while the *Red Book of Hergest* sits in the Bodleian Library at the University of Oxford. Together, they represent two of the most valuable Welsh literary artefacts ever created. In the 17th and 18th centuries, they were kept and protected by leading Welsh antiquarians at a time when the intelligentsia were starting to reappreciate the importance of Celtic heritage and history. But it's unlikely that the wider English-speaking world would ever have heard of the Mabinogi if it hadn't been for the enthusiasm of a young Englishwoman named Lady Charlotte Guest.

Lady Charlotte was born into the English aristocracy. She might have become the wife of a prime minister – she had an early courtship with Benjamin Disraeli – but instead, when she was 20 years old, she fell in love and married a budding industrialist called Josiah John Guest who was 27 years her senior. Her family was disappointed – Guest was not of noble rank. Instead, he was part of a new breed of 19th-century entrepreneur intent on harnessing nature for personal fortune and for the advancement of modern society. In 1815 he had taken over the Dowlais Ironworks near Merthyr Tydfil from his father and pitted himself against the Crawshays and their Cyfarthfa furnace.

Lady Charlotte was somewhat of a paradox. She immediately demonstrated a business acumen that helped her husband build the Ironworks. Yet, at the same time, she was a passionate humanitarian, an early environmentalist and an aficionado of the Welsh language and its literary heritage. She learned Welsh upon moving to Dowlais and soon was introduced to *The Four Branches of the Mabinogi* by her friend and fellow member of the Abergavenny Literary Society, John Jones (who was known by his Welsh pen name, Tegid). In 1837, Tegid lent her a copy of the *Red Book of Hergest* that he had been commissioned to recreate when studying at Oxford. Lady Charlotte set about translating into English not just the *Red Book of Hergest* but also a series of other important Welsh poems and romances – many emboldening the legend of King Arthur. The result was *The Mabinogion*, published in seven volumes between 1838 and 1845.

One character in Guest's Mabinogion would prove to be particularly important in terms of Wales's cultural connection to the forests and nature even though he was not included in either the original *White Book* or *Red Book*. His name was Taliesin, a 6th-century poet who is generally accepted to be one of the earliest documented Welsh poets, or bards. Guest included a homage to him called *Hanes Taliesin* (*The Tale of Taliesin*), written in the 16th century.

In fact, some medieval literature refers to Taliesin as 'Chief of the Bards'. How much of his story was real and how much was the imagination of later bards is impossible to say, but the result is a historical character who also exists as the stuff of legend.

Some of poems attributed to Taliesin put him at the very heart of the Mabinogi legends. No more so than *The Battle of the Trees* which first appeared in another 14th-century book called *Llyfr Taliesin* (*The Book of Taliesin*). In this poem, Taliesin tells the story of how the sorcerer Gwydion (slayer of Pryderi) brings the trees of the forest to life to fight a battle on his behalf:

> Alder, front of the line,
> formed the vanguard
> Willow and Rowan
> were late to the fray.

Lady Charlotte Guest's Mabinogion, along with other ancient Welsh stories such as Taliesin's, intrigued Victorian readers at a time when their own connection to nature was being eroded by the new industrial and urban way of life. Even today, the poem's influence seemingly endures in modern popular culture. Can you ever read J. R. R. Tolkien's *The Lord of the Rings* again without wondering about his inspiration for the Ents – those trees that come to life and march to war against Sauron and the kingdom of Mordor? What about the enchanted forest in *Frozen II* or the Forbidden Forest of the Harry Potter novels? All have that same sense of magic and power that the bards imbued in the forests long, long ago.

The Natural Legacy of the Bards

I had got lost in the rich history of Strata Florida and had forgotten the time. The sun was starting to set on the horizon over Cors Caron and the entire western side of the wide Teifi Valley was bathed in a soft, yellow light. I walked out under the great stone arch and prepared to wander back to Pontrhydfendigaid where I was staying the night. But before I said farewell to the abbey, I wanted to make one final stop in the churchyard next door where another famous poet and a spiritual descendant of Taliesin was buried.

His name was Dafydd ap Gwilym and his fame came not just from the racy, sometimes pornographic, imagery in his poetry, but from the belief that he was the embodiment of the ancient Welsh bardic tradition – possessing a skill set of storytelling, wisdom and mysticism inherited and passed down through the centuries from the Druids to the saints to the likes of Taliesin.

Ap Gwilym died around 1380 and was said to have been buried underneath a great yew tree in the graveyard of the church next to Strata Florida. Yews are some of the oldest trees found in Wales – many in graveyards. Some believe they are a legacy of the Druids who planted yew trees near their temples and sacred spaces as a symbol of the regeneration of the natural world and the spirit. As Christianity replaced pagan religions those spaces became graveyards. Others have a more pragmatic explanation: yew trees are highly poisonous to animals and so are an excellent way of stopping livestock trampling over the graves or scavengers digging them up. Given that some yew trees are said to be thousands of years old, I quite liked the poetic idea that the Druids had planted them.

George Borrow also came to visit ap Gwilym's grave on his *Wild Wales* walk. Borrow was flummoxed however when he found not one but two giant yews in the graveyard. He surmised that the tree located at the northern wall of the churchyard must have been the poet's final resting place because it looked older than the second tree and even though 'either lightning or the force of wind had splitten off a considerable part of the head and trunk, so that one part of it looked strong and blooming, the other was white and spectral.'

Borrow took his trip in the middle of the 19th century, at a time when the writings of Dafydd ap Gwilym, and the role of the bard in

Celtic and British identity, were of increasing interest to the intelligentsia of the Romantic movement (his book was published just 15 years after Lady Charlotte Guest finished the last volume of *The Mabinogion*). One person who helped influence the Victorian infatuation with Dafydd ap Gwilym and the tales of ancient bards was Edward Williams. He, under the pen name, Iolo Morganwg, had dedicated his life to making the case that Welsh Druidic traditions underpinned the modern Romantic movement.

A Rattleskull Genius

Born in Glamorgan, Williams was a man of few means and grew up learning stonemasonry skills – a trade he would fall back on to survive throughout his highly eventful life. His real calling, however, was as a writer, a poet, a philosopher, an amateur arborist, a fighter against slavery and inequality and a leader in the Unitarian movement. More than anything else, he was a passionate advocate for the reaffirmation of a Druidic lineage – passed down through the bards and closely aligned with nature – that could define and shape a cohesive Welsh identity. He wrote his first piece of poetry in Wales but soon moved to London to be part of the Welsh expat intellectual Gwyneddigion Society and the growing Romantic movement.

Iolo's devotion to the bardic tradition was impressive; obsessive even. He named his own son Taliesin and even adopted the fictitious suffix of BBD (Bard by the Privilege and Rite of the Bards of the Isle of Britain). He devoted himself to translating the work of his hero Dafydd ap Gwilym so that it could be enjoyed by new audiences both in Wales and in England. In 1789 he published *Barddoniaeth Dafydd ab Gwilym*, a collection that included a large number of ap Gwylim's poems that had never been seen before (for reasons that will become clear soon). Iolo's investment in the Druidic/bardic tradition was so intense that he even developed a runic system based on an ancient Druid alphabet, similar to the Ogham of the Irish Druids.

Iolo's most audacious attempt to cement the Druidic/bardic legacy endures to this day, celebrated each year at Wales's National Eisteddfod – the Welsh-language cultural festival of singing, dancing and bardic recital that can be traced back to the rule of The Lord Rhys, the original benefactor of the monks at Strata Florida.

In the October 1792 edition of *Gentleman's Magazine*, a story described how on September 23 'this being the day on which the autumnal equinox occurred, some Welsh Bards, resident in London, assembled in congress on Primrose Hill, according to ancient usage … The wonted ceremonies were observed. A circle of stones formed, in the middle of which was the Maen Gorsedd, or Altar, on which a naked sword being placed, all the Bards assisted to sheath it.'

This supposed long-lost Druidic ceremony – harking back to the oak grove celebrations of Silurian times – had been organised by Iolo Morganwg, He'd conjured the idea out of thin air – inspired perhaps by the mystical abilities of Taliesin and probably fuelled by his addiction to laudanum, the opiate tincture of choice for many a Romantic writer looking for inspiration.

The theatrical stunt didn't end there. In 1819, Iolo pitched the idea of the Gorsedd to the organisers of the Eisteddfod. Perennially challenged to drum up enough interest in the event, the organisers gave him the go-ahead. At the end of the festival, Iolo produced a stone circle of pebbles from his coat pocket in the garden of Carmarthen's Ivy Bush Hotel and recreated the Gorsedd ceremony that he had first imagined in London nearly 30 years before. In his 1968 study, *The Druids*, Stuart Piggott wrote, 'The Gorsedd, which Iolo originally had hoped might supersede the Eisteddfod, was now assured of a future as an integral part of it, nicely calculated to appeal to nationals and romantics, the credulous and the pompous.'

Piggott's derisive description isn't surprising given how Iolo's reputation became tarnished after his death. In the late 19th century, a new breed of Welsh academics began investigating Iolo's literary output and discovered that many of the medieval manuscripts (including those marvellous new works of Dafydd ap Gwilym) were fake. Iolo was branded a charlatan and a forger. Yet perhaps his only real sin was being a dreamer and a true romantic – a man passionate about his heritage, his land and an ideal. He certainly saw no financial gain from his fabrication of history. Most of all though, Iolo seemed to have been emulating (if also embellishing) that liminal storytelling space between history and legend that his heroes were most celebrated for. In that context, surely he was a true bard?

The two yews described by Borrow were still in the churchyard when I visited. Today, it is the one to the west of the Abbey and close to St Mary's Parish Church that has been officially ordained as Dafydd ap Gwilym's grave, denoted by a large plaque made out of pebble that sat perched on a low stone wall supporting the tree's base. The trunk of the great tree, once estimated to have been 24 feet wide, had been reduced to two large fragments with a hollow middle.

Before you head to Strata Florida to shed a tear or recite a poem like Borrow (and perhaps Iolo) keep in mind that there is, however, a caveat to the Dafydd ap Gwilym yew tree story: Dafydd might not be there at all. A rival monastery, Talley, some 10 miles south, also claims to be his resting place. That's Welsh history for you.

11

Environmentalism's Romantic Past

A walk from Pontrhydfendigaid to Borth

I checked into the Red Lion pub in Pontrhydfendigaid (which translates as 'the bridge over the blessed ford') a mile from Ystrad Flur. The next day I would walk to Devil's Bridge and then onto Borth, following a 36-mile-long walking path called, appropriately, the Borth to Pontrhydfendigaid Trail (though I was walking it in reverse). It was also known as the Mal Evans Way, after the chairman of the Aberystwyth Group of the Ramblers' Association.

The Red Lion was a simple, no-nonsense place that had been catering to local farmers and drovers for hundreds of years. Back in 1837, the Liverpool writer Thomas Roscoe described 'stopping at the small hostelry, where a rampant red lion swings and creeks its invitation to man and beast'.

Roscoe settled into the pub and made notes on the décor, notably:

Carefully pinned to a curtain hung a very knowing lace cap, with boarders of that extraordinary width and abundance seen only among the Welsh belles, and most beautifully 'got up' as the ladies say. On a corner table, too, lay a hat, which, by its gloss, newness, and clever shape, evidently intended to invite the cap to church the following Sunday, and the entrance of a tight, blooming, dark-eyed, and sprightly-looking Welsh girl with my intended repast, soon enabled my calculating curiosity to supply a face worthy of the becoming national costume.

The landlord, a slight Hungarian man called Roland, could have done with a bit of help right now – even without the addition of what has become established as the traditional Welsh national dress. He looked rushed off his feet as he struggled to keep up with the drinks and food orders being thrown at him on this summer evening. By 8 p.m. however the pub was almost empty and, as I enjoyed a pint of Wye Valley Brewery Butty Bach, I asked what had brought him to a remote village in the heart of mid-Wales.

'I came here 14 years ago. I have a Welsh fiancée and we bought the pub a couple of years back,' he said. Roland had lived in cities for many years but now craved the quiet life. 'It's nice here. No one is going to rob you,' he added matter-of-factly.

It was a reassuring thought though perhaps not one the local tourist board will be adopting as their new slogan any time soon.

The next morning, I said goodbye to Roland and headed off through the village onto the Borth to Pontrhydfendigaid Trail. It was a grey but dry day and the dark clouds created a moody backdrop as they sat behind the craggy Pen y Bannau hill in the distance. The trail weaved its way through the back of the village and past a number of gardens – I'm not sure who was more surprised when I walked past one family enjoying an 8.30 a.m. hot tub.

Outside of the village I came across a farm campsite where a middle-aged man dressed in a grey bathrobe was sipping tea and smoking a breakfast cigarette. He pointed me in the right direction up the track and I continued to climb through fields of sheep and disused, rusting farm equipment. The Borth to Bont walking trail required me to head due east but I could see on the map there was a perfectly good public footpath that led straight on in the northerly direction I needed to go. So, of course, I took the short cut.

A few weeks later when I looked back at notes of the walk I could see I'd written in block capitals: 'JUST COS IT SAYS THERE IS A PATH DOESN'T MEAN ANYONE HAS USED IT.'

Indeed, what should have been an easy stroll turned into a dance through stinging nettles and brambles that tore at my legs. I vowed that from now on I would stick to the official walking paths I'd planned to follow.

For the first hour I followed a desolate rough stone and mud track over the northern fringe of the Elenydd leading from Ffair Rhos towards Pen Rhiwlas. The path resembled a minor torrent – so much water was running down it from the hillsides.

Still, my only real obstacle this morning was a very large flock of sheep. There must have been more than 200 of them ambling in front of me, making a mess of the dirt track, their legs and long white tails stained muddy brown. I was forced to wade through churned-up puddles of mud. This could have been a very slow and depressing slog in the rain. Luckily the sun was out and the temperature was starting to rise – along with my spirits – so I could see the funny, if slightly smelly, side of being stuck behind a sheep convoy.

Finally I was rid of them and free to pick up the pace once again. It was midday now and the sun was warm on my back. I reached an old farmhouse now spruced up and converted into what had the appearance of a high-end holiday cottage. The gate was padlocked so I climbed over and continued on the footpath as it snaked back behind the property through a grove of mixed oaks.

Back when I began this long journey, I had struggled to recognise these most majestic of trees but, slowly, my mind was awakening to the natural world around me. I still was no expert but at least I could recognise sessile oaks as they hugged the steep sides of craggy ravines. I could spot the mountain-loving rowan trees by their bright red berries and I could identify alder in the low-lying waterlogged areas it thrives in. I also was starting to pay attention to the rhythms of other wildlife – how the ubiquitous red kites hunted in pairs and how what looked like chiffchaffs picked their way through the grassy tussocks of upland raised bog looking for insects as I picked my own way in search of dry, flat ground. Admittedly, I still needed to consult a bird-spotting app but it was a start.

The more I experienced nature first-hand the more I realised that I wasn't learning about this world for the first time but more rediscovering a knowledge that I once had and had lost. I'd studied all the trees of Wales when I was a child in school. At the same age, I'd practised spotting local birds in my garden and on cub scout outings. Yet, at some point in my teens, other more urban priorities (bars, cars, gigs, etc.) took over and my own connection with nature started to falter. Now, my fresh commitment to explore nature was making me realise the wealth of what I'd turned my back on.

At last the thick woodland of Coed Bwlchgwallter came into view. At points, sunlight broke through the cloud cover, casting its light on sections of conifer leaves and creating what looked like a green patchwork from afar. I followed a road down to a farmhouse that had a mini conifer plantation where its front garden might once have been. The public footpath skirted around the property and past a herd of shaggy-haired Welsh longhorn cows. They looked very overdressed for such a warm day. Ahead of me was another thick forested valley and running down the middle was an expanse of landscaped fields and gardens.

I had arrived at the Hafod Estate – an enduring visual embodiment of the Romantic movement's embrace of nature.

Picturing the Picturesque

In 1780, a young aristocrat named Thomas Johnes travelled from his ancestral home in Ludlow, England, just over the Welsh border, to a wild, unkempt valley in the Cambrian Mountains known as Hafod Uchtryd. Five hundred years before, this had been the summer grange of the Cistercian monks at Strata Florida but it had fallen into disrepair over the centuries. The hillsides had been mined for lead and the land had been extensively grazed by tenant sheep farmers, stripping it bare of vegetation.

Furthermore, most of those farmers were close to destitute. It was as unappealing a piece of rural real estate as you could imagine.

Johnes had inherited Hafod Uchtryd on the death of his father. But while most other well-to-do young men would have balked at what life was like in the Ystwyth Valley, Johnes fell in love with its rugged beauty and saw the potential to create something special.

A few years earlier the artist and travel writer William Gilpin, had published his influential 'Essay on Prints'. It expanded on the philosophies of the new, highly popular Romantic tradition to the natural world, creating a new artistic and aesthetic movement that would become known as the Picturesque – one that could be defined as 'that kind of beauty which is agreeable in a picture.'

In 1782 Gilpin laid out his philosophy in a book, *Observations on the River Wye and several parts of South Wales, etc. relative chiefly to Picturesque Beauty*. Gilpin encouraged his readers to undertake 'picturesque travel' and discover beauty created solely by 'Nature'. This, he explained, involved celebrating that which was considered unspoiled or created in harmony with the natural landscape.

Gilpin's choice of the Afon Gwy (River Wye), running up the border between England and Wales, generated great interest in visiting Wales with an educated set of tourists who in previous generations had looked to the Grand Tour of Europe for aesthetic inspiration and to provide sophisticated dinner conversation. With much of the European continent off-limits because of war and revolution, the natural beauty of Wales offered a good substitute.

Gilpin had already started to influence the way some wealthy landowners were shaping their estates. Two Hereford-based landowners in particular, Richard Payne Knight and his friend Sir Uvedale Price, heartily embraced Gilpin's ideas and, through their work and writing, helped elevate the Picturesque into mainstream consciousness.

Knight was Thomas Johnes's cousin and it wasn't long before the Hafod heir reached out to Gilpin for advice on how he could make his own estate picturesque. Johnes travelled to England to meet Gilpin in 1787, taking a portfolio of sketches with him. His goal was to have the Hafod Estate included in the second edition of Gilpin's Wye tour.

Gilpin was impressed by Johnes's vision for Hafod, even more so when Johnes explained his ideas were influenced by a book written by Gilpin's great friend, William Mason, titled: *The English Garden*.

Thomas Johnes got what he wanted. Gilpin included Hafod in later editions of the Wye Tour, writing that, 'the views shift rapidly from one to another; each being characterised by some circumstances peculiar to itself.' It was the only entry in Gilpin's tours not based on first-person observations.

The planting of trees was central to both Mason's and Gilpin's picturesque aesthetic so Johnes's transformation of Hafod involved an aggressive and sustained policy of afforestation. From 1782 to 1813 more than three million trees were planted over the estate – initially to offer employment to Johnes's tenants and to protect the crops he was growing on the lower ground but also to create a vast natural relief for the mansion and grounds he built in the valley. Johnes's approach to planting was very much in sync with Mason's Picturesque principles – the valley's jagged peaks were left to project from hanging woods.

Conifer was the preferred tree species of choice for planting across all of Wales's estates at the time and larch was particularly popular because its early growth rate was superior to pine and spruce. Also, it was believed to be less attractive and palatable to sheep than most of the other trees being planted. Larch accounted for well over half the total woodland acreage of the estate. Such was Johnes's prodigiousness, he received the Royal Society of Arts medal for tree planting on five occasions.

At its peak Hafod's picturesque charms attracted many hundreds of visitors each year – so many that Johnes was forced to charge admission to help cover the running costs of the estate. These early tourists would often visit Hafod on a day trip from Aberystwyth that also took in the Devil's Bridge waterfall a few miles to the north of the estate. Other more adventurous souls would continue their journey to Pontrhydfendigaid and the abbey at Strata Florida.

In 1794, a group of Cambridge Students made part of this journey through mid-Wales. Among them was Samuel Coleridge. Four years later, he would publish what became one of the most celebrated of Romantic poems, *Kubla Khan, or, A Vision in a Dream: A Fragment*. Could Hafod have been the inspiration for Coleridge's opium-inspired homage to the Mongol summer palace of Xanadu? That certainly was the argument made by literary critic Geoffrey Grigson in his 1947 essay, *Kubla Khan in Wales: Hafod and the Devil's Bridge*.

Nowadays the Hafod Estate looks a little different to how it did in Johnes's day but not completely. The original great house has gone, having burned down in 1807 and, while it was rebuilt, Johnes was forced to sell Hafod in 1814, bankrupted by his devotion to creating his own Xanadu. Over the years the estate fell into disrepair and the main house was demolished by the Forestry Commission. The estate fell on hard times during the 20th century but, since the early 1990s, a charitable enterprise, The Hafod Trust, has worked to restore its designed landscape.

Part of the Trust's focus was on restoring two signature walks created by Johnes. They are the Lady's Walk and the Gentleman's Walk and their differences say quite a lot about how 18th-century society viewed the abilities of what they might have referred to as the 'fairer sex'. The former is a two-and-a-quarter-mile gentle stroll along the valley floor and Ystwyth River as it generates volume and picks up speed on its rendezvous with the sea at Aberystwyth. Along the way, ladies got to choose between exploring the Garden Walk – a tight woodland path that passes through the flower garden – or the meadow path that hugs the river.

By contrast, The Gentleman's Walk is a six-mile 'manly' walk – rising high into the thick and steep mixed woodland hillsides running down the valley. It mirrored the route I was walking through the estate so I climbed up into the tall forest, past lines of trees that had been snapped at their trunks or, in some cases, ripped up by their roots in severe winter storms earlier that year, and wandered the tight dirt trail as it hugged the mountainside, went past a series of mini waterfalls and through tunnels carved out of the side of the rock. At some points I had a bird's-eye view of the Hafod Estate while at other times it was as if I'd been swallowed up by the forest.

Today, the 200-hectare Hafod Estate remains a mix of wild and nurtured spaces. Its forested flanks are in sharp contrast to the neatly planned and recently restored flower garden, valley walking trails and the central lawn-turned-meadow that today provides a pastoral home to a flock of particularly plump and well-coiffured sheep who graze among the tourists walking through.

And it wasn't just a few tourists sharing space with the sheep. In the late summer of 2020, Hafod (and all of Wales for that matter) was packed with visitors from all over the UK as nearly all international travel stopped because of the pandemic. Two hundred years after Wales first became a haven for Picturesque tourists, a new generation of British holidaymakers were connecting with the estate's natural beauty.

As I made my way through the grounds, a steady procession of families explored the trails while others enjoyed picnics on the lawns of the ornate gardens. In the flower garden, two little girls played hide-and-seek around a miniature hedge while their parents watched contentedly from a bench. Down by the river, families made their way past the tall green reeds that lined both banks so they could paddle in the cool water. On a much grander scale, Hafod's gardens and lawns reminded me a little of playing in Insole Court as a child. I paused for a while to appreciate the fun the little kids were having playing in nature – and the break it gave their parents!

On one of the larger tracks, near the obelisk monument built in 1805 in honour of the 5th Duke of Bedford, a renowned agriculturalist and friend of Johnes, I stopped to chat with another walker who waved and said hello as we approached each other. He had travelled from Hereford on the English border and was dressed in serious looking hiking gear. He was even carrying a pair of binoculars.

'I'm retired but my wife has kicked me out for a few days so she can have a summer holiday at home with her sister,' he explained. 'I'm a keen gardener so Hafod was a good choice – I love all of the Picturesque stuff.'

I mentioned that I was just passing through the estate on my way north to Devil's Bridge.

'You'll make it easily, it's not far,' my fellow walker said, before adding: 'Mind you, I drove down.'

On to Devil's Bridge

The Borth to Pontrhydfendigaid walking trail headed east on the south side of the Ystwyth River and weaved its way around the village of Cwmystwyth before heading north through Coed yr Arch and Coed y Ceuleth woodlands towards Devil's Bridge. It looked like a great walk but it was nearly 3 p.m. and I had to make up time if I was going to make it to Ponterwyd, a village seven miles north where I was staying the night. Hafod had taken me down a very enjoyable rabbit hole of history and scenery but had thrown my walking schedule off track.

After consulting my map, I decided to take a more direct route by following a road that led from Hafod up towards The Arch, a stone structure built in 1810 to mark the Golden Jubilee of King George III and which had also served as the northern gateway to the estate.

It was raining and, as I walked up the side of the road, car after car raced by me – so many that I had to jump out of the road onto the uneven bank by its side and pick my way up the steep incline to avoid getting run over.

The Arch sat at the top of a mountain pass. It was here that I stumbled on a marker for The Cambrian Way. If you'd asked me yesterday if I would ever get on that trail again, I'd have said you were crazy but now, outnumbered and outgunned by the cars racing by, I was thrilled to take my chances once more with Tony Drake's vision of mountain walking.

This stretch of The Cambrian Way followed a bridleway running directly above the main road to Devil's Bridge. To begin with, I trekked over open ground, snacking on the early ripening blackberries growing in the hedgerows by the side of the path.

Soon the trail led into an unnamed wood and the sounds of the traffic below became muffled before disappearing completely. Purple heather mixed with bright green moss at the foot of the pine trees. A lone dog howled in the distance. On the horizon, I could just make out the roofs of houses nestled above a valley. This had to be Devil's Bridge.

There's a good reason this one small village in the heart of Welsh-speaking mid-Wales has such an eye-catching English name: tourism marketing. Its original Welsh name, Pontarfynach, simply means 'bridge on the River Mynach' (Monk). It's thought that the monks of Strata Florida first constructed a stone bridge to connect both sides of a steep gorge back in the 11th century – possibly to connect a pilgrimage trail between their abbey and another Cistercian seat of worship and learning called Cymer some 50 miles north.

In the late 18th century, as increasing numbers of wealthy English tourists started to visit the Hafod Estate, Thomas Johnes decided to build a hunting lodge (he called it a 'little public cottage') for visitors, overlooking the gorge and the spectacular waterfalls that cascade into it. Visiting the lodge in 1799, the English physician, antiquarian and travel writer George Lipscomb described his view in true picturesque prose:

> In front of the principal room a huge chasm penetrates into the bosom of the opposite mountain, and displays the rough surfaces of mossy rocks, whose summits are clothed with wood. A winding road borders the edge of it, and soon loses itself among the mountains.

To add to the allure and mystique of this wild Wales experience, Johnes helped inject new life into a local legend about how the bridge across the Mynach was constructed. It recounted how the Devil had made a pact with a local woman, promising to build a great bridge in just one night. In return he demanded the soul of the first living thing to cross the bridge. In the morning the old lady arrived at the bridge with her dog and was met by the Devil. He expected her to walk across the bridge and forfeit her soul but, instead, she threw a loaf of bread she was carrying across the bridge and her dog sprinted after it. Outwitted, the Devil disappeared in a huff.

Through the 19th century, increasing numbers of tourists came to see the waterfalls and the Devil's Bridge. Over time, the name stuck. I stopped outside Johnes's old hunting lodge. Just a few years ago, it had featured on the TV-noir drama, *Hinterland,* as a bleak and spooky old hotel. Recently, though, it had been completely refurbished and renamed as The Hafod Hotel. This afternoon, it was full of tourists enjoying a meal or a drink in the afternoon sun.

I joined them, sitting on a wall opposite the hotel sipping a beer and gawking at the steady convoy of tourists in luxury cars – Bentleys, Range Rover Vogues, fancy Porsches and low-slung Lamborghinis – snaking their way over the bridge and up past the hotel. Surely, this set would normally have decamped to Tuscany, Provence and other European destinations, plans presumably scuppered by Covid. I wondered if they even bothered to get out of their cars to appreciate the landscape they were driving through – or even noticed it amid the roar of the supercharged engines or the boom of the sound system?

It was time to move on. My hotel for the night was still five miles away so I rejoined the Borth to Pontrhydfendigaid Trail and walked down through green pastures and into the woodlands that led to the valley floor. Above me, four red kites circled looking for food.

The trail hugged the side of the valley until I crossed a narrow gauge Vale of Rheidol railway line that brings tourists to Devil's Bridge from Aberystwyth. There was a swing gate and walkway across the line with signs warning you to take care crossing. There was nothing to worry about today, though, the steam engine service suspended because of the pandemic.

I was now in Coed Rheidol, an ancient oak wood that was heavily coppiced in the First World War to provide pitwood for the south Wales mines. It was a jumbled, contorted playground of regrown sessile oaks, their trunks and branches spread at all angles as if the entire forest was taking part in a game of Twister.

By the time I'd reached Ponterwyd I was exhausted; I had walked 15 miles through the hills that day and I was very grateful to check into the George Borrow Hotel.

This was the place Borrow stayed on his walk some 150 years ago and, while it would be unfair to say the Borrow Hotel hadn't changed at all since his visit, it certainly could have done with a refresh. Neither did the landlady, a lady in her 50s or 60s, appear overly thrilled to have guests (though the strict Covid rules on staying in hotels couldn't have made hotel life easy). Trying to lighten the mood, I asked her what it was like running such an iconic hotel. 'We've been trying to sell it for the past eight years but no one wants to buy it,' was her reply.

The Right to Roam

The next morning I rejoined the Borth long distance walk at Bwlch Nant yr Arian Forest. I climbed up the footpath known as the Miner's Trail over Pen Darren. A giant wooden chair was positioned on the brow of the ridge, looking out across the valley towards the sea.

To my left I could just make out the hazy outline of Cardigan Bay while to my right was the peak of Pumlumon, the highest point in mid-Wales at 752 metres and the source of two of Wales's longest rivers, the Hafren and the Gwy.

Bwlch Nant yr Arian was another part of the National Forest plan. It was easy to see how people might embrace these woodlands. The forest park was already well known for its red kite feeding centre and for its biking and walking trails. On one, the Elenydd Trail, wooden sculptures celebrated local folklore and legends including the Knockers of Cwmsymlog – the name given to the faeries who were said to help miners locate seams of lead by making knocking noises.

As I wandered through the elevated woodland, I thought about all the Romantic writers and poets who had flocked to Wales. How their travels through the natural beauty and landscape had shaped their appreciation of the importance of connecting with nature – and how their creative expression of this connection has influenced millions of others all over the world.

There was the poet William Wordsworth who composed *Lines Written a Few Miles Above Tintern Abbey* in his head as he walked through the Wye Valley back to the house he shared with Samuel Coleridge near Bristol. Coleridge, in turn, found the muse for his poetry while walking miles along the Somerset coast in a laudanum haze, gazing across the Bristol Channel at south Wales. I imagined how the artist J. M. W. Turner must have felt the first time he set eyes on Carreg Cennen and marvelled, as I had done, at how its craggy ruins sat in stark contrast to the rolling farmland of rural Carmarthenshire. And I also spared a thought for Iolo Morganwg whose passionate embrace of the ancient Welsh Druidic tradition helped inspire the Romantic tradition, even if his legacy became tarnished by his own embellishments.

The Romantic tradition was very much a reaction to industrialisation and the resulting pollution, urbanisation and social inequalities that accompanied it. It was a rejection of the idea that science, technology and man-made accomplishments should be considered superior to the natural world even as a new era of business sought to tame and exploit the environment for its own gain – principally through the use of fossil fuels.

As the 19th century progressed, what had started as a cultural reaction to the new industrial age transformed into a movement committed to conserving and protecting the environment on both sides of the Atlantic. The Royal Society for the Protection of Birds was founded in 1889 followed six years later by the National Trust for Places of Historic Interest or Natural Beauty (which was originally established as a conservation group to protect green spaces). In the US, meanwhile, the influence of poets like Henry David Thoreau and Walt Whitman, along with the writing of George Perkins Marsh (in particular *Man and Nature*, his 1864 polemic attack on humankind's 'reckless destructiveness' of the natural world) helped infuse new environmental sensibilities in the educated classes. In 1892, conservationist John Muir founded the Sierra Club and this was followed by the Audubon Society in 1905.

It was lunchtime and I had made it to Talybont, a mere two miles from Borth, the end point of the trail. I was hungry having walked nonstop for the past four hours so I stopped for a sandwich and a quick pint of beer at the Black Lion pub. I didn't linger – I was keen to reach my destination before the storm clouds gathering in the Irish Sea made it to shore. Anyway, today was definitely not the right day to hang around Talybont. In the half hour I'd been in the pub, a sewage pipe had ruptured in the centre of the village.

I pushed on, walking slowly but steadily through the woods on the north side of the Afon Leri until the trail emerged into an open field and I saw something I'd yet to encounter on the 150 miles I'd walked so far. The field was full not just of sheep but also seagulls. As I reached the top the long coastline of Cardigan Bay and the town of Borth came into view. Finally, I was in sniffing distance of my destination. I skipped my way down through the fields and onto the lane that would lead to the final footpath of the day – a straight flat shot across the coastal plain into town.

Except the footpath no longer existed. Instead, on the metal gate that once provided access to the route there was a sign screaming: PRIVATE – THIS IS NOT A PUBLIC RIGHT OF WAY. I had no choice but to trudge further down the lane about half a mile and then scramble through boggy track before picking up the trail again.

My boots and feet were soaked and I was annoyed at having been denied access to what looked like a perfectly good entrance to the public footpath. I felt it was my right to walk this beautiful land – especially when the map established I was walking on an official right of way.

I wasn't alone in my anger at being shut out. The blocking of public rights of way has long been a complaint among the walking community. Lockdown, however, had spurred a new impetus in England and Wales to reclaim people's right to roam the countryside. There was even an online campaign, supported by leading figures in the arts and the environment, calling on the government to expand the 2000 Countryside and Rights of Way Act that had granted unrestricted access to over three million acres of countryside across England and Wales. Ninety-two per cent of land still remained off-limits to walkers, however, and the campaigners were demanding improved access to woodlands, rivers and Green Belt land. They pointed to Scotland, which passed a law in 2005 giving people the right to access most land and inland water for recreational purposes.

The new Right to Roam movement drew inspiration from the 1932 Kinder Scout protest. That saw some 400 walkers organised by the British Workers' Sports Federation (an offshoot of the British Communist Party) stage an organised trespass on a moorland plateau in the Derbyshire Peak District owned by the Duke of Devonshire. This mass action – the largest ever seen in the UK – had been sparked by a growing sense of resentment against the way wealthy landowners prevented ordinary people, the majority of whom lived and worked in Britain's polluted towns and cities, from enjoying large tracts of the countryside.

When the walkers reached Kinder Scout they clashed with gamekeepers. Several of the ramblers were arrested. Five were convicted and imprisoned. At the trial, the leader of the group, a young man named Benny Rothman, gave this impassioned defence:

> We ramblers, after a hard week's work, in smokey towns and cities, go out rambling for relaxation and fresh air. And we find the finest rambling country is closed to us. Our request, or demand, for access to all peaks and uncultivated moorland is nothing unreasonable.

The severity of the prison sentences (ranging from two to six months, even though trespassing was not a crime) received a great deal of newspaper coverage. People across the country were shocked by what they read and soon other walking protests were taking place. The Right to Roam movement was born.

I had reached the halfway point of my journey, having covered nearly 150 miles. Along the way I'd attempted to trace the history of deforestation in Wales and I'd seen how industrialisation, and the widespread migration to the cities that it brought about, had broken the strong connection to the forests and to nature that we as society once possessed. But I'd also seen how local communities were trying to regain that connection for their physical and mental health. How through our legends and folklore, we continue to celebrate and be in awe of the power of nature. And how we are just starting to learn the importance of trees in maintaining the well-being of our planet.

I could see that it was critical that we rebalance our relationship with nature, but how could we even start given the damage that had been done over many centuries? A piecemeal approach was not going to work. The PRIVATE sign illustrated how great ideas like the Borth to Pontrhydfendigaid walking trail can falter if just one part of the system doesn't work. If we were really going to address the problems that threatened all our futures we needed systems – legal, political, economic and cultural – that were designed to work with nature, not against it.

Part Three

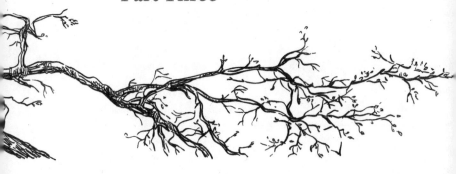

The Rise
of the Trees

12

A National Forest is Born

Walking from Borth to Machynlleth

A long, long time ago (or so the story goes) there was a rich and fertile kingdom situated on the lowland flood plains of west Wales. The land was so valued that one acre there was worth four elsewhere. It was called Cantre'r Gwaelod (the lowland or sunken hundred) and was ruled by King Gwyddno Garanhir, whose palace was located near modern-day Aberystwyth. The land lay below sea level and was protected by a complex system of sea walls. The guardian of these defences was a friend of the king, a prince named Seithennyn. Every night he shut the gates to protect Cantre'r Gwaelod from the sea flooding in. But, one night, Seithennyn got drunk at a feast and forgot to close the gates. It was a stormy evening and the spring high tides flooded all of the land and the 16 villages within it. Cantre'r Gwaelod was lost. But sometimes, at very low tide after winter storms, you can see the remnants of an ancient oak, pine and birch forest protruding from the sands on the beach at Borth, a seaside town five miles north of Aberystwyth. And it is said that on a clear day, you can sometimes hear the peel of a submerged church bell ringing out across Cardigan Bay.

This tale was first written down in the *Black Book of Carmarthen* (though, as with many local legends, there are different versions of the story of this Welsh Atlantis, as it is often called). For antiquarians like Iolo Morganwg who resurrected it in the late 18th century, it offered yet another narrative that pointed to Wales's historic importance and sense of identity.

I would have loved to have seen the sunken forest but it was not to be that morning. I stood on the seafront watching an angry black squall moving in from the bay. I scoffed my bacon and egg sandwich and gulped my coffee so that I could start walking and escape the storm. I had 15 miles of mostly uphill walking ahead and I wanted to reach my destination, Machynlleth, by late afternoon. There, I was meeting up with a group of friends who were going to join me for a few days walking in north Wales.

I crossed the railway track that cut through the centre of town, walked past St Matthew's Church and arrived at the signpost for the Wales National Coastal Path just as the squall chased me down on this flat, coastal plain with no tree cover and no place to shelter.

Rain comes in many different shapes, sizes and speeds in Wales. But it can be relied upon to turn up most days in one of those forms. Rain is so prevalent in Wales that, over the years, local folk have come up with more than 20 different words to describe it. There's *glawio* (raining), *dafnu* (spotting), *sgrympian* (a short sharp shower), *cawodi* (showering), *tollti* (pouring), *brylymu* (pouring very quickly) and my personal favourite, *mae hi'n bwrw hen wragedd a ffyn* (it's raining old women and sticks).

The storm was over almost before it started but, over the course of a couple of minutes, I had got soaked to the skin and felt like I'd experienced all 20 different descriptions in one go. Pissed off, very, very wet and still clutching my now-soggy takeaway coffee cup, I squelched through marshy fields, trying not to slip on the wooden plank micro-bridges that had been laid down to help walkers navigate the path.

The weather quickly improved, however, and soon I was stripping off my wet outer layers as the heat of the sun transformed me into a walking steam room – one that was leaving a trail of evaporation across the middle of Cors Fochno, an ancient coastal raised peat bog that many thousands of years ago would have been connected to what became the sunken forest of Cantre'r Gwaelod.

Once, there were over 4,000 hectares of raised bog in Wales but today just over a quarter of that is left. Cors Fochno is one of the largest actively growing raised bogs in the lowlands of the UK. It is also considered one of the finest in the UK – part of the 324-square-mile UNESCO Dyfi Valley Biosphere Reserve – and is home to many different types of moss including *Sphagnum fuscum* and *imbricatum*. The mosses can hold more than eight times their own weight in water. One of the local species, *sphagnum cuspidatum*, is called 'wet kittens' because it looks like soaked fur when removed from the water. In the centre of the bog, far from the encroachment of any human activity, a very rare species called *sphagnum pulchrum* resembled a yellow lawn.

These mosses also help engineer the workings of the bog. As the plants grow upwards their remains decompose under the waterlogged conditions, eventually forming peat – the peat at Cors Fochno is eight metres deep in places.

That's how the experts describe the wonders of Cors Fochno anyway. All my untrained eyes could make out was a hodgepodge blanket of light green, mustard yellow and dark mustard brown wetland grasses, reeds and fern. One part of the marsh looked like it was inhabited by green smurfs, there were so many tussocks popping up amongst the short grass.

If the finer points of coastal flora still escaped me, I was getting better at spotting some of the fauna that lived there. Directly above me, two crows were squabbling and pecking at each other in mid-air. In the distance what looked like a flight of swallows were scouting the flat landscape while, around the channels of water cutting through the bog, small yellow and brown sedge warblers ducked in and out of the reed beds. Hundreds of orange-brown butterflies fussed around and there was a constant hum of bees, flies and what looked like some very large horseflies going about their buzziness. Later, I also discovered I was walking through a party zone for adders and grass snakes.

Cors Fochno is part protected nature reserve and part agricultural land. A cow scratched an itch against a solar panel. Further on, a sheep dog corralled a flock of ewes while the farmer watched on, his young daughter by his side.

Cors Fochno, like Cors Caron outside of Tregaron, also plays an important role in helping combat climate change. These peatlands are some of the most effective carbon sponges on the planet – it can take around 1,000 years to make just one metre of peat, and this slow process makes the raised peat bog extremely effective at absorbing and storing carbon.

However, when peat bogs are damaged they lose their ability to hold carbon and they switch from being a carbon sink to a carbon spewer. Currently, drained peatlands (much of it appropriated for agriculture) contribute an estimated at 1.9 gigatonnes of CO_2 annually to the atmosphere. That's the equivalent of nearly six per cent of all human-related CO_2 emissions.*

Climate researchers believe the world may have lost as much as 87 per cent of its wetlands since the start of the First Industrial Revolution and much of the loss has occurred since 1900.[†] Back in 1971, the United Nations passed the Ramsar Convention on Wetlands, an intergovernmental treaty promoting wetland conservation. Today, the convention is believed to protect 2,413 wetlands encompassing some 985,000 square miles and has been ratified by 170 countries.[‡] Yet despite this global action, peatland and wetland destruction continues. One recent scientific study estimates that at least 35 per cent of wetlands globally have been lost since Ramsar was adopted.

Cors Fochno was part of a four-year initiative to restore seven raised bogs in Wales. The project aimed to repair 50 per cent of Welsh raised bog habitat by improving water retention, cutting down invasive species, removing scrub and, where relevant, introducing light cattle grazing, all in partnership with local communities and landowners.[§]

That's if climate change doesn't intervene first. Cors Fochno and the entire area around the town of Borth sit at sea level. Scientists project

---

* https://www.iucn.org/resources/issues-briefs/peatlands-and-climate-change
[†] https://www.wwt.org.uk/our-work/threats-to-wetlands/#:~:text=Unsustainable%20development,for%20housing%2C%20industry%20and%20agriculture
[‡] https://earth.org/researchers-urge-better-protection-as-wetlands-continue-to-vanish/
[§] https://naturalresources.wales/about-us/our-projects/nature-projects/new-life-for-welsh-raised-bogs/?lang=en

that, if greenhouse gas emissions aren't dramatically reduced, the oceans could rise as much as four metres over the next 200 years. According to the scientific modelling, even a half-metre rise in the Irish Sea would flood much of the land around the Dyfi estuary. By comparison, the legend of Cantre'r Gwaelod would seem like a drop in the ocean.

Blazing a Coastal Trail

I wandered inland to the nearby village of Tre Taliesin. Legend had it the village got its name because the famous poet/bard was buried in a mound called Bedd Taliesin high on a hill nearby. In *Hanes Taliesin*, a 16th-century account of the poet's life, the infant child Taliesin is discovered by Elffin, son of King Gwyddno Garanhir, having been abandoned in a basket and pushed out to sea by the witch Ceridwen (she was furious because Taliesin had sipped her magic potion and so gained great powers of prophecy). Elffin and his wife adopt Taliesin and the child brings great joy, and wealth to the family – which is just as well seeing as most of their lands have been swallowed by the sea.

But the truth of the matter was that no one really knew where he was buried. It was unlikely to be in a burial mound dating back to the Bronze Age. I did like one spin on the legend however. It said that anyone who was brave (or foolhardy) enough to sleep in the grave for one night would become either a poet or an idiot.

That wasn't a risk I was ready to take so I pressed on, climbing steadily on a woodland track that snaked its way out of the village and up onto a coastal ridgeway. The footpath was dry and all felt well again after the morning's deluge. Wild lavender grew at the side of the grass track next to the bracken and oak; birch and the odd apple tree rose above them.

The path led through Coed Llechwedd, gateway to the secluded and secretive Cwm Einion – a wild, winding stretch of Celtic Rainforest located on the steep banks of the Afon Einion. It has prospered for centuries because of its intimidating terrain. The woodland hugs the craggy sides of the Afon Einion Valley, making it near inaccessible for both humans and, importantly, grazing animals. Further upstream was Artists Valley, home to an eclectic community of artists, musicians, environmental advocates. Years ago, Led Zeppelin's lead singer Robert Plant lived in the valley.

Cwm Einion is one of three areas of natural beauty that comprise the UNESCO Dyfi Biosphere, the other two being Cors Fochno and Pen Llŷn a'r Sarnau a large coastal and estuary area to the north of the Dyfi Valley rich in marine wildlife. The Biosphere is the type of grand conservation project that would have pleased the Romantics and early Victorian environmentalists. (In fact, just five miles north is the National Trust's first piece of land. Back in 1895, Mrs Fanny Talbot, donated 4.5 acres of cliff top at Dinas Oleu, near the town of Barmouth.) Yet it may also have puzzled them a little: unlike traditional nature reserves whose sole focus tends to be ecological conservation, Dyfi Biosphere is focused very much on striking the right balance between human activity and nature's needs.

There are some 700 UNESCO Biosphere projects globally and all put a focus on sustainable development and management of the land through environmental and biodiversity conservation, encouraging economies and communities to grow while respecting and benefiting from nature, and developing education resources so that all involved can learn the benefits of a nature-focused economy and pass on that knowledge.

Sustainable tourism was a key focus of the project but it was also important to include and win over areas of the local economy that traditionally had viewed big environmental projects as a threat – notably the local farming community. Furthermore, the Biosphere emphasised improving the well-being of local communities by giving them greater access to, and involvement in, woodland planting and walking.

Tying the well-being of local communities to the well-being of the environment they live in and depend on seemed obvious in the middle of a pandemic when getting back to nature provided a mental lifeline for so many people. But back in 2009, when the Dyfi Biosphere Reserve first launched, the understanding that business and agriculture had not just a responsibility but a vested interest in environmental conservation was hardly part of mainstream thinking.

The ethos behind the Dyfi Biosphere project echoed a much bigger and ambitious idea that the Welsh government launched in 2009. Called One Wales, One Planet, it envisaged Wales as a nation that would live within its environmental limits, have healthy and sustainably managed eco-systems and a resilient and sustainable economy (rather than viewing the environment and economy as two separate and unconnected entities). The manifesto was unapologetically aspirational – it's sort of the utopian vision Romantics like Samuel Coleridge or Iolo Morganwg might have embraced.

Where the Romantics committed their dreams to poetry or let them drift away in an opium haze, the One Wales, One Planet team wanted to cement a lasting sustainable living vision. However, while many people were working hard towards different parts of the One Wales, One Planet agenda, it still wasn't adopted in core policy decisions. New ideas tended to break through the bureaucracy on an individual basis. As a result, their impact was piecemeal.

One of the pioneers of One Wales, One Planet (but who also under-stood its limitations) was the then Environment Minister for Wales, Jane Davidson. She had already introduced the first plastic bag charge in the UK, had been instrumental in launching a Climate Change Commission for Wales and had pioneered and championed the creation of the 870-mile Wales Coast Path walking trail. She and her colleagues, like many people in the sustainability movement at this time, understood that the only way to succeed was to completely change the systems that determined how Wales operated. That would require enshrining One Wales, One Planet into law. Davidson would be instrumental in campaigning for this to hap-pen. Finally, in April 2015, after years of lobbying, the Welsh Assembly passed a new, landmark law: the Well-being of Future Generations Act.

As we've seen, the Future Generations Act has already made its mark on a number of policy decisions that would likely have been very different before it was passed – such as the M4 motorway relief road described in chapter two. The creation of a National Forest for Wales potentially could become the most influential of all, reshaping the balance between Welsh communities and the forests, mitigating carbon emissions, opening a new chapter in Welsh tourism and, most radical of all, helping the nation prosper while also living within its natural means.

The National Forest for Wales

Cwm Einion felt completely different to most of the woods I'd encountered so far (perhaps with the exception of another Celtic Rainforest, Gwenffrwd-Dinas). Later, I would learn that I had descended into one of the best examples of something called Tilio-Acerion woodland. Here, small-leaved lime trees grew in the rocky sites of the ravine and shared space with ash and weeping wych elm. It was also home to other ancient semi-natural mixed broad-leaved woodland such as sessile oak, rowan and downy birch. Together, these trees provided a home to a rich mix of biodiversity. These included 177 species of lichen (including the very rare *Parmotrema robustum* which looks like a cross between kelp and some lettuce that you've left in the bottom of the fridge for too long) and more than 150 species of mosses and liverworts. Lichen is often referred to as the coral of the rainforest, such is its importance in supporting biodiversity.

Amid this tapestry of ancient trees and the plant life below them, the Einion River rushed through, bubbling and breaking into white foam as it encountered the many rocks and boulders in its path. Some of the larger oaks had grown and twisted until they almost touched their neighbours on the other side of the river in a surrealist guard of honour.

Coed Cwm Einion looked majestic and magical to my untrained eye but actually it was slowly being nursed back to health after many decades of neglect, overgrazing and a concerted attack by invasive species that bully the natural ecology (*Rhododendron ponticum* being a major culprit). The woodland was part of a seven-million-pound multi-year ancient forest conservation and restoration initiative. And it was a prime example of the type of woodland that the new National Forest for Wales aimed to nurture and protect.

The National Forest was a bold strategy to embed an appreciation of nature and biodiversity at the very heart of what it meant to be Welsh.

The multi-year plan involved planting new forests and restoring ancient woodlands with an emphasis on nurturing native deciduous trees, breathing new biodiversity life into the hedgerows that line the country-side and working with the farming community to improve tree cover on their land.

And it couldn't have come at a more important time for the country. Just under 20 per cent of the Welsh landscape had any tree cover (compare that to nearly 30 per cent on average in mainland Europe). Only 15 per cent of the total landscape was actual woodland – the remainder a hodgepodge of agricultural landscapes, urban areas and transport corridors that, while still valuable, didn't deliver nearly the same degree of environmental bene-fits as connected woodlands could.

Even as the Welsh government was pledging £15 million over the next five years to bring the National Forest idea to life, its own State of Natural Resources annual report was sounding the alarm – warning that Wales was using up its natural resources, including rivers, forests and farmland, at a completely unsustainable rate. If everyone on Earth used natural resources at the same rate as people in Wales, two and a half planets would be needed.

The National Forest plan also aimed to educate communities and schools about the importance of nature and to create a network of walks, trails and paths that will connect people to the forests and woodlands of Wales – some huge expanses like Wentwood, Brechfa and Bwlch Nant yr Arian along with other small woods like here in Cwm Einion.

My goal in setting off on this walk had been to map one such poten-tial National Forest route that could help people reconnect with nature and, in doing so, understand its importance in their daily lives. I'd be the first to admit that my route would need a few tweaks if it was going to become a viable walking trail. But, having made it this far – some 150 miles of connected woodland walking from my start point back in Wentwood Forest – I was more determined than ever to complete the plan, even though my legs ached, my ankle felt bruised and my back had all the flexi-bility of a slab of Welsh slate.

The Last Prince of Wales

I left the leaning trees, crossed the river by way of a sturdy wooden footbridge, and climbed out of the valley up onto Foel Fawr, the big hill that sat high above the Dyfi estuary.

Below me sat the village of Furnace, so named because, in the early 18th century, it was the site of one the very first industrial-scale iron foundry blast furnace operations. Next to it, on the southern banks of the estuary, lay the 550-hectare Ynys-Hir (Long Island) nature refuge, one of the premier bird-watching sites in the UK where twitchers flock to see pied flycatchers, lapwings, wood warblers and redshanks to name a few.

Sunlight glinted off a stone just ahead of me. It was a weather-beaten metal directional dial of the Dyfi Valley built and installed on the trail by the Royal Society for the Protection of Birds. The dial covered a 15-mile expanse of landscape. It pointed to the Dyfi Valley National Nature Reserve opposite Ynys-Hir on the other side of the river and the rounded peak of Cadair Idris, one of Wales's highest mountains at 893 metres, in the distance. At the far right of the dial, and out of my view, sat Dyfi Forest – one of the largest in Wales and one of the foundation forests for the National Forest project.

A small posse of wild white ponies joined me as I gazed across the valley at the hazy, faded green, yellow and brown shaded foothills of Snowdonia. They parked themselves about 20 feet away, some grazing the short hillside grass while others laid down for a rest. They seemed completely unfazed by my presence – probably because they were so used to seeing walkers, such was the popularity of the Wales Coast Path.

The path led down from Foel Fawr into the Llyfnant Valley where I passed a family hiking up the hill. The father was about my age. He had a short grey beard, wore a baseball cap and was kitted out in expensive looking hiking gear. The mother looked less prepared for what I imagined the father had suggested was just going to be an easy afternoon stroll. Still, she was practically ready to scale Everest in both her clothing and attitude when compared to their teenage daughter who dawdled 20 yards behind her parents, sliding her way up the trail in no-grip white tennis shoes, and displaying an expression of pure loathing towards the whole experience.

I passed a farmhouse near the bottom of the valley. Smoke billowed from the chimney but there were little signs of any other activity. The Coast Path cut through a meadow behind the farm. I saw a herd of cows moving in the next field but thought nothing of it. A minute later, they appeared en masse in the meadow. That's when they started running right at me.

I rapidly weighed up my options. Should I stand still? Should I run back to the farm? Would I make it before the herd trampled me to death? There had already been at least two cases of walkers killed by cows in the UK this summer, probably due to the increase in people discovering the countryside in lockdown. That was a tiny number in the big scheme of things but I had no intention in becoming just another statistic. I knew I wasn't trespassing – this was the official coast path – but there was no point explaining that to the cows. So I took evasive action, sprinting as fast as my middle-aged, tired legs would carry me up to the top of the field. My strategy worked. The cows had no interest in chasing me uphill. I watched them come to a halt at the far end of the field. From my elevated perch I looked across at where they'd come from. The gate connecting the two fields had been left wide open.

The final four miles to Machynlleth were the hardest I'd encountered so far on my journey. The route proved to be a steady, grinding climb on dusty forestry roads through the monotonous conifer plantations of Coed Garth-Gwynion. At one point I had to clamber over a large fallen pine tree that blocked the forest road.

Finally, the trail joined a paved country road. I took this as a good sign that I was getting close to Machynlleth. Instead, I was faced with yet another ridiculously steep ascent. Maybe I hadn't eaten or drunk enough today, or maybe I was just fatigued by multiple days walking but I felt light-headed and a little feverish as I climbed. I had to stop every few hundred metres to catch my breath. After 15 minutes, and with much relief, I finally made it to the top of the hill and sat down on the grass to rest.

I'd been walking, off-and-on, for nearly a month now but today was the first time I'd felt like stopping and trying to call a taxi to get me to my hotel. I know I would have kicked myself if I had but that's how exhausted I was. This was strange and deflating because, for the most part, this journey had invigorated me and lifted my spirits in a way they hadn't been for a long time. It had been weeks since I'd been gripped by any feelings of anxiety and I was sleeping better than I had done in years. Part of the reason must have been that I was so tired at the end of each walk that I positively craved going to sleep. But it was more than that. For the first time in at least five years, I felt I had a purpose again – a project that fascinated me, that I wholeheartedly believed in and that I thought I could do a good job of documenting when the time came to sit down and write.

As I sat on the grass hill I reminded myself of how much fun this journey was and how different my life was to just a few months before. As an extra reminder, below me was a lovely sight in the form of Machynlleth. The town sat just removed from the banks of the Afon Dyfi in the heart of a wide flat and lush green valley – it was easy to appreciate why its name translated to 'the slope on the fair plain'. Once I'd recovered my wits, I soon realised that the Coast Path had merged with Glyndŵr's Way, another long distance walking trail named after Owain Glyndŵr, a true revolutionary hero who became the last independent ruler of Wales. The doldrums banished, I descended on the path into the town with a lot more energy than I'd felt possible half an hour before.

In 1400, Glyndŵr, a nobleman who had served in the English King Richard II's army, launched a rebellion against the new English King, Henry IV, which would last for 12 years. For part of that time, Glyndŵr established his own parliament in Machynlleth and outlined his vision for Welsh independence including establishing an independent church in Wales and two Welsh universities. Glyndŵr's bravery and ambition captured the hearts and spirits of many people in Wales as well as Welsh expatriates living in England. It was said that young Welsh men studying at Oxford University left abruptly to join the rebellion and Glyndŵr also drew support from veteran Welsh soldiers in the English army. Significantly, his followers considered him the true Prince of Wales.

I followed the Glyndŵr's Way as it weaved its way down the hill into Machynlleth. It emerged on the main street opposite the strikingly robust brown and yellow stone medieval building where Glyndŵr assembled his parliament. As I looked at this important piece of Welsh history, I started to contemplate whether the National Forest also could help forge a new sense of national identity – one built on reconnecting the people of Wales to nature.

To outsiders it might seem that Wales already has a strong national identity given how proud most of us are about being Welsh. In reality, Wales is a disconnected nation in many ways. We have a national language but it is spoken by a minority of the population, having suffered centuries of neglect – sabotage even. We are disconnected geographically due to woeful transportation infrastructure as anyone who has to travel regularly between the north and south knows. The political centre of power, the Sennedd, is located in the capital city of Cardiff in the south but many people in north Wales likely identify more with the nearby English cities of Liverpool and Manchester.

Where Wales does come together as one is around sport. The national rugby team, to an extent, though football might well be the sport most people in Wales find common cause with. Could a national embrace of the great Welsh outdoors develop a similar sense of pride?

There is a precedent for what might at first seem a far-fetched idea. In 1994, Costa Rica enshrined into its constitution the right of 'every person […] to a healthy and ecologically balanced environment'. This built on a decision taken a decade before to stop the reckless deforestation of Costa Rica's tropical rainforest by investing in large-scale afforestation and forest restoration schemes. Since then, Costa Rica has also shaped its economy and its global image around environmentally conscious tourism – putting the appreciation of nature at the very heart of its national identity. Ticos (as native Costa Ricans call themselves) even adopted a phrase – *Pura Vida* (pure life) – to describe this national sensibility.

Wales had already enshrined a commitment to well-being of its people and future generations into law. And, as I'd seen by walking just halfway through my country, this beautiful land had untapped potential to inspire its own people and visitors. If we could tap into a bit of Glyndŵr's vision, then Wales might yet unite around nature and the Forest. At the very least, one of the walking trails in the National Forest surely had to be named after the last Prince of Wales.

13

The Rights of Trees

A walk from Machynlleth to Dolgellau

For the next two days, four old friends from my university days, Rob, Neil, Dale and Ross, would be walking with me as we headed north from Machynlleth into Snowdonia National Park. Our route would lead through the vast Coed y Brenin Forest ending up in the village of Maentwrog where, if you remember back to the Mabinogi, Pryderi, was slain by the trickster Gwydion.

I was glad to have company once again. A week of walking on my own had been rewarding but also quite challenging. I'd appreciated being able to lose myself in the landscape of Ceredigion, to escape my everyday existence and take stock of my own sense of well-being. But you can get too much of a good thing and I'd definitely spent more than enough time in my own head.

My friends all lived in or close to London and were eager both to explore this part of north Wales and to see first-hand the project I'd embarked on. All were keen walkers – Dale and Ross in particular. Both had tut-tutted a little when I confessed to relying on a digital OS map on my phone, quickly unfolding their 1:250 000 paper maps to double-check my proposed routes. I don't mind admitting that I felt under pressure at the very real prospect that I might get us all horribly lost. If I did, I already knew I'd never hear the end of it from them.

The next morning, the five of us set off from under the big clocktower at the top of Machynlleth's main street. This was once a meeting point for temperance campaigners; in 1907 hundreds gathered here to greet General William Booth, founder of the Salvation Army, as he passed through town.

We were not the best representatives of temperance this morning, thanks to a few bottles of red wine the night before. So we left before besmirching General Booth's legacy, starting out at a brisk pace towards the stone bridge over the Afan Dyfi at the very edge of town. The river was high and swollen – cresting just a foot below the bridge's supporting arches – and in places had started spilling over into the fields.

Our route today would follow the steep and winding Afon Dulas Valley north towards the town of Dolgellau. But for the first 200 metres, we had to contend with walking on the hard shoulder of the main road that cut through the valley. Trucks, motorhomes, and cars packed with holidaying families roared by – so it was with some relief that we reached a turn-off onto an almost deserted country lane.

Dale, an avid birdwatcher, had brought his binoculars with him. Within minutes he'd spotted clusters of swallows and house martins swooping into a field.

'They're feeding off the flies hanging around the cows. Where there's shit there's flies,' he said, matter-of-factly.

The lane wound through a dense patch of woodland. Two different woods to be precise. Above us on the hillside was a conifer plantation packed with hundreds of thick rich, dark green pine trees. However, the forest floor below their towering crowns was bare and devoid of life, there being few opportunities for light to penetrate the canopy. In contrast the valley below us was a rich, tangled mass of sessile oak and rowan. Here, the forest floor was alive with moss and lichen.

A man, who must have been well into his 80s, emerged out of the lower wood carrying a large log that was almost the same size as him.

'Bloody hell, that looks like hard work,' I said to him as we walked by. The old guy laughed: 'It keeps me fit. Until it kills me, that is.'

The lane led to an old mining village called Corris. On the other side of the steep valley we could see little farmhouses and cottages dotted on the side of the hill.

The conversation turned to music. It was this group of friends with whom I'd been compiling those collaborative playlists and having weekly Zoom chats through lockdown. By now we'd put together nearly 20 different lists covering genres as diverse as Pub Rock, Brum Beat (music originating from the greater Birmingham area), Folk, Heavy Rock, New York Salsa, Africa, the Caribbean and South America. Each one featured over 100 tracks (some many more). This week we'd selected the music of Wales as our choice. As we walked we debated the relative merits of 1970s rockers, Budgie, the underrated 80s band, The Alarm, and our love of Gruff Rhys's work. I made an educated and impassioned defence of the Manic Street Preachers even though my walking companions were lukewarm about them.

'Did you know that Robert Plant and Jimmy Page wrote most of Led Zep III while staying in a farmhouse somewhere near here,' said Rob.

I had heard the story before of how the two songwriters had spent time at Bron-yr-Aur, a farmhouse where Plant had holidayed as a child. They'd even named one of the songs on their third album after the place. But I'd never given any thought to where in Wales it was. I took out my phone and searched the OS app. Rob was correct. Bron-yr-Aur was only a mile or so over the next valley.

In the early 1970s, this part of mid-Wales became a haven for many young artists, musicians and self-described hippies, who were looking to check out from mainstream society and embrace nature. The Hippie movement had many counter-cultural influences but its commitment to nature was very much influenced by the work of Rachel Carson. Her 1962 book, *Silent Spring*, a damning investigation of the US chemical industry and the effect pesticides were having on the environment, had provided a catalyst for a new movement of environmental activism and thinking.

In 1970, the US government created the Environmental Protection Agency following years of lobbying off the back of Carson's findings and it passed the first ever Clean Air Act to legislate pollution. That same year the Natural Resources Defense Council was founded and the first Earth Day, organised by Senator Gaylord Nelson, took place. In 1971 Greenpeace sprang up in Amsterdam and Friends of the Earth was established in the UK. In 1973, just a few hundred metres from where we now stood, the Centre for Alternative Technology (CAT) opened its doors to a generation of alternative thinkers who were passionate about protecting the environment.

At the time CAT definitely was seen as a 'way out there' type of hippy experiment. There weren't many people, even in mid-Wales, willing to live completely off-grid in an experimental community for alternative types of eco-friendly technology. For decades, this reputation endured. Yet, some of CAT's early experiments around scalable solar and wind power would prove instrumental in driving the development of commercial renewable energy. Nowadays, CAT's long-held philosophy of balancing the needs of both society and nature finally is reaching the mainstream.

In recent years CAT had developed a strong research and educational reputation – notably through a comprehensive report into how the UK could drastically reduce energy demand and reach Net Zero carbon emissions. It provided a blueprint for the ways businesses could act and how people could adapt their own way of life.

The Net Zero goal was inspiring but, in order for it to ever have a chance of working, it was clear that a major shift was needed. One where society radically rethinks its systems of governance and law to give nature a fighting chance of achieving parity with the modern, industrial and increasingly technologically driven world. To put it more simply – we need laws that make sure we treat nature as equals. That's not as crazy as it might sound. In fact, the blueprint for doing so is as old as the Centre for Alternative Technology itself.

Back in 1972, amid the bustle of the energetic new environmental movement, a young academic published a paper in the Southern California Law Review titled: *Should Trees Have Standing? – Towards Legal Rights for Natural Objects.* His name was Christopher Stone and though 'green' in terms of legal experience his heritage stood him in good stead for the battle against institutional power he was about to wage – his father was the legendary muckraking journalist I. F. Stone.

Stone carefully outlined how, over the centuries, Western legal tradition had gradually expanded the definition of legal personhood from exclusively white adult men to women, children, people of colour and indigenous communities. He also argued that, as companies are afforded the same legal rights as humans, why not trees or other parts of nature? Crucially, a person, in legal terms, cannot be owned. That meant no individual, corporation or government could claim ownership of an environmental entity that had been acknowledged as an established legal personality.

Stone wrote his article in response to the US Supreme Court case involving the Sierra Club, one of the US's most prominent environmental groups. It had filed a lawsuit to block the Walt Disney Company from building a ski resort in a remote valley of California's Sierra Nevada Mountains. The Sierra Club argued that the Disney resort would cause 'irreparable harm to the public interest.'

The US Supreme Court rejected the suit because the Sierra Club had not shown it had any specific legal interest in the case. Stone argued that the Sierra Club didn't need to prove it was personally impacted. Instead, it was acting as a good steward of nature – whose voice couldn't be heard in a court of law (for fairly obvious reasons). It was an argument that resonated with at least one of the justices. In what would become a famous dissent Supreme Court Justice, William Douglas, wrote that, 'Contemporary public concern for protecting nature's ecological equilibrium should lead to the conferral of standing upon environmental objects to sue for their own preservation.'

Douglas's argument went on to build on Stone's own thinking and become a catalyst for the new, growing field of environmental law, and a blueprint for a new legal concept, the Rights of Nature, that looks set to reshape our relationship to trees and nature in the decades to come:

Inanimate objects are sometimes parties in litigation. A ship has a legal personality, a fiction found useful for maritime purposes. The corporation sole – a creature of ecclesiastical law – is an acceptable adversary and large fortunes ride on its cases. The ordinary corporation is a 'person' for purposes of the adjudicatory processes, whether it represents proprietary, spiritual, aesthetic, or charitable causes.

So it should be as respects valleys, alpine meadows, rivers, lakes, estuaries, beaches, ridges, groves of trees, swampland, or even air that feels the destructive pressures of modern technology and modern life. The river, for example, is the living symbol of all the life it sustains or nourishes – fish, aquatic insects, water ouzels, otter, fisher, deer, elk, bear, and all other animals, including man, who are dependent on it or who enjoy it for its sight, its sound, or its life. The river as plaintiff speaks for the ecological unit of life that is part of it. Those people who have a meaningful relation to that body of water – whether it be a fisherman, a canoeist, a zoologist, or a logger – must be able to speak for the values which the river represents and which are threatened with destruction.

Over time Stone's argument and Douglas's expansion of it have started to resonate around the world and filter into national and regional laws.

In 2008, the government of Ecuador added new articles into its constitution called The Rights of Nature Ecuador. Based on the *Sumac Kawsay* (good living) worldview of the country's Quechua indigenous people, the laws recognised the inalienable rights of *Pachamama* (mother earth), gave people the authority to petition on the behalf of nature, and required the government to address violations of these rights. It must be said that Ecuador continues to struggle with protecting nature. However, in 2021, its highest court ruled that plans to mine for copper and gold in a protected cloud forest were unconstitutional because they violated the rights of nature.

A number of other nations, states and regional governments have embraced the Rights of Nature as part of law and regulation. The Inter-American Court of Human Rights has declared that its regional human rights treaty protects the rights of the environment. In New

Zealand, the Māori nation worked with the federal government to secure legal rights for the Whanganui River. By doing so it helped reassert the traditional Māori world view that the land can't be owned by any human.

In France, Spain, Switzerland and other nations the legal Rights of Nature are gaining traction and have helped protect rivers, lakes and forests win legal status. And in Colombia, the Supreme Court has declared the Amazon to be a legal person with rights – to be protected, conserved and restored – and ordered the state to reduce deforestation. The case was brought by 25 children and, to protect their future rights, the court set up an 'Inter-Generational Pact' for the rainforest.

The Rights of Nature movement is a direct challenge to the centuries-old commoditisation of nature and the concept that humans have ownership of it. It also embraces the greater sustainability philosophy that humans have to integrate the needs and well-being of nature into their systems – be they legal, political or economic – if future generations are going to survive.

Good Stewards Needed

At the entrance to Corris, where the Dulas and Deri rivers meet, we paused for a snack on a sturdy old bridge riddled with old, faint graffiti that I could neither read nor translate. Surrounding us on a triangle of mountainside were tall pine forests.

As we chewed on energy bars, Haribos and nuts I brought up the idea that trees and nature should have legal rights. All of my friends were highly experienced lawyers, working in the fields of company law, creating financial funds, maritime law and white-collar crime respectively. I'd been party to many of their conversations about aspects of law over the years and had done my best to seem interested. Now I was genuinely interested to get their insight on the pros and cons of whether trees should have legal standing.

'To be honest, the only encounter I've had with a tree recently was when a 70-foot Scots pine came crashing down in my garden,' said Rob.

'But it did almost crash into my neighbours' house. That certainly would have been a legal issue!'

In fact, none of my learned friends had any real direct experience dealing with legal rights of nature. It wasn't an area of expertise most lawyers had ever needed to consider.

That, undoubtedly, will change in the coming years as the legal implications of climate change and loss of biodiversity become mainstream concerns for business and society. All of us, not just environmental lawyers, will need to have a greater appreciation of the importance of providing legal safeguards for nature, whether it be through the Rights of Nature movement or the growing movement to add ecocide to national statute books around the world.

We left Corris, headed up a very narrow footpath that veered off the country lane and followed the Afon Dulas north. The river had flooded the fields close to where we were walking and, in a number of places, the path was bisected by little streams that flowed down from the hillside above us. We jumped over the first few or tiptoed across stones that hadn't been submerged. Now, though, we faced a flooded section where there was no choice but to get wet.

It was one of those classic hiking dilemmas: remove your socks and boots and wade bare feet or put your faith in the waterproof pedigree of your boots and hope the water didn't go over your ankles?

The decision for me was simple. I was wearing below-the-ankle summer boots so I took them off; the cold stream water on my bare feet felt refreshing after a couple of hours walking. Rob, Dale and Ross did the same but Neil decided to take his chances with boots on – he'd joined the walk with a dodgy knee and was having difficulties bending it. Removing his boots was not a decision to be taken lightly.

So, as the four of us balanced on one leg trying to dry our feet on the other side of the stream, Neil, a six-foot-four man who was now fairly immobile in one leg, tried to navigate the crossing, picking out submerged rocks to aim for in the hope of minimising getting his feet wet. I've never seen a baby crane try and take its first steps but I imagine it might resemble the stumbling, lurching spectacle we were now watching – though the crane would have a less colourful vocabulary.

The flooded footpath brought us to an old mining village called Aberllefenni. We picked up a new trail that carved its way through piles of discarded slate. On the other side of the valley we could make out a gaping hole that had been blasted out of the mountain side and we walked past old rusting winching gear that once would have hauled slate wagons up and down the mountain. We were in a graveyard of sharp, clean-cut black and grey slate – another world compared to forest and hillside grazing lands we'd left behind just a few minutes ago. It felt like an open wound – one created by quarry owners then abandoned with no attempt to help it heal. The only signs of life were sloe bushes that, somehow, had found a way to prosper amid the mineral carnage.

When Christopher Stone wrote about the legal standing of trees, he was clear that nature needed good human stewards to help fight for its rights. As we left behind that graveyard of slate it also struck me that, if we really were going to embrace the rights of nature, we'd need stewards who had the creativity to reimagine and reshape the dysfunctional relationship we'd created – making use of natural resources without leaving a trail of destruction in our wake. After all, it wasn't as if mining was about to disappear. As we start to transform to a fabled green economy, many of the environmental and ecological tensions that haunted the fossil fuel age will still be with us – just consider the environmental impact of the new rush for lithium and so-called rare earth minerals that are key components in EV batteries.

The People's Rights to Experience Nature

We had reached another threshold – we were about to cross the invisible boundary that marked the start of Parc Cenedlaethol Eryri (Snowdonia National Park).

Snowdonia is one of three national parks in Wales – the others being the Pembrokeshire Coast and the Brecon Beacons (part of which I'd hiked through when discovering the Physicians of Myddfai). Together they account for nearly 20 per cent of the total landmass of Wales.

The idea of creating a national park system in the UK had first been proposed back in the late 19th century and was driven by the popularity of Victorian nature tourism – itself inspired by the words and sketches of the Romantic poets and artists like Wordsworth, Coleridge and Turner and the influence of the Picturesque movement embodied by Thomas Johnes's Hafod Estate.

The problem, however, was that the majority of land in the UK was privately owned, fiercely protected by the aristocracy and enforced through the past few centuries by the thousands of land enclosure acts. In 1884, a member of the UK parliament named James Bryce introduced the first 'freedom to roam' bill. It failed (perhaps unsurprising given that both the House of Commons and House of Lords were packed with heredi- tary landowners) but it kick-started the campaign for public access to the countryside that took on new impetus after the end of the Great War as the country grew ever more industrialised and more people found them- selves bound by life in Britain's overcrowded, polluted cities.

Following the 1932 Kinder Scout Trespass, ramblers and nature con- servationists joined forces to campaign for the creation of national parks where anyone could walk. Their campaign was embraced within parlia- ment and, in 1949, the UK government passed an Act of Parliament to establish a national park infrastructure to provide recreational opportun- ities for the public while conserving the natural beauty of the land.

Three years later, Snowdonia National Park came into being – an area of 827 square miles covering mountains, beaches and hillside farmland. Unlike many national parks in other parts of the world, the UK system makes use of both public and private land and allows commerce such as farming and some artisanal work to take place within its boundaries. It does so out of necessity. The UK has very few areas left that could be considered truly wild. There is no equivalent to Yellowstone in the US or Kruger in South Africa. But what the UK's national parks lack in true wilderness they make up for in popularity. Snowdonia alone receives some

10 million visitors each year – which creates its own problems as we will discover later.

By now we had climbed halfway up Craig Hengae on a steep, dusty and not exactly pleasant forestry track that headed in a series of switchbacks through spruce plantations over Mynydd Hengae. Which was a problem because, according to the route I'd mapped out the night before, we were supposed to be walking on an easy-going path that meandered up the valley floor some 300 metres below us, tracking the Afon Llefenni as it flowed towards Dolgellau.

I admitted to my friends that, just perhaps, we'd taken the wrong route. Neil, having noticeably limped the last couple of miles because of his knee, didn't say much but his silence spoke volumes. Rob looked tired and slightly irritated while I could tell that Ross deeply regretted not having taken charge of map reading in the first place. Only Dale seemed unfazed by our predicament but I suspected that was because he'd spotted some lesser spotted warbler off in the woods. Such was the karma of twitchers.

Neither did the collective mood improve after it became clear (having consulted both the digital and paper versions of the map) that there was no shortcut back down the mountain. Our only option was to press on up the dusty road until it descended back onto the path we were supposed to be on.

It was at that point that I was saved by the Royal Air Force. Not by a helicopter rescue crew winching me away from the predicament I'd created. But rather the deafening and anger-defusing roar of a pair of RAF fighter jets as they swooped down the valley on combat manoeuvres. This particular part of Snowdonia was known as the Mach Loop – the fighter jets flew through here at least once a day. It was an impressive and slightly scary experience – certainly enough to shock a person or four out of any amicidal intentions they might be entertaining at the time.

With the jets gone and good humour somewhat restored we made it over the crest of Mynydd Hengae and rejoined the paved track – part of the ancient Sarn Helen Roman road. To the west we could just make out the summit of Cadair Idris – the Chair of Idris (a mythical giant) and the dominant peak in this southern part of Snowdonia National Park. At the bottom of the valley was an equally inviting landmark: the Cross Foxes pub where we would stay the night. Despite having sore legs and feet, I felt buoyed by the prospect of a cold beer after nearly 14 miles of hard walking.

After just over a mile, we joined a walking trail known as the Mary Jones Path as it wound its way through woodland and farmland not far from the base of the giant's chair. It was named in honour of 15-year-old Mary Jones who, in 1800, walked 25 miles across the Welsh mountains to Bala, to receive a Bible from the Reverend Thomas Charles. It is said that Mary had saved six years to afford the Bible and Charles was so impressed by her commitment that it spurred him to establish The British and Foreign Bible Society four years later.

No one was naming any society after us today but we had put in quite a shift. There was just one more trail to follow – an easy stroll by the side of the Afon Clywedog that led directly to the pub. Just as we were about to join the path a group of four dirt bikers, their engines revving hard, emerged out of the woods. They were covered head to toe in wet mud.

'We do have right of way – I checked,' said the lead biker defensively, a heavyset man with a strong Manchester accent. 'Don't go down there yet, there's one more still to come,' he added.

We heard the lone straggler long before we could see him – revving hard and swearing even louder which was quite some feat and some indication of his frustration. Finally he came into view. He was a quite a bit older than the other bikers – in his mid 60s I would think – and his motorbike was stuck between two rocks on the path. He was cursing the world and looked absolutely exhausted. His mates erupted in laughter, ridiculing him for being so old and slow. Finally, the man revved hard, and freed his bike causing a splatter of mud Jackson Pollock would have admired. Reunited, the bikers disappeared in a cacophony of high revving diesel engine noise.

By the time we arrived at the Cross Foxes pub we were covered in the mud churned up by the bikers. The landlord gave us a look that said, 'where the hell have you been?' His mood soon improved though as five fatigued and thirsty middle-aged men began investing in his beer and food supplies. He obviously knew a good thing when he saw it.

14

Forest Politics

A walk from Dolgellau to Maentwrog

We left Cross Foxes after a hearty breakfast on what was going to be a strenuous day's uphill trek north through the vast Coed y Brenin Forest towards the village of Trawsfynydd. It was one of the most significant forests in all of Wales, attracting walkers and mountain bikers from all over the UK. It would also be one of the main arteries of the new National Forest for Wales. I'd driven through it many times on my way to north Wales but I'd never walked in the forest. The drive was a long, steady climb so I suspected today's hike was going to be just as challenging as yesterday.

We started at an easy pace following a deserted country lane known on the map as Gwanus. It was a dry, overcast morning and we were happy to amble and chat, taking stock of the various aches and pains we'd accumulated after yesterday's hike. Neil's knee was bothering him (not helped by yesterday's detour, as he reminded me). Rob, who had been walking up to 10 miles a day in Norfolk in preparation for this trip, was finding that 14 miles through the foothills of Snowdonia National Park quite a different proposition. My left knee and ankle felt particularly stiff – collateral damage no doubt after yomping so many miles but probably not helped by my misadventure back in the raised bog of the Elenydd. Only Ross and Dale seemed sprightly.

We joined the Cross Britain Way, a 280-mile-long hiking trail that starts on the east coast of England and finishes in Barmouth, a few miles down the coast from our current location. This was a relatively new walking route, launched in 2014 as part of the Macmillan Ways – a series of paths created to help walkers raise money for the cancer charity of the same name. In recent years, group hiking for charity had become a competitive challenge for people all over the UK, especially a younger generation who might consider the Ramblers' Association uncool but were keen to embrace a fundraising walk (particularly when it could be organised, mapped, recorded and shared via apps and social media.)

Most weekends, thousands of these digitally driven hiking challenges take place across Wales, whether it be conquering parts of the Wales Coast Path and Offa's Dyke or accomplishing the Welsh Three Peaks Challenge – hiking to the summit of three signature Welsh mountains (Yr Wyddfa, Cadair Idris and Pen y Fan) within a 24-hour period.

One hundred and fifty years ago, visitors to Dolgellau also came to explore planned trails, though the picturesque nature walks mapped out for them tended to be less strenuous and adventurous. It was one of those trails, Torrent Walk, that we had stumbled on right now.

The Torrent Walk was a circular route that ran either side of a steep gorge through which the Afan Clywedog flowed. It was created in the 1800s by Baron Richards, a famous local magistrate, to extend the gardens of his Plas Caerynwch family estate and quickly became a popular destination for both locals and early Victorian tourists. In recent years, the Snowdonia National Park Authority had restored the three-quarter-of-a-mile-path on the eastern side of the gorge because of its significance as a Site of Special Scientific Interest rich in biodiversity.

Descending into the Torrent Walk from the modern paved road felt like entering Annwn, that mythical otherworld of the Mabinogi. The sounds of cars vanished amid the rushing of the river as it navigated the steep banks of the gorge and the large boulders that had broken off from the hillside above and become lodged in the riverbed – smoothed and shaped over millennia by the rushing waters.

It was dark and cool but occasionally shafts of sunlight broke through the oak, beech and ash canopy above, casting a Polaroid-like glow on the green and yellow leaves and electrifying the already brilliant green moss that made its home at the base of the tree trunks.

Halfway down the trail we encountered three enormous moss-covered rocks while, just beyond, a collection of vines hung down from the branches of gravity-defying sessile oaks as if they were stretching every sinew to drink from the rushing river. This felt more like we were walking in the Monteverde cloud forest of Costa Rica than a wood outside Dolgellau.

According to the Snowdonia National Park website, the Torrent Walk had other secret natural treasures. It described how the gorge was home to 'a wealth of wildlife and special plants – there are otters, dormice and lesser horseshoe bats not to mention an important collection of lichen, ferns, mushrooms and liverwort.' And it asked the reader: 'How many of these will you find?'

To tell the truth, not that many. We definitely talked about mushrooms as we walked but only in the context of what we'd had for breakfast that morning – part of a larger discussion on the merits of cooked breakfasts around the world, the pros and cons of bacon versus sausage, black pudding, baked beans (we all agreed this was a good invention) and whether grilled tomato constituted a crime against cooking. None of us could quite get our heads or taste buds around laverbread, the salty cooked seaweed that is considered a delicacy here in Wales.

We'd maintained this conversation for a good part of the morning off-and-on. Caught up in this banal but enjoyable group chat I'd really not paid as much attention to my surroundings as I would have if I'd been walking alone or perhaps even with just one other person. In those situations the experience is shaped by your surroundings but when you're walking with a large group – especially when they are old friends – the experience is no less enjoyable but very different.

And so it was that, through a combination of rambling and rambling conversation, we arrived at the gates of Nannau, one of north Wales's great old estates. In its heyday, visitors were taken by carriage up the grand main drive to the mansion but those days were long gone. Today, the main gate had a sign attached that read: PRIVATE – KEEP OUT. The driveway behind the gate was overgrown with bushes and completely impassable.

The Georgian-style Nannau mansion was built by Sir Robert Howell Vaughan, with work starting in 1788 and completed around 1796. However, at least five other properties had existed on this piece of upland before then and the original house was built in the 11th century by Cadwgan, son of Bleddyn ap Cynfyn, the Prince of Powys. His descendants, the Nannaus,* were one of the most influential families in north Wales and retained the estate until 1701 when the land passed to the Vaughan family – who also were related to Cadwgan. This was the same Vaughan family that had lived in nearby Hengwrt and whose antiquarian ancestor, Robert, had acquired the *Red Book of Hergest* that intrigued Iolo Morganwg and later became a foundation of Lady Charlotte Guest's *Mabinogion*. The Nannau family were renowned for maintaining the bardic tradition so revered by the antiquarians. In the 17th century, it was the last remaining household in Wales to retain its own in-house poet and storyteller.

But it was another slice of history related to Nannau that I was most interested in. It was here, in either 1402 or 1404, that Owain Glyndŵr burned to the ground the home of his arch-rival (and cousin) Hywel Sele.

According to the story, Glyndŵr had discovered that Sele had pledged allegiance to King Henry IV (who he opposed). Glyndŵr travelled to Nannau to confront Sele but the local Abbot of Cymmer, hoping to reconcile the two men, suggest they go out hunting together.

The 18th-century Welsh writer and antiquarian, Thomas Pennant, recounted what happened next:

---

* Surnames were not really used in Wales until Tudor times when the English courts insisted on them. To conform, some Welsh families assumed an existing nickname, such as Gwyn or Wyn, meaning 'white'. Others shortened 'ap Hugh' to 'Pugh' or 'ap Rhys' to 'Prys'. The name Nannau was taken from the Welsh name for stream while Vaughan is derived from 'Fychan', meaning 'Younger' or 'Junior', used to distinguish a man from his father or uncle of the same name.

While they were walking out, Owen (Glyndŵr) observed a doe feeding and told Howel, who was reckoned to be the best archer of his day, that there was a fine mark for him. Howel bent his bow, pretending to aim at the doe, suddenly turned and discharged the arrow full at the breast of Glyndŵr, who fortunately had armour beneath his clothes and received no hurt. Enraged at this treachery, he seized on Sele, burnt his house, and hurried him away from the place; nor could anyone learn how he was disposed of.

Years later, when on his deathbed, Glyndŵr is said to have asked his friend and right-hand man, Madoc, to return to Nannau and tell Sele's family what happened to him. Madoc met with Hywel Sele's widow and led her out to a great oak tree on the Nannau estate. Her husband's skeleton was stashed in its vast hollow trunk, still clutching a rusty sword. Ever since, the great oak has been known as Derwen Ceubren yr Ellyll (the hollow tree of the ghost).

No one knows for sure where the great tree once stood. It finally fell on the night of 27 July 1813 and apparently a sundial was placed to mark the spot. But that has long disappeared. Parts of the tree, however, endured: its wood was used to create a set of six silver-mounted acorn-shaped cups along with a silver-mounted oak table seal. Some of these items can be seen today in the National Museum of Wales in Cardiff.

I was determined to see the place where Glyndŵr murdered his rival. So we walked around the perimeter of the estate up a country lane until we reached what the OS maps indicated was another track leading to the mansion. To begin with it seemed promising but soon shrank to a single file path through long grass and thick brambles before disappearing completely amid the undergrowth. It was only with the help of our maps and GPS that we could now pick our way through the woodland, scrambling over fallen trees and through boggy terrain, until, at last, we reached open land and the four stories of a tall, grey stone mansion came into view.

The building was completely derelict and the grounds neglected. We peaked inside the ground floor windows – the interior had been gutted. Yet from the outside it still retained its grandeur and commanded one of the most amazing views of any property in Wales – a clear Picturesque view of the entire valley leading up to Cadair Idris some 10 miles away.

Into the Forest of the King

We entered Coed y Brenin Forest at Coed y Pandy wood and began the long, steady ascent to the village of Trawsfynydd. The forest is considered one of the finest mountain biking centres in the whole of Europe – a complex network of technical and more leisurely trails along with numerous walking routes as well. We were on the main mixed-use path that headed directly north and walked single file as an assortment of families, couples and lone daredevils in protective heavy-duty plastic armour shot by on their bikes at varying speeds of insanity.

The UK Forestry Commission purchased this area from the Vaughan family in 1923. It was called Vaughan Forest until 1935 when it was renamed, along with one forest each in England and Scotland, as Coed y Brenin, or the King's Forest, in celebration of King George V's Silver Jubilee. Over time, the Forestry Commission acquired thousands more acres of surrounding hillside.

The sun was bright and we stopped from time to time to enjoy the day and have a swig of water. At one such stop, just after we'd crossed a bridge over the Afon Gain near the village of Ganllwyd, we stopped near an elderly walker with reading glasses perched on his nose. He was seated on a boulder by the side of the path, consulting a very faded green OS map – it looked like it had been in constant use since the 1960s.

'That map has seen some action,' I said.

'Yep, it will just about see me out, I suspect,' he said with a smile.

Coed y Brenin, along with Wales's other major forests, is set to play an important role in helping combat climate change as the Welsh government makes protecting existing forests and planting new trees a policy priority.

Nowadays, with the climate emergency focusing minds like never before, it's easy to think of mass tree planting as a new solution to the damage we've done to our forests. But in Wales, forest conservation and demands for new planting has been a significant issue ever since the 15th century.

In 1482, the government passed the Statute of Enclosure to counter centuries of military deforestation and felling of woods for private profit. The act, which only applied to Royal lands, allowed landowners to enclose their lands against deer and cattle for seven years so that the trees would have a chance to grow without being eaten.

By the 16th century, as timber became ever more important for building military ships and as a raw material in early mining and other industrial work, the British Crown began to lease land on terms that obliged tenants to plant specific numbers and types of trees. One 1564 lease in Wales required the tenant to plant 180 trees, either oak, ash, elm, poplar or walnut.

Over the next couple of centuries, the owners of new large private estates like Hafod, Chirk Castle and Gnoll in the Vale of Neath experimented with intensive planting not just of fast-growing softwood timber trees like spruce and larch but also other exotic imports such as cedar of Lebanon, Italian cypress and Portugal laurel.

By the 19th century, just four per cent of the United Kingdom was covered by woodland. Most of the damage had been done thousands of years before. Since that time some remaining deciduous woodlands have been cleared then chomped into submission by sheep and cattle while other ancient woodlands endured through coppicing for timber then regrowth. A few remained relatively untouched by human activity.

Given the growing industrial demand for timber, however, in 1885 a parliamentary committee was set up to consider whether, 'by the establishment of a Forest School, or otherwise, our woodlands could be rendered more remunerative.'

One of its key findings was that 'there is probably a larger area of unplanted land in Wales that would pay for planting than in any other portion of the kingdom.' Over time, large chunks of upland of Wales would be transformed into new conifer forest plantations but the urgency of reforestation only really took hold at the start of the First World War when Britain's lack of ready timber became a matter of national security.

At the time, wood alcohol was a key component of cordite, which was essential for igniting the British Army and Navy's firepower. Britain was forced to import millions of tonnes of timber to support the war effort – a mistake the generals and the government vowed must never happen again.

The UK government established the Forestry Commission in 1919. It purchased large amounts of land – a lot of it in Wales. By the time the Second World War began in 1939, the Commission controlled some 28,000 hectares and was the single largest owner of land in Britain.

Land purchases continued throughout the war. While some of that land had been bought from old estates like the Vaughans', much had been wrestled from sheep farmers through compulsory purchase orders. This fostered animosity towards the Forestry Commission and to central government that continues to this day.

The Commission compounded local anger with its determination to generate a fast-growing timber resource. This meant it focused on vast plantations of non-native conifers set out in rigid, straight assembly lines of trees – a very different aesthetic to the wild beauty of Wales's native deciduous woodlands. The timber-industry driven approach reshaped the look of much of Wales's forests to the extent that, today, the remaining mixed deciduous woodlands feel like an oasis of biodiversity compared to a desert of soulless conifers.

Over the past 40 years, however, the Forestry Commission started to change from having a commercial focus on timber production to one of conservation and the planting of native forest lands. Today, it is the Commission's successor, Natural Resources Wales, that is charged with helping bring the National Forest project to life.

As with so many government and private schemes all over the world, the National Forest plan seeks to encourage and fund farmers, foresters and local communities to plant new trees to help combat climate change, improve water management and maintain and enhance biodiversity.

In terms of climate change, the case for planting new trees seems pretty straightforward. As trees grow, they absorb and store the mostly man-made carbon dioxide emissions that are driving global warming and radically changing our climate. Hence, if we keep planting more trees then we stand a better chance of limiting climate change.

A concerted push to increase forest cover (especially tropical forest cover) around the world has been underway for over a decade. Under the 2011 Bonn Challenge, a global restoration goal started by the International Union for Conservation of Nature and the German government, 59 nation states, private associations and other organisations pledged to restore 350 million hectares of degraded and deforested landscapes by 2030.

In 2019, Ethiopia claimed to have planted some 350 million trees in just 24 hours by encouraging every citizen to plant at least 40 seedlings – part of a national 'green legacy' initiative to grow four billion trees in one year. Ethiopia had seen its forest coverage shrink from 35 per cent a century ago to just four per cent a few years ago. Pakistan recently achieved a 'Billion Tree Tsunami' – converting 350,000 hectares of degraded and deforested land – one and three quarter times the size of Wales – into 'restoration areas' where land and forest could recover.

There are similar stories the world over with countries like China, Canada and the UK, companies like HP, Salesforce and Lloyds Bank, and charities like Trillion Trees (a partnership between WWF, BirdLife International and the Wildlife Conservation Society) and the National Trust all racing to increase global tree cover. (Even as I was finishing writing this book, the Welsh government announced a plan to give every household a free tree to plant as part of its commitment to tackle climate change.)

A concerted effort to reforest our planet makes good sense. As long as it is done properly. The reality though, as many communities are finding to their cost, is that the wrong reforestation policies can be worse than no reforestation at all.

Take China's Grain-for-Green mass planting programme for example. In 1998, severe flooding caused by heavy rains and made worse by deforestation killed more than 4,000 people in southern China. In its wake the government launched ambitious reforestation policies to help stabilise the soil and shore up the land. By 2015, farmers had planted more than 69.2 million acres of trees on what once was cropland and scrubland and the country's tree cover had increased by 32 per cent. Unfortunately, a lot of what was planted wasn't actually forest. Farmers all too often planted just one species of tree creating a monoculture that failed to help increase biodiversity or strengthen the quality of the soil and the resilience of the land. To make matters worse, farmers sometimes felled existing woodlands to plant the types of trees the government was promoting.

In the UK, the Forestry Commission has also got its planting wrong from time to time. In 2020 it admitted it was a mistake to grant permission for a new plantation on peatlands in Cumbria that threatened an ecologically fragile blanket bog and grassland, which included 100 species of plants. That same year, a report by the UK government's own Natural Capital Committee (NCC), warned that planting more trees on peat bogs would prove a serious mistake because they dry out the peat and can end up releasing more greenhouse gases than they can absorb.

In Canada, planting on peat bogs caused a natural disaster of epic proportions when a 2016 wildfire nearly destroyed the town of Fort McMurray in Alberta, burning down 2,400 houses and forcing almost a hundred thousand people from their homes.

The problem began in the 1980s when the Canadian government experimented with converting peat bogs to timber-producing forests, draining large areas of Alberta's swamps to plant black spruce. The new trees sucked up groundwater out of the swamps and their wide canopies further starved the peat moss of the moisture it needed. In its place a different, drier moss grew. When the wildfire started, the dry moss acted as kindling and all the carbon that had been stored in both the forest and the peat bog was released back into the atmosphere. The wrong type of planting turned a potent carbon sink into a deadly carbon emitter.

Even the much vaunted Ethiopian 350-million-tree plan didn't go to plan. Heavy rainfall washed away more than one-third of the seedlings.

Those that survived struggled to grow because they'd been planted in holes filled with poor soil.

Clearly, the global effort to supercharge tree planting is going to be both complicated and very expensive, though nothing like the costs to our economy and society of climate change. In many cases though, forests have the potential to regenerate without any tree planting (as centuries of woodland regrowth after coppicing proves). Seeds naturally spread to land next to existing forests and local communities can protect young trees from fires and over grazing. In Brazil, it is estimated that almost a third of its Atlantic Forest – where 70 million hectares of land have been degraded – could regenerate on its own without the need for new planting.

Power and Priorities

We had left Coed y Brenin, walking down part of the Sarn Helen Roman stone road into the wide Afon Eden Valley. To our left stood the intimidating Rhinogydd mountain range. In front of us, Llyn Trawsfynydd, the largest man-made body of water in Wales. Just over a hundred years ago a young, exceptionally talented poet-shepherd named Ellis Humphrey Evans grazed his flock in these hills. Evans was a poet in the Romantic tradition. He gave himself the bardic name, Hedd Wyn, which means Blessed Peace in Welsh, and was inspired by the way sunlight pierced through the mist in the valley where he lived. He celebrated and captured the beauty of what he saw in verse, continuing the long and close connection of Welsh bards to the natural world.

Evans wouldn't have recognised the landscape we were looking down on. The green fields and rolling hills that once led down to the Vale of Ffestiniog at the bottom of this wide glacial valley were flooded and eradicated in 1924 to create a deep-water reservoir for a new hydro-electric power station.

We'll never know just how this great young poet might have described the destruction of his valley because he didn't live to see it. Earlier, we had walked by his memorial in the centre of Trawsfynydd, the village that gave its name to the lake. It explained how Hedd Wyn was awarded the highest accolade, the Bardic Chair, at the 1917 National Eisteddfod. But he never collected his prize. Earlier in the year, Evans had enlisted to serve in the 15th Battalion of the Royal Welsh Fusiliers. On 31 July that year, he was killed on the first day of the Battle of Passchendaele in Belgium. Evans's winning submission was an anti-war poem, 'Yr Arwr' (The Hero).

We were on the final stage of our group walk that had started some fifty miles back in Machynlleth. The sun was out but there was a chill in the wind flowing up the valley from the coast. It foretold that summer was coming to an end. We didn't have quite the same levels of energy as the previous couple of days – the long climb through Coed y Brenin had taken its toll. At one point, as we walked on the six-mile circular hiking and biking path that ran around the lake, I suggested we scramble up one of the hills to get a better view of the entire valley. 'I'd rather cut off my own legs,' said Rob, bringing the discussion to a swift conclusion.

Soon though, the path did start ascending up the side of Cwm Moch as we navigated our way around Coed y Rhygen nature reserve. Ahead of us, a tall, wiry, elderly man with a white beard walked slowly but purpose-fully, his arthritic black and white retriever lagging behind. When the dog saw us approaching it dallied even longer.

'She'll take any chance she can to have a rest,' the man said of his old dog. Judging by his accent, he was originally from the north-west of England, but he'd been living in this area for nearly 20 years.

'I'm just off up to be with my wife at the top. I do it every day at midday,' he said. He kept walking for about 200 metres until he reached a wooden bench and took a seat. On it was a plaque in memory of his wife, Sue.

'It's such a nice, quiet place. You know, you're the first people I've seen all week,' he said, in a way that made me a little sad.

The path down from Cwm Moch led us through thick fern and bracken. At one point an adder slid across the dry mud path in front of us. In the distance, on the far side of the water, we could clearly see the twin reactor towers of the old Trawsfynydd nuclear power station – the only nuclear power plant in the UK ever to be built inland. It could only operate thanks to the deep cooling waters of the reservoir. Built in 1965, the plant was decommissioned in 1991 but the hulking twin nuclear reactor towers still loomed over the lake like mutant Norman castles.

We had reached the concrete dam at the far end of the reservoir. It was an arresting sight. On one side was 40 million cubic metres of water occupying the flooded valley. On the other side, a couple of hundred metres below, was the jagged narrow gorge called Ceunant Llennyrch through which the Afon Prysor River flowed. Unlike other parts of the surrounding woodlands that had been farmed or exploited for local industry, this gorge was so inaccessible that it appeared trapped in time. Its sides were cloaked in a contorted display of oak, rowan and birch. Ash, hazel and elm grew in the lower, less treacherous parts of the wooded valley. Even from this height it felt like having an aerial view of a mysterious and magic kingdom.

All I could think about was what if the dam ever failed. Llyn Trawsfynydd had already eradicated the land of Hedd Wyn, I found it hard to contemplate that this monument of humanity's attempt to 'tame' nature might destroy the woodland below as well.

Not least because, if we are to inspire present and future generations to reassess their relationship to the forest and seek a new balance with nature, we will need woodlands like the two that sat on either bank of the river. Together, Coed Felenrhyd and Llennyrch occupied some 310 hectares and linked the Coed y Rhygen nature reserve to the Dwyryd estuary down in the Vale of Ffestiniog.

Our route took us down the valley through Felenrhyd on a simple grass path that hugged the side of the ravine. It was dense woodland to pick our way through and very wet underfoot so we were more than a little surprised to meet a cyclist – on a road bike at that – halfway down the valley path. He was kitted out in full white racing lycra and wearing cycling cleats – completely the wrong type of footwear for the trail he found himself on. He was looking for a hidden lake he'd heard of, Llyn Llenyrch. We couldn't help – being as new to the wood as he was. At least we didn't have to carry a bike through it.

When Coed Cadw (the Welsh branch of the Woodland Trust) took over stewardship of the Felenrhyd in 1991 it was deeply infested with the invasive shrub, *Rhododendron ponticum*, and had a dense conifer plantation. It had taken several decades to reduce this dual threat to the ancient woodland but now the dividends were plain to see. The oaks were able to thrive once more and the forest floor was alive with brilliant green combinations of Bryophytes including liverwort and spectacular bunches of barnacle lichen. Prostrate Signal-moss (*Sematophyllum demissum*) clung to the rocks in the ravine – a species native only to north Wales and parts of the Atlantic coast of southern Ireland.

The wood's qualities were only enhanced by its place in legend and folklore. According to the fourth branch of the Mabinogi, it was here in Coed Felenrhyd, that the malevolent sorcerer, Gwydion, killed Pryderi, Prince of Dyfed, after stealing his magical swine of pigs. Pryderi's body was said to be buried in the nearby village of Maentwrog at the foot of an ancient yew tree.

I felt overawed by the power and, yes, what I thought might really be the wisdom of this ancient forest. It exuded peace and calm yet also power and authority. And it embodied everything I imagined writers and artists like Tolkien and Turner as well as a whole host of Disney animators might have dreamed of when bringing enchanted forests to life in their art.

I imagined bringing the world's decision makers and opinion formers – the CEOs of major companies, the politicians, the media and even social media influencers on a walk through woods like Coed Felenrhyd. I was convinced that opening their eyes to the magic of these forests could change the way businesses, governments and the media act and think. If our leaders didn't want to make peace with nature after a walk in these woods then there really wouldn't be any hope for the rest of us.

15

The Business of Nature

A walk from Maentwrog to Penmachno

My friends had headed back to London and I was alone once more. I'd really enjoyed walking with them – the last stretch had felt a bit like a holiday after the solo hike through the Cambrian Mountains and the Coastal Path to Machynlleth. But I was also happy to be alone again to give my full focus to the final stretch of my long walk through Wales. Ahead of me lay 55 miles of footpaths, bridleways and tracks over the eastern hills of Snowdonia National Park, up through the wilds of Clocaenog Forest before descending into the rolling farm lands around Corwen, hugging the Afon Dyfrdwy (River Dee) Valley into the Vale of Llangollen and finishing in the town of Chirk, near Wrexham, on the English border.

I started out on a warm September day with a visit to the graveyard at Maentwrog church. I wanted to see the yew tree where Pryderi was said to lay.

The church was situated in the heart of the village on a small ridge looking out over the Vale of Ffestiniog and the Afon Dwyryd as it flowed to Porthmadog and the sea. Just out of view down the coast was Portmeirion, the dream village of architect Sir Bertram Clough Williams-Ellis (one of the original forces behind Snowdonia National Park). His Italianate buildings had captured the imagination of tourists for generations but were probably best known for where the 1960s cult mystery drama, *The Prisoner*, was filmed.

There were two great yew trees at the foot of the graveyard, both of them at least six feet wide with gnarled bark. It was impossible to tell which one might have been Pryderi's resting place (if indeed he existed at all). But at least from here I could enjoy the view across the valley. In the distance, a grand old Victorian mansion sat high on the hill. The Gothic castellated, thick stone-walled and slate-roofed Plas Tan y Bwlch was once home to slate mining barons, the Oakeley family, until their hedonistic lifestyle and serious gambling debts collided head-on with a decline in the demand for the product that had given them their wealth.

Nowadays Plas Tan y Bwlch is the main education and training centre for Snowdonia National Park. Instead of hosting champagne parties bank-rolled from the riches of slate, the mansion now entertains school groups learning the importance of biodiversity, sustainable tourism and preventing deforestation.

I left the graveyard and headed out of the village with Plas Tan y Bwlch dominating my view as I walked. I started thinking about how, in our never relenting drive to create wealth we have forgotten just how much our own fortunes are tied to those of nature. This was particularly true of the mining history I'd encountered on my walk so far, as the excesses of the Oakeley family clearly demonstrated. But whatever form of industry has been involved, for over 250 years the engines of economic growth have treated all the riches of nature – be they trees, fresh water, wildlife and minerals – as commodities to be used without any consideration of their value and cost outside of what it means to a company's bottom line.

In the vast majority of companies today, the environmental impacts caused by their business activities are still considered an 'externality' – an outside factor that isn't accounted for in a company's financial performance. That's not surprising when you consider how so many of the world's major companies – the ones many of us depend on for our food, clothes, household products, even toilet paper – still haven't taken any meaningful action on their own connections to deforestation, either through their own activities or, more often, the work they subcontract out to suppliers. One influential report published in 2020 showed that over half of

350 multinationals whose business benefits from forest products either had no policies against deforestation or had policies but failed to enforce them. More recently, the NGO Global Canopy found that two-thirds of the world's major investment banks have no policies to prevent deforestation caused by the companies they invest in and lend to.

Most of the CEOs of those companies and banks would no doubt express great platitudes about caring for the planet and all their 'stakeholders'. But how can the world of business really claim any leadership when some school kids in north Wales probably know – and care – more than they do about sustainability issues like climate change and biodiversity?

With those thoughts churning in my mind I picked up the pace to the village of Llan Ffestiniog where I joined a mountain road leading up through a valley known as Cwm Teigl. It was only 11 a.m. but the sun was hot on my back as I climbed the single-track path. I could see the ruins of old stone crofting cottages on the hillsides. Years ago, these would have been home to sheep farmers or workers from the old slate quarries. Many were now abandoned shells but one or two were being renovated. On a particularly tight bend in the lane I hopped out of the way to let a delivery truck go by. I caught up with it a few minutes later as it stopped at one of the cottages being renovated. Its cargo – slate to repair the roof.

I was in the shadow of Manod Mawr, a 661-metre mountain that forms part of the Moelwynion range within Snowdonia. All I could see was a wall of scree. No vegetation grew on its bare rock and thousands of years of wind rushing up the valley had chipped away any rough edges, sending them scuttling down as tiny rocks that gathered at the foot of Afon Teigl. The river trickled down the valley, making easy work of cutting through the tufty grass and bog that flanked its banks. In the distance I could see the northern end of Cardigan Bay hemmed in by the Llŷn Peninsula. It resembled a pickaxe pointing out into the Irish Sea.

My surroundings looked like a Sublime portrait of desolation so it was a surprise when I passed upon a small patch of tended garden by the side of the river, a dense miniature wood next to it and, next to that, a small orchard. Behind this oasis was an old stone house. Only later I would discover it was Hafod Ysbyty, the summer hospice of the Knights of St John, but more of that later.

The road zigzagged up the valley until it reached Cwt y Bugail Quarry, one of the few remaining active slate mines in Wales. A century ago, slate quarries extended for miles across Manod mountain to the town of Blaenau Ffestiniog. The tunnels dug to extract the slate were so deep and so extensive that, in 1940, at the height of the Second World War, the British government used Manod to hide the National Gallery's art collection to protect it from the German bombing blitz of London. The initial plan had been to ship the collection to Canada but the Gallery's director feared it could be sunk by German U-boats. So he wrote to Prime Minister Winston Churchill outlining his fears. Churchill wrote back saying, 'Hide them in caves and cellars, but not one picture shall leave this island.'

The quarry in Manod Mawr was perfect. Sixty metres underground, its cave system ran throughout the mountain and was big enough to house the entire collection. Special wooden 'elephant' cases were constructed to transport the paintings, which came to Wales on trucks. Some paintings were so large that the entrance to the mine had to be enlarged using explosives. The artwork remained safely in Manod until the end of the war.

Here's a little footnote to that tale. Remember J. M. W. Turner and his tours through Wales with his sketchbook? The ones that helped shape his Romantic sensibilities? Some of them were sketches of Snowdonia. When Turner died in 1851 he left all of his works to the National Gallery. So when those trucks brought the artworks up to Manod, Turner's memories of Snowdonia came home.

I found a footpath that led away from the slow, monotonous ascent of the quarry road. It hugged the opposite side of the valley before emerging onto a high, flat ridgeway where it met an official walking path, the Snowdonia Slate Trail. I followed the path avoiding the, by now, inevitable boggy sections, until it reached the boundary fence of a large conifer plantation. To my left I could see the heavy loaders working the slate quarry while in front of me there was a broken wooden stile straddling a rusty wire fence and an old, weathered map with a sign that read:

> Public access on foot to the area outlined on the map is allowed
> unless care of the wood necessitates closure under an agreement
> between the owner and Snowdonia National Park.

This was clearly a private woodland within the confines of the National Park – perhaps part of Manod quarry land? There was another interesting feature on the map. It denoted that the footpath running through the middle of the wood was Sarn Helen – the old Roman road that I'd first walked outside Neath and then had picked up again outside of Machynlleth. Surely this was serendipity. Admittedly, the official Slate Trail veered left up the hill. But this unnamed, mystery wood, was begging to be explored.

And so, against my better judgement, I climbed the broken stile and started down the overgrown grassy track into a gap that disappeared into the dense forest. Immediately, I sensed something wasn't quite right about this route. For one thing it felt too quiet. That might sound ridiculous when describing a forest. After all, part of the joy of escaping into woodlands is the silence and the calm they can bring. But this wood didn't calm me. It put me on edge.

It soon became clear there was no path through this wood. The wide track I'd ventured onto was blocked every 50 metres or so by fallen trees. The path itself was a brilliant green colour – inviting in principle but, as I now knew after hiking for weeks through stretches of Celtic Rainforest, that green was a carpet of moss and the thing that moss loves more than anything is water. This was no walking path. It was a boggy 10-metre-wide stream. Not only was I likely to get soaked but trying to walk even on the sides of it would be courting disaster.

The only choice was to retreat deeper into the forest and pick my way through the tightly clustered spruce trees, avoiding the sharp eye level branches as I went. The forest floor was empty apart from colonies of red and white mushrooms growing at the base of the trees and a network of mini streams. As I searched for dry footholds, I would slip into the water. By the time I spotted light at the edge of the forest my feet were sodden and my wits frayed.

To get out of the forest I had to hop over a battered wire fence – never a good sign for what is supposed to be a footpath. In front of me was a sheer drop of about 50 feet and beyond it a landscape that bore no similarity to either the forest or the hill country I'd been walking in before. I was staring down at the abandoned slate quarry of Rhiwbach.

The quarry was one of the most remote in all of Wales. When it opened in 1812, its only connection to the outside world was a dirt track leading back down the valley. So, unlike most quarry operations, the owners built a village at the site, including houses, barrack-style quarters for lodging workers, a shop and a meeting room that doubled as both school and chapel. The workers had to pay rent to stay in the barracks, which were overcrowded, filthy, and lacked decent toilet facilities. From where I was standing at the top of the ridge, I could see the ruins of the houses and the long barrack buildings among discarded slate.

I heard voices in the distance – a conversation taking place about which way to go next. I peered down into the quarry site and saw two mountain bikers threading their way along makeshift slate paths and heading up towards me.

We met halfway down the path that navigated the east side of the quarry wall. The bikers, Peter and Andy, were riding high-end electric mountain bikes. They were staying in nearby Cwm Penmachno (where I was headed) but they lived in the north Wales town of Conwy. They asked me about the forest I'd just walked through as they were trying to find a way down to Llan Ffestiniog for the day. I told them about my experience and they quickly agreed it was no route for a mountain bike – especially a 20-kilo electric one.

It was clear they weren't used to running into lone hikers in abandoned slate mines so they asked me what I was doing. I explained my journey and how a walking route for the new National Forest for Wales could be as important as the Wales Coast Path for enticing walkers to reconnect with the forests and nature. 'Don't forget the cyclists,' said Peter. 'We don't want those ramblers to have all the fun,' added Andy with a laugh.

The Need for a New Way to Value Nature

I left Rhiwbach and rejoined the Slate Trail path that took me through a small piece of forest down into the village of Cwm Penmachno, but I couldn't rid my mind of the image I'd seen up on that mountain – how the ghosts of an abandoned industry still haunt the landscape.

The quarry had been shut down in the 1950s, admittedly a different age in terms of environmental responsibility, but it was still another shocking reminder of just how detached we as society had become from the natural world we depend on. I wondered if the owners had ever stopped to appreciate the value of the fresh mountain stream water they relied on to wash their slate? Or of the timber they took from the forests and the wildlife that depended on the health of that forest?

The answer is, of course, no. They didn't have to consider these questions because they had no concerns about having enough raw materials or how using those materials might alter the health of our planet and, in turn, our own lives. A century ago we weren't overshooting our sustainable use of the earth's natural resources by 29 July (as we'd done just a couple of weeks before).

Even in the mid-2000s, when I first began reporting on issues like climate change, access to fresh water and deforestation, no major company was accounting for them in their financial projections or corporate reporting. Planting trees, to give one good example, was seen as a way to give employees a corporate social responsibility task that would play well in the community. The idea that investing in trees could help improve that company's carbon footprint or improve employee well-being (and hence reduce health insurance costs) didn't even register.

Today though, there's not a company in the world that can afford to ignore the impact their operations is having on the natural world or the debt it owes our planet. The more I walked the more convinced I became that understanding and accounting for the value nature delivers to our lives was essential to rebalancing our relationship to the natural world.

In the midst of a global pandemic, it seemed that a mind shift was starting to take place. Shocked by the way one virus could bring their world to a halt, companies were finally waking up and taking note of just how great and disruptive a threat climate change, diminishing supplies of natural resources and the decline of biodiversity posed to their business and their profits.

Two important factors seemed to be pushing business to act. The first was the realisation that, in the wake of the pandemic, governments are starting to demonstrate some resolve in making good on climate and biodiversity promises. Second, and tied to the first, was the actions of the global investment community.

Follow the money was the advice given to journalists Bob Woodward and Carl Bernstein during their Watergate reporting for *The Washington Post*. Today, that same mantra had corporate executive boards looking anxiously at how their investors judge what success looks like, and where their companies were vulnerable to climate change and other sustainability risks.

In 2020 three important words were radically changing how investors started to act and how companies scrambled to satisfy those investor demands. They were Environmental, Social and Governance (ESG). In a world on the threshold of a new sustainable business revolution, ESG was becoming not just a buzzword for a new greener way of investing but also pointed to what the future of evaluating corporate success will look like.

Which sounds great right? After decades of dragging its feet and ignoring science, the greater business and investment world was starting to come to its senses over the climate and nature emergency. Except, it's not that simple because, for the most part, the business and financial community didn't have a clue how to value nature, and still didn't appreciate how completely intertwined our lives are with the complex and interconnected rhythms of the planet.

The economist Kate Raworth, in her 2017 zeitgeist book, *Doughnut Economics*, clearly spelt out the complexities:

Take, for example, what happens when hillsides are deforested. Land conversion of this kind is likely to accelerate biodiversity loss, weaken the freshwater cycle, and exacerbate climate change – and these impacts, in turn put increased stress on remaining forests. Furthermore the loss of forests and secure water supplies may leave local communities more vulnerable to outbreaks of disease and to lower food production, resulting in children dropping out of school. And when kids drop out of school, poverty in all its forms can have knock-on effects for generations.

It probably sounds ridiculous that the most important companies in the world had spent decades making a fortune off access to a steady supply of natural resources yet never bothered to work out the full impact in financial terms of their activities on nature (or the people whose lives also depend on it). But that's the reality of how, until recently, companies operated. For far too long, environmental and social issues have been viewed as separate to the core business of a company.

However, in the last few years, economists have started employing a new concept called natural capital to solve the business problem of how to value nature. Simply put, natural capital refers to our planet's stocks of natural resources: its minerals, soil, air, water and biodiversity. We draw down on these stocks when we produce our food, drink or clean with water, make fuel to power our machines, use raw materials to build with and even create medicines.

In traditional financial thinking, when we overspend we run into debt. The same is true with natural capital except that the debt owed presents itself in the form of threatened ecosystems like clear-cut forests, polluted rivers and acid oceans. If we keep going into debt with our natural capital the planet runs the risk of local, regional or even global ecosystem collapse.

In natural capital accounting, economists look at the financial cost to the environment and to society of running up these debts, but they also seek to put a financial value on the benefits that so-called ecosystem services provide the world. These include the way forests help with climate regulation and provide natural flood defences, how peat-lands store billions of tonnes of carbon and how insects pollinate crops and plants.

For example, it's estimated that California's street trees provide $1 billion per year in economic value to the state through atmospheric regulation and flood prevention. Mexico's mangrove forests, meanwhile, provide an annual $70 billion to the economy through storm protection, fisheries support and ecotourism. Taken as a whole, global ecosystem services have been estimated to be worth $125 trillion each year. Current global gross domestic product (GDP) is only two-thirds that amount.

How Much Is That Tree Worth in the Forest?

It was a slow but pleasant walk this warm day down the valley to Cwm Penmachno's sister village, Penmachno. Both hamlets sit within Gwydir Forest Park, a 28-square-mile expanse of mountainous woodlands – much of it spruce, fir, larch and pine planted by the Forestry Commission after the First World War. Once there would have been native oak (in 1778 Thomas Pennant recalled that 'the noblest oaks in all Wales' grew in Gwydir) but most was felled to fuel the war effort.

A long ridge of conifers kept watch over me as I walked. As I looked at these human-planted substitutes I felt a little queasy about the prospect of our global financial sector deciding the value of nature. By placing a financial value on the services nature provides humanity, and conversely on the negative impact business activities have on its ability to provide those services, companies will be forced to account for, and be judged on, their relationship to nature.

Many of the world's biggest investment banks now demand companies disclose their natural capital risk and have vowed not to support businesses that compromise ecosystem services – not necessarily out of any tree-hugging sympathies but rather because they are deemed a bad investment as governments around the world vow to finally fight climate change and biodiversity loss.

As investors look for better places to put their money, and as companies look for ways to reduce their own climate risk, a sexy new financial product has emerged – the tree.

In 2020, carbon offsetting (the financial process whereby companies fund forest conservation projects as a way of reducing their own carbon footprint) was still a relatively small market worth about $600 million worldwide. But that is about to change as governments and businesses scramble to meet the terms of the hugely ambitious Net Zero carbon emission pledges they have eagerly made in the last couple of years.

Many will find it impossible to reach those goals by eliminating all their own carbon emissions in time and so they are looking to the carbon absorbing forests and wetlands for help. One study estimates the carbon offset market will be worth more than $200 billion by 2050. Part of this new economic 'tree rush' explains the explosion in tree planting over recent years but, if you want to trap carbon dioxide, protecting an old forest trumps growing a new forest every time. And that's where a new economic vehicle called carbon offsetting – essentially paying forest owners not to cut them down – has taken hold.

The idea of protecting forests through carbon offsetting is not a new concept. Back in 2007 the United Nations launched a global programme aimed at ringfencing tropical rainforests from being chopped down. It was called Reducing Emissions from Deforestation and forest Degradation (REDD) and it matched countries eager to reduce their total carbon footprint with nations that had tropical forest in need of protecting.

The idea was sound and jump-started lots of other smaller scale forest carbon-offsetting alliances between companies and landowners. Unfortunately, it's much harder to prove that the money pledged is actually having the right impact. Too often, over the past 15 years, REDD projects have proved to be ineffective. Sometimes it's due to lack of enforcement resulting in supposedly protected rainforest being cut down. Other times, not enough due diligence was done and money pledged was being directed at forests that were already being protected or, worse, were being employed for cash crops.

One 2020 report by University College London also demonstrated that the offsets market is padded with old legacy carbon credits. These old credits – representing 600 m tonnes of carbon – were from projects that already happened so purchasing them provided no additional climate benefit.

Ultimately, carbon offsetting raises a troubling question. Is it really helping reduce global climate emissions or does the whole system simply give major corporations, governments and ourselves as individuals an excuse to avoid, or slack off on, their own carbon cutting responsibilities? What's the point of having a company pledge billions to plant new trees or protect rainforest if all it really achieves is buying them more time to delay reducing their own carbon emissions?

What Is the Value of Nature?

The road leading into Penmachno hugged the side of Afon Machno River. Down in the valley, all was calm – it felt like a world removed from the scarred landscape I'd been through today to get here.

As I meandered, I kept thinking of just how much now rides on our ability – and desire – to put a value on nature. I imagined how natural capital accounting and the explosion in sustainable investment could turn whole industries on their head and transform the economic value of rural areas that only recently had been written off in the mass flight to the cities.

Looking at the forests and the river valley around me I realised I was staring at a whole new form of economic wealth. Imagine what that could mean for a people and nation like Wales?

And then I got scared, because every time we as society start putting a price on nature it quickly becomes commoditised and abused. Trying to protect nature under the terms of our existing economic systems only makes sense if we believe that those systems offer us the best path to a better future. But what if our entire sense of economic value is wrong?

In Māori, Quechua and other indigenous cultures the notion of owning land didn't exist. These communities knew that they could only survive and prosper if they treated nature as equals and co-dependants. We had seen this during the pandemic in a newfound appreciation of how trees and nature improve our mental health. How, though, do you start quantifying that benefit? How could we honestly hope to rebalance our relationship with nature if we reduced it to a numbers game like we do everything else?

In *Doughnut Economics*, Kate Raworth lambasts our infatuation with economic growth at the cost of everything else valuable in life. Indeed, her whole theory rests on the idea that we must live within boundaries where the needs of both everyone on the planet and that of the planet itself are being met.

Raworth rails against our modern quixotic quest for ever greater economic growth when it is exactly that pursuit that prevents us from putting our relationship with nature back in balance. Economic growth is good, she argues, but only to the point where it starts damaging other parts of the system we depend on to survive.

As I thought about her words, I also remembered how Peter Wohlleben described a healthy forest. He talked about the way different trees, even different species, in the forest support and nurture each other as they grow, and how, after a certain number of years, mature trees – notably the oak – stop growing up so that they don't compromise their own stability and sustainability. In doing so, they not only ensure their own longevity but they give younger trees a chance to flourish and grow – improving the quality of life for all the forest.

> Why do [trees] share food with their own species and sometimes even go so far as to nourish their competitors? The reasons are the same as for human communities: there are advantages to working together. A tree is not a forest. On its own, a tree cannot establish a consistent local climate. It is at the mercy of wind and weather. But together, many trees create an ecosystem that moderates extremes of heat and cold, stores a great deal of water, and generates a great deal of humidity. And in this protected

environment, trees can live to be very old. To get to this point, the community must remain intact no matter what. If every tree were looking out only for itself, then quite a few of them would never reach old age.

Not for the first time on this long journey, I felt the forests were demonstrating a wisdom we humans could only hope to emulate.

16

Sheep and Trees

A long walk from Penmachno to Corwen

I left Penmachno by way of an old stone bridge that headed north towards the famous Conwy falls and the Victorian artists' colony of Betws-y-Coed, now a tourism hub for those looking to hike and climb in Snowdonia National Park. The good weather of the previous days had disappeared – there was a thick mist over the hills around me and I could sense the menace of rain in the air. As I walked over the bridge I glanced back up the valley towards Cwm Penmachno and was amazed to see a giant dragon standing in a field next to the river. It looked to be about 30 feet tall.

Initially, I thought this might be an opportunity to practise the Welsh I'd learned through my online course. But on closer inspection it was clear this dragon was no conversationalist. It was carved from a large tree. I was in no great rush so I turned back into the village to see if I could learn more.

A lady was sweeping the pavement outside of a cottage on one of the side streets and I asked if she knew anything about the dragon.

'Oh, that's in Dion's place. Just walk down the lane to the last house and you'll find him,' she said.

Dion wasn't in but his dad, Ivan was. He was standing at the bottom of his garden, clearing up wood shavings from the bottom of the dragon sculpture and dragging on a cigarette. I introduced myself to Ivan and he invited me into the garden to take a closer look at the work of art.

Up close I could see how intricate the handiwork was. The dragon was carved out of ash and had ornately detailed scales, claws and wide wings. The sculptor, Ivan said, was a friend of his son called Edward 'Woody' Parkes.

Next to the dragon stood another ash sculpture in the shape of a large standing bear. It was just as detailed and intricate as the dragon. Ivan had spent most of his life around this area of north Wales. Now retired, he'd previously worked as a gold miner. Two rich seams existed in Wales. One just south of here around the town of Dolgellau and another in the foothills of the Cambrian Mountains along the banks of the Afon Cothi. The latter had been mined going as far back as the Roman Conquest.

Ivan looked at the two beautiful sculptures that now took centre place in his garden. 'Ash dieback is killing our trees – at least this way they can live on after death,' he said, taking another puff of his cigarette.

Life after death. I pondered on Ivan's words as I climbed over the hills towards the village of Ysbyty Ifan. Time and time again during this journey, I'd come across people and places that had been forced to reinvent themselves after the old ways had gone. The coming years were only going to increase the pressure on all of us to move forward – to embrace new life after death so to speak – no more so than the community and landscape I now was walking through.

From the foot of Foel Gopyn (coppiced hill) I could see the expanse of the Vale of the Conwy below. Everywhere I looked there were sheep grazing – Badger Face Welsh Mountain breed by the looks of them. This part of Snowdonia National Park, an agricultural estate comprising some 20,316 acres, was owned by the National Trust and home to some 50 tenant farmers who tended sheep or cattle or both. It was a tight-knit community bound together by hard work and the Welsh language. According to the 2011 government census, 80 per cent of the community spoke Welsh.

Just a mile or so away was the childhood home of Bishop William Morgan, the man whose accomplishment of translating the Bible into Welsh (first published in 1588) helped keep the language alive after

King Henry VIII had tried to outlaw and eradicate it through the Acts of Union. His home, known as Ty Mawr, sat on the banks of the Afon Wybrnant in a small, but very pretty sessile oak wood in the heart of Gwydir Forest. Today, it is the most isolated historic building maintained by the National Trust.

I met one of the farmers as I was walking down to Ysbyty Ifan. Her name was Gwyneth and she had been farming this patch of land for over 40 years. She was a grandmother but still rode a Honda TRX quad bike to get up to the high grazing pasture – her elderly black, white and brown sheep dog, Jim, running by her side on a leash.

I'd seen a lot of farmers with sheep dogs over the past few weeks and all of them rode red Honda quads – it was the de facto way of covering the rugged high ground they farmed. Normally though the sheep dog would hop up on the quad bike and enjoy the ride. Not Jim.

'Oh no, he's such a softie he's too scared to get on the bike with me. That's why it takes an age to get up here,' said Gwyneth.

We'd met because, at first, Gwyneth had confused me with someone else. 'Oh, I thought you were the man who was coming to fix my fences,' she said after driving across her field to chat with me. She wore a dark blue anorak, frayed blue waterproof trousers and her blonde hair was being swept in all directions by the strong wind coming through the mountains. She'd originally taken on the farm with her husband, but he died of cancer 16 years ago. They used to have a herd of cattle but nowadays she could only handle the sheep.

I asked Gwyneth what it was like keeping a sheep farm running on her own. 'It's a real worry you know,' she said. 'All of us around here – we're all worried about the future of hill farming.'

She told me that, from time to time, she has contemplated giving up and retiring. Then she looked around at the valley below, with Snowdonia over my shoulder and the large expanse of forest behind her and said, 'But why should I stop when it's so lovely up here?'

I left Gwyneth and Jim to wait for the fence man and headed back down through the fields. I could hear the sound of children playing outside at the local school, birds cheeping in the trees around me and the diesel engine of a farmer's tractor hard at work in the fields close by. As I picked my way down the muddy stone track I thought about all the work Gwyneth had dedicated to farming these hills and I wondered if she may be part of the last generation to work this way.

As Wales starts to make tough choices about how it fights climate change, the role of the highland sheep farming is coming under increasing scrutiny.

Sheep have been an ever-present part of life in Wales since the days of the early Celts. The Cistercian monks of Strata Florida helped make sheep farming a thriving industry, selling wool throughout Europe. In the 18th century demand for wool increased dramatically as it was used to make the durable 'Welsh plains' or 'Negro Cloth' that slave owners in the West Indies dressed their captives in. Nowadays we would consider this blood wool but, at the time, it was a lifeline for the subsistence hill farmers.

There are 10 million sheep in Wales. They outnumber people by more than three to one. Indeed, you could argue that sheep are as important a cultural symbol to Wales as the dragon or daffodil or the leek. Economically though, sheep farming has struggled for decades and has long been subsidised by government grants. And when you consider the industry through the lens of climate change, hill sheep farming appears unsustainable on the scale it operates now.

That's not because it has a particularly large carbon footprint. Hillside sheep and cattle farming contribute just 12 per cent of the total emissions from Welsh agriculture. Rather, it's what the sheep eat, not what they emit. For thousands of years, sheep have been consuming whatever tasty green foliage they can get their herbivorous jaws around. When Wales was covered with mature woodland they might have picked away at the plants on the forest floor. But the early farmers recognised the sheep's need to eat lots of grasses and small plants and so cleared the woods to increase grazing land. From then on, the sheep did what sheep do best – eating everything they found tasty in sight, including any new saplings that might have grown into trees.

It's not just that widespread sheep farming is hampering nature's ability to reforest and counterbalance climate change. Climate change is also threatening the sheep. Rising summer temperatures and longer dry spells are starting to compromise the quality of the pasture and hillside land Welsh sheep and cattle still graze on and put at risk their access to water.

Given the precarious economic and environmental standing of sheep farming, there's growing pressure to rebalance and reshape the way hillside pasture and grazing land is employed. Some environmental campaigners have even questioned the entire viability of the sheep farming industry in Wales – going so far as to call for widespread rewilding of Welsh hillside farmland.

Simply put, rewilding aims to let nature recover from centuries of agriculture and industry and then develop with minimal human input. It means giving nature the time and the space to repair damaged ecosystems such as native woodlands, wetlands, riverbanks and estuaries. It can also involve the reintroduction of native predator species like the lynx and wolf – to give a few examples – that had been forced off the land by farming or hunted into extinction.

Among Wales's traditional farming community the idea of rewilding has been embraced with about the same enthusiasm as a plate of New Zealand lamb. Many farmers have fervently and vociferously defended themselves against what they perceive as an all-out attack on a livelihood and a way of life that has endured for many, many generations. Spend any time in mid-Wales for example and you'll soon see the stickers on the backs of farm tractors and Land Rovers that read 'Conservation not Rewilding'.

The farmers argue that they, not outside environmentalists, know more about looking after this land – their families having had a working relationship with this land for hundreds of years. They ask: how can the rewilding advocates really know what the Welsh landscape looked like thousands of years ago or how it functioned on an ecological level? They point to other radical rewilding projects that went terribly wrong – the poster child of how not to do it being a Dutch effort to rewild a large tract of reclaimed marshland outside Amsterdam that disastrously backfired when the animals imported to help the rewilding plan starved to death during a particularly harsh winter. After thousands of years of humans working and looking after the landscape, simply abandoning it to nature could do far more harm than good, they say.

Part of the community's hostility comes from a long history of being bullied by government and authorities (consider the Forestry Commission's land grabs in the early 20th century). Part of it also comes from a grudge against high-minded urban intellectualism. And another part of it is a fear that, if farming disappears, so will their culture and their community's ties to the Welsh language. In one instance, a leading member of The Farmers Union of Wales even compared the idea of rewilding the farmlands of mid- and north Wales to the forced displacement of native American communities that took place in the 19th century to pave the way for the establishment of Yellowstone National Park.

Nevertheless, despite farmers' concerns, the future of Wales's upland farms looks set to involve a return to woodland as carbon offsetting and tree planting becomes increasingly important for government and business. How that afforestation occurs may yet reshape local communities in ways that were unimaginable to farmers just a few years ago. It may well make rewilding look desirable by comparison.

Finding Common Ground among the Hedgerows

I arrived at Ysbyty Ifan (hospital of St John), a little village located on the banks of the River Conwy. I crossed the bridge and walked by the local church. The village was deserted apart from a man tending his garden next to the river and a lady putting her washing out to dry next door.

The village had been called Dôl Gynwal until the end of the 12th century. That's when the Knights of St John turned up and set up a hospice and resting station for pilgrims and other travellers (the village sat at the crossroads of a number of important Cistercian pilgrimage routes as well as droving roads, including the route I'd just followed out of Penmachno).

The Knights of St John first came into being in 1080 when Benedictine monks established a hospital in Jerusalem to care for pilgrims of all faiths who had travelled to the Holy City. The people working at the hospital were inducted into a new religious order of Catholicism and became known as the Hospitallers. When the Christian crusaders took control of Jerusalem the Hospitallers took on a military role and became the Knights of St John.

At the end of the 13th century Muslim armies overran Jerusalem and the Knights fled first to Cyprus then Rhodes before finally establishing a base on the island of Malta and founding the famous walled city of Valletta. During all this time they quietly went about their business in Ysbyty Ifan until King Henry VIII fell out of love with Catholicism just as he was falling in love with Anne Boleyn. Unable to secure permission from the Pope to divorce his first wife, Catherine of Aragon, Henry decided to break away from the Catholic church and, in 1534, declared himself head of a new Church of England.

He dissolved and tried to destroy all the monasteries in England and Wales and he outlawed the Knights of St John. That's when life in Ysbyty Ifan took a decidedly dark turn. With the Knights gone a new order moved into their hospital – a dastardly, murderous group of outlaws known as Gwylliaid Cochion Mawddwy, or the Red Bandits of Mawddwy (a village about 30 miles south of Ysbyty Ifan). The bandits got their name because of their long, wild red hair and a reputation for rage, robbery and pillage that terrorised the local community.

Their infamy was assured on 12 October 1555 when the bandits murdered Baron Lewis Owen, the Sheriff of Meirionnydd, in cold blood. He had been targeted because, in an earlier raid, his men had captured 80 members of the outlaw group including two young boys and then hung them, one by one, in front of their families. The mother of the two boys was called Lowri and she had begged the sheriff for mercy. Instead – according to local lore – he kicked her to the ground and instructed the executioners to 'hang the two boys next'.

Lowri vowed to gain revenge, warning the sheriff: 'These hands will be washed in your blood.' On that October day, the remaining members of the gang ambushed Baron Owen as he rode through Bwlch Oerddrws, a valley a few miles from the Cross Foxes pub where my friends and I stayed. They rained arrows down on his entourage – who fled – and they dragged the sheriff away to a forest, lashing him to a tree. Then, as the story goes, an old man named John Goch (Red John) took a dagger and slit Owen's throat. As the dying sheriff looked down, he saw Lowri at his feet. She was washing her hands with the blood gushing from his throat.

I left Ysbyty Ifan still trying to distinguish the good guys from the bad guys in that particular tale. Thankfully the village had another less gory claim to fame that I could remember it by. On its outskirts, as I headed towards the village of Pentrefoelas, I passed near an old farmhouse called Bryngwyn. In the early 17th century, this was the home of John Morris: Abraham Lincoln's great, great, grandfather.

The possibility that farmers and environmentalists could work well together to protect biodiversity, encourage new woodlands and save upland farming often gets lost in the heated arguments over who would be the best stewards of the Welsh hillsides.

The harsh reality for the farming community is that they, like the rest of us, find themselves on the threshold of change whether they like it or not. The trade barriers erected in the wake of the UK's decision to leave the European Union (a decision that the majority of Welsh farmers supported in the 2016 referendum, it has to be said), along with the subsequent removal of EU farming subsidies, threatens to destroy their livelihoods far quicker than any government policies or academic ideas about combating climate change. Simply put, the future of Welsh sheep farming is going to involve less sheep and more stewardship of new woodland.

But, just as with coal miners in West Virginia, oil and gas workers in the Dakotas and Canada, and even ranchers in Argentina and Brazil, helping a community move from a dependency on stranded assets (for that is what many of Wales's sheep will soon be) to new industries that will be sustainable in the future is not going to be easy.

Some progress is being made. Stump Up for Trees, a charity based in south Wales, has an ambitious plan to work with the farming community to plant one million trees in the Brecon Beacons, on land that has been cleared for agricultural use but is not being employed that way. Here, in the hills above Ysbyty Ifan, the National Trust was working with its tenant farmers to diversify away from a dependency on sheep farming and embrace new sustainable methods. One large 54-hectare farm, Blaen Eidda Isaf, was working to reduce its sheep numbers by 70 per cent but achieve economic viability and sustainable farming through new cattle rearing matched to the natural qualities and capacity of the land – grazing cattle in the summer helps restore the habitat for ground nesting birds such as curlew. And even though fewer lambs were being produced, they achieved better weights in a shorter time period – making the sheep enterprise viable and improving the quality of moorland and biodiversity.

Blaen Eidda Isaf also was planting more farmland trees and hedgerows to protect riverside habitats to help reduce soil erosion and downstream flood risk. This mirrors initiatives by the Woodland Trust and the Welsh government to help farmers plant new trees and co-opt them into the larger idea of its National Forest network by working with them to boost biodiversity in the thousands of hedgerows that line country lanes and mark the boundaries of their fields and land.

I'll admit I'd not really given hedgerows a lot of thought up until now even though I'd been walking alongside them every day since I started this journey. Now though, as I meandered down the lanes outside Ysbyty Ifan I started to study the hedgerows, looking for blackberries and marvelling at the massed tangle of branches and leaves that comprised what environmentalists consider to be essential corridors for biodiversity. At one point a wild hare jumped out of the hedge 20 feet in front of me. It stopped, stared at me then darted back into the undergrowth.

Have you ever stopped to study a hedgerow on a countryside walk? They can be amazingly dense and complex combinations of small trees, bushes and flowers – often comprising of hawthorn, blackthorn, field maple, hazel or spindle and sometimes they include pollarded ash or oak (a pruning system whereby the upper branches are removed to encourage a dense crown). Within the skeleton of the hedgerow, ramblers such as bramble and rose often thrive along with honeysuckle and wild clematis. And at the foot of the hedge you often find herbaceous vegetation such as cow parsley and hedge mustard. Sometimes woodland flowers like blue-bells and greater stitchwort can grow.

In this part of north Wales the rich mix provides an ideal habitat for small animals such as the dormouse and birds like the yellowhammer, whitethroat, blue tit and great tit, as well as bees and other insects like butterflies and hoverflies. Hedgerows also perform an important environmental function for the farmers – they reduce soil erosion and water run-off on arable land.

The history of hedgerows goes back to the Bronze Age but it was the Romans (never ones to shirk a project around creating order) who embraced the practice of planting trees and bushes to line their roads and delineate land ownership. The practice of forming and tending to hedgerows continued well up until the height of the Industrial Revolution (many of the hedges in this part of the country first got their start in medieval times) but, in the 20th century, many were destroyed as the roads and lanes were widened to accommodate motor vehicles and as farming became more industrialised.

With that industrialisation came pesticides and fertilisers. These not only damaged the quality of hedgerows but also threatened the habitat of the wildlife that lived within them. Now, by working with farmers to reduce their use of chemicals, the Welsh government hoped to breathe new life into the hedgerow network.

Sustainable initiatives (for both the environment and local communities) like the ones being run by Stump Up for Trees and the Welsh government with The Woodland Trust are going to be crucial in helping the upland farming community survive and thrive. As the economic value of nature skyrockets because of the need to increase forest cover and offset carbon emissions, those farmers who own their land might yet be sitting on a green goldmine. How they handle that newfound investment will shape the future of rural Wales. Already among the Welsh farming community there was talk of London-based investment and real estate firms offering large sums of money to purchase local farmland to turn it into private carbon-offsetting forest plantations. These deals might benefit individual farmers but they could end up being more damaging to the local environment and the social cohesion of local communities than any rewilding project. The companies currently scouring the hills of Wales for carbon-offsetting opportunities threaten to repeat the mistakes of the Forestry Commission during the early 20th century – creating new tracts of private forest off-limits to local people and doing so with fast-growing conifer plantations that degrade the environment.

Surely, if Wales was so committed to the idea of a National Forest, then the economic value and wealth being ascribed to trees and other natural resources should serve all the people of Wales?

It was late afternoon and I was starting to tire so I was very happy when I saw the sign for Y Giler Arms, the pub where I was staying the night. I checked in and then returned to the bar for a well-earned beer.

I'd brought my notebooks and laptop down so I could collect my thoughts from the day's walk over dinner. That way I would be ready for a good night's sleep ahead of tomorrow's challenge – a long walk through the imposing Clocaenog Forest that had dominated the horizon ever since I'd left Gwyneth and her sheep dog Jim on the hills above Ysbyty Ifan.

Two couples were sitting together at a nearby table. They'd arrived making quite a bluster, talking loudly in very correct clipped English accents, and they'd made no secret to anyone else in the pub of their disappointment in Wales so far. As I sat listening to their gripes about the standards of the public footpaths – 'They're just not well marked. You get in a field and you don't know where to go!'; the slow service in the local pubs – 'Really, it was like something out of Fawlty Towers!' and the mediocre wine list they had to choose from – 'what self-respecting restaurant doesn't have a decent claret?' – it was like I'd been transported back to Victorian times where I imagined the well-to-do tourists who'd come in search of the Picturesque would have held their noses at having to interact with the peasantry (as George Borrow describes in some of his *Wild Wales* encounters).

There were two young women serving in the pub that night and I could see them glancing at each other and chatting in Welsh. I was livid at the boorishness of the four tourists but held my tongue. Later, however, when they had left, I sympathised with the two girls for having to put up with people being so condescending about their home. 'Ah, don't worry it doesn't bother us. We're used to it from people like that,' said one of the girls with a laugh.

Her name was Siwan. She was 17 years old and studying for her A-Levels at a local Welsh-language school. She lived on a nearby farm and worked at the pub a few nights a week for spending money.

She asked me what I was working on and so I started telling her about the National Forest for Wales, why it was important in terms of climate change and shaping a national identity in tune with nature. But I also said it asked tough questions of the way we have lived and worked up until now – especially when it came to farming.

Siwan was fascinated with the idea but also made clear how local people were wary of any government plans for their land.

'Lots of farmers are mad that Natural Resources [the government agency in charge of rural and environmental affairs] want to plant more trees on farmland rather than letting them get on with farming,' she said.

At the very heart of local community distrust was the memory of how government had treated this part of Wales some 60 years before.

'Around here, we've all grown up learning about what happened at Tryweryn and we never want it to happen again,' said Siwan.

She was talking about one of the most egregious public policy decisions ever taken in Wales – the flooding of the Tryweryn Valley and the village of Capel Celyn to create a reservoir and water supply for the city of Liverpool in England.

In 1956, Liverpool City Council sponsored a Private Member's Bill in the UK parliament to develop the reservoir in the valley, a few miles outside the town of Bala and about 12 miles from where we were now. The village, consisting of 12 houses and farms, a post office, school, and a chapel with cemetery would be sacrificed and its residents relocated.

By getting approval through an Act of Parliament, Liverpool City Council would not require permission from any local authorities in Wales to flood the valley. In the subsequent House of Commons debate, 35 out of 36 Welsh MPs opposed the bill but a majority of English MPs voted in favour.

The destruction of Tryweryn to satisfy the needs of an English city gave new fuel to demands in Wales for greater political devolution and sowed the seeds for the modern independence movement. It even spawned a short-lived paramilitary organisation, Mudiad Amddiffyn Cymru (Movement for the Defence of Wales), to which was attributed a series of bombing incidents in the first few years after the flooding of Tryweryn. In the mid-1960s, a new rallying cry around Welsh nationalism emerged – Cofiwch Dryweryn (Remember Tryweryn) – when it was immortalised in a graffiti mural painted on a stone cottage in mid-Wales. Liverpool did apologise for its actions in 2005, but today you can still see replicas of that mural painted outside homes throughout Wales.

On the Hiraethog Trail

In 1824, the poet Wordsworth visited the village of Llanfihangel Glyn Myfyr to see his friend, the village vicar, Robert Jones. This morning I was following in Wordsworth's lonely footsteps as I prepared to join the Hiraethog Trail, a 44-mile circular walk around the local countryside. I would only be on the trail for a few miles but the route would take me into the heart of Clocaenog Forest.

Just outside the village a footpath led up a steep ravine and onto a high flat plain. At the top of the ravine was a large boulder. It was called Maen Cred and, according to local folklore, it was placed there in the 17th century as a waymarker to help guide travellers into a nearby farm that provided shelter. How the locals moved the boulder uphill is anyone's guess – the thing must have been about the size of a VW Campervan!

Ahead of me lay Clocaenog Forest, a conifer centurion guard that stretched as far as the eye could see. Much of the original Clocaenog woodlands, like Coed y Brenin and Gwydir, had been cut down in the First World War only to be replaced with conifer plantations. And as with those other forests, when the Forestry Commission began its mass replanting schemes after the war it took over many hill farms to expand the forest's original footprint. Today Clocaenog covers more than 5,500 hectares. The sign at the entrance where I was standing said it was the size of 10,000 rugby pitches – a very Welsh comparison.

I could hear heavy machinery at work as I walked briskly down the wide forest track. I didn't linger to find out what they were doing – something about this forest gave me the creeps and I wanted to move through it as quickly as I could. Perhaps it was the pure size of Clocaenog that I found overpowering. Despite having my map and GPS I still felt it would be easy to get lost up here. And then there was its tragic history.

Back in the 1990s a serial killer by name of Peter Moore murdered a young man named Edward Carthy and dumped his body here in the forest. Then, in 2002, a schizophrenic artist, Richard Sumner, handcuffed himself to a tree in the forest and threw away the key. Three years later his skeleton was found by a woman who had got lost in the forest while walking her dog.

So I was relieved when I reached a main road that ran through the southern part of the forest. Next to it was a car park and a series of mini walking trails around a small lake. Getting out of their cars and preparing for what looked like an important mission were Vic, Rhiannon and Penny – part of a red squirrel conservation group named 'Red Squirrels United' (which would be an excellent name for a football team).

Clocaenog, along with the island of Ynys Môn and a few woodlands in the Tywi Valley of mid-Wales, is one of the last refuges for the native red squirrel – having been driven out of the rest of the forests by its interloping cousin, the grey squirrel. Originally from the US, the grey squirrel was introduced to the UK, at the end of the 19th century. Since that time the grey squirrel population has ballooned to a current estimate of over 2.5 million while poor red has dwindled from a high of 3.5 million to under 140,000 today.

There were some 16 red squirrels known to be living in this small section of the forest and Red Squirrels United had come to check that the cameras the group used to monitor the animals' well-being were working properly. Vic, a wiry man of about 70, had a map of the cameras on his iPad – 'I can't share where they are because it's quite secret,' he explained. Rhiannon, a middle-aged woman wearing a blue rain jacket, was carrying a clipboard and proudly holding a pen. Penny, the newbie of the group, seemed happy just to tag along for the walk. 'Every time I enter the forest, I just take a deep breath and relax,' she said.

I left the southern edge of Clocaenog and emerged at the head of the Afon Clwyd River Valley. Below me was miles of pastureland dotted with small farmhouses. I looked at my map to see how many there were. Directly below me was Pendre Bach and Pendre Fawr. Ty hen was a little further down the country road leading into the village of Melin-y-Wig. On the other side of the valley sat Foelas and Tai Teg.

At the village of Betws Gwerful Goch I joined the Brenig Way, another walking trail that would guide me south through farming country down to the market town of Corwen. I thought about how the beef and dairy farmers in this part of Wales would fare in the coming years as the world is forced to adapt its diets to counter the climate emergency.

Wales's farmers represent just a tiny fraction of the global agricultural industry and have a minuscule environmental impact compared to the big agribusinesses that produce much of the world's food. Yet, as climate change increases, they will find themselves even further embroiled in what may yet be the most important and influential debate of this century: how can we feed the planet without destroying it?

At present the world's food system – from farming to transportation to grocery store packaging – is responsible for approximately 30 per cent of total greenhouse gas emissions and is the main cause of deforestation worldwide. Beef alone accounts for over half the total amount of forest lost to agriculture in just 15 years – some 45 million hectares (an area more than 20 times the size of Wales). Meanwhile, when you take into account how much energy and raw materials go into rearing one cow (it takes 1,800 gallons of water to produce just one pound of beef, for example), the whole process is wholly unsustainable on the scale it currently operates.

The solution is obvious – we need to reduce the amount of meat, especially beef, and dairy that we eat. Already, that is starting to happen. Consider the increase in consumer appetite for plant-based foods over the past five years and its projected growth – Bloomberg estimates the sector will make up 7.7 per cent of the global protein market by 2030. We also need to source the food we do eat from regenerative farming, which looks to put more back into the environment and society than it extracts whether by employing less intensive grazing techniques for cattle and other livestock or by planting cover crops to help improve soil quality and reduce erosion.

Some of the most innovative farming in this part of Wales takes place at the Rhug Estate, situated on the main A5 road that leads into Corwen and on my route. It is owned and run by Robert Wynn, known by his formal title of Lord Newborough. The Wynn family have been a power in this part of north Wales for centuries (though not to be confused with the Wynn family that once owned the entire Gwydir Forest).

Today, Rhug is the last of the many grand estates once associated with the clan. It covers 12,500 acres in Denbighshire and a further 8,000 in Gwynedd, including the 6,700-acre organic farm here on the outskirts of Corwen. Lord Newborough, now in his early 70s, has spent the last three decades turning it into a centre of excellence for sustainable farming. Transforming the Rhug Estate into an organic farm started in 1998 and took two years to complete. It involved introducing a seven-year rotation, to include cattle, sheep, grain, forage and root crops. In 2000, the Soil Association certified Rhug Estate as organic and the farm continues to innovate with ways to avoid pesticides and to produce high-quality food.

Here, one of the oldest parts of the Welsh establishment has embraced change in the form of organic farming to survive. The explosive growth of plant-based foods in the US and Europe shows how quickly people's tastes can also shift when they want to. Much like trees, the economic value of beef is set to change as its production increasingly is linked to carbon emissions. In a short time, beef may become a true luxury item. That idea horrifies many red meat fans now, but people don't complain when they spend top dollar for a lobster meal or a dozen oysters – both delicacies that were considered poor man's food just a few centuries ago.

17

Making Peace with Nature

A final walk from Corwen to Chirk

I had reached the final leg of the journey – a 25-mile walk through the Vale of Llangollen towards Chirk Castle, one of the Marcher fortresses built in the 13th century to keep the unruly Welsh in their place. It promised to be a beautiful stretch of countryside – a slalom navigation following the Afon Dyfrdwy (River Dee) as it weaved its way out of Wales, hemmed in on the north side by Llantysilio and Ruabon mountains and on its south by the Berwyn range.

I passed a battle-ready statue of Owain Glyndŵr in the centre of Corwen – straddling his horse with sword raised – and headed out of town along a country lane that followed the north side of the river. Three hundred metres above me, Caer Drewyn, an old Iron Age hillfort that Glyndŵr is said to have used as a base, stood watch over the valley.

I started to reflect on my experiences on this long walk – what the history of Wales and its world-changing pursuit of industrial progress had done to nature and how it had altered people's relationship to the land and forests around them. That change hadn't just come with the Industrial Revolution – it had been taking place ever since the first Celts arrived and started clearing the forests to make a place to live and farm. The arrival of the Romans and, later, the Normans, continued to reshape that relationship even though throughout these periods (and for hundreds of years

afterwards) people practised woodland management in the form of coppicing and pollarding (a method of pruning mature trees) to maintain
the remaining woodlands. The Acts of Enclosure, which started in the
1600s but really took hold in the late 18th and early 19th centuries, formal-
ised a system of private land ownership unlike anything that had come
before – supercharging agricultural modernisation and driving many rural
inhabitants to the new towns and cities. By the time that the Industrial
Revolution had started to transform life across the United Kingdom, the
natural world was increasingly seen as little more than a commodity to
profit from, or a hindrance to progress.

While we needed to reboot and rebalance our relationship with
nature, it couldn't just be done with the flick of a switch. From what I'd
seen walking through the old coalfields of south Wales, the lead and slate
mines of the north and the sheep farms dotted throughout the country, it
was clear that we had to get the balance right between nature and society
if we stood any chance of reinventing our systems and – crucially – of
winning over those who feel they were going to lose out at the expense
of nature.

Take the way we eat and produce our food. Throughout my journey
I'd heard the concerns of the farming community about their future, and
their suspicions about what nature-focused and tree planting policies
might entail. I'd read the arguments for and against plant-based proteins
and meat substitutes and the pros and cons of mass rewilding on Wales's
hillsides. There was so much noise on either side of the meat versus the
environment debate that any sense of balance and nuance had been lost.
As a result, despite nearly everyone agreeing that we needed to move in a
truly sustainable direction, the pervading sense of mutual distrust meant
that there was a lack of agreement on how to do so.

After about an hour's walking I reached the village of Carrog, a few
miles east of Corwen.

In the 19th century it became popular as a holiday home getaway for
wealthy Liverpudlians. I stopped to read some local tourist information
about the village. It proudly recounted how, in 1968, Paul McCartney's

brother got married in the local church. Positioned high above the Afon Dyfrdwy, Carrog still retains a certain grandeur both in its architecture and its stature. Directly across from the village, on the other side of the river, it was just possible to make out the canopies of two trees rising above what is known as Owain Glyndŵr's Mount, a 12th-century motte fortification that the Welsh leader made his stronghold.

It was still early in the day but I felt weary and low on energy despite the (by-now mandatory) full cooked breakfast I'd consumed just a couple of hours before. I perked up though when I saw the sign for the Dee Valley path – the walking route that would take me through the foothills of Llantysilio mountain.

That enthusiasm was short-lived as it became clear the Dee Valley path shown on the map no longer existed. The signs for what appeared to be its new route didn't connect with the path I was on. I persevered on the old route nonetheless – it was an official public footpath after all – and climbed steadily up the mountain through the pine forest plantation of Coed Tir-Llanerch. The path emerged onto high sheep grazing land that provided views of the Vale of Llangollen below me and the Berwyn mountain range rising up above the other side of the valley.

I had a decision to make. The new Dee Valley path clearly headed further north, climbing and looping around the summit of the mountain. The original path, however, headed due east and, importantly given how I was feeling, it was all downhill. It was an easy decision.

All went fine until, suddenly, it didn't. The field I found myself in was fenced off apart from one kissing gate, and the path I was supposed to follow to get there was blocked by a path of stinging nettles. Much as I hated to admit it, I was starting to agree with the English tourists back at Y Giler Arms – these footpaths did have a habit of disappearing into the ether.

When I finally hacked my way through the nettles, I was well and truly stung and in the worst mood of the entire trip. Maybe I should have been grateful that it had taken nearly 300 miles of walking to get this misled by an official footpath but I had a glass-half-empty worldview at this point.

I made a pact with myself – no more speculative footpaths for the next few miles. Instead, I would stick to paved country lanes and gravel farm tracks. My mood improved as I walked along these established byways and immersed myself in the bustle of the countryside. In one field a flock of sheep were enjoying a lunchtime natter. In another, a couple of geese were bathing in a stream next to a farmhouse. Acorns that had dropped from the oaks lined the side of the lane and crunched under my feet as I walked. At one point a moorhen darted from a hedgerow directly in front of me and then ran for its life down the lane trying to find an escape route back into the hedge. It bounced three times off the thick low branches – as if it was in some animated cartoon – before finally scurrying to safety.

Just before the village of Rhewl, I left the road and climbed up an old hillside track. A large ash tree stood alone in the field ahead of me. One of its boughs had been torn off and hung limp by its side. There was no one else here – even the sheep had clocked off for the morning – so I sat myself down and opened an energy bar for lunch.

I had a view across the entire valley. I could see a large bird of prey circling above a field in the distance. I could hear the buzzing of insects in the grass around me and I could follow the flow of the Afon Dyfrdwy even if I couldn't hear the running water.

Every part of the natural world was working together, sometimes feeding off one other and sometimes supporting one other to create a series of functioning and complex ecosystems. Looking and listening at nature going about its business I couldn't help think just how much stronger our connections and respect would be if only we had more time to study what lies around us and appreciate nature's intricacies, and to work with it rather than thinking we can control it.

In some ways, I'd already seen the beginnings of that new relationship on my journey as I'd explored community woodlands, learned about fledgling rewilding initiatives, heard about new regenerative and organic farming ideas and seen how well planned forestry can support local communities and the environment. Nature can teach us so much more, however – particularly in terms of the way we design and build in the future.

A few years before, I had attended a talk given by Janine Benyus, author of *Biomimicry: Innovation Inspired by Nature*. What she said that day changed my worldview. She spoke of how life has existed on earth in one form or another for 3.8 billion years. In that time, life – in the form of nature – has learned what is required to survive on earth. Given nature's proven track record in adapting, surviving and prospering, Benyus offered this philosophy: we humans should be looking to these biological elders for guidance because they have figured out how to create a sustainable world.

The concept of mimicking the way nature functions has been understood ever since Leonardo da Vinci studied the mechanics of birds in the air to invent his flying machine. That idea never left the sketchpad but when the Wright Brothers finally got airborne in 1903 their success was partly rooted in their study of how pigeons flew.

Janine Benyus's book, however, kick-started the modern nature-inspired innovation movement. Today a new generation of designers, engineers and planners are developing biomimicry in the form of buildings such as the self-ventilating Eastgate Centre in Zimbabwe that was inspired by the cooling architecture of African termite hills, and transportation like the Japanese bullet train whose aerodynamic nose was modelled on a kingfisher's beak.

Trees have played their own part in inspiring innovation. Modern car engineers have learnt how the fibre composition of tree trunks helps maximise both strength and flexibility and have applied that thinking to design chassis that withstand impact just as well as conventional vehicles but are up to 30 per cent lighter – hence boosting fuel efficiency. Architects have also studied how the interconnected root systems of trees provide them with balance and support during major storms and hurricanes, and how the leaf pattern of sunflowers can help design better solar panels. Even the rain jacket in my backpack was inspired by biomimicry. Its Velcro fasteners were developed in the 1950s after inventor George de Mestral analysed the way cockleburs from the Burdock plant hooked onto his clothes and the fur of his dog while they were out walking.

I left the top of that tranquil hill and descended back down into the valley and into humanity. This side of the river was home to a cluster of caravan parks and campsites. Steve Winwood's *Higher Love* blasted from one of the tents while groups of kids swam in the river and played on a makeshift swing that been strapped to a thick tree branch above the water.

I was getting close to Llangollen and a well-deserved meal. Before that, I decided to make a quick stop at Horseshoe Falls, where I could follow the canal towpath into town. Horseshoe Falls aren't really water-falls at all. They are a series of weirs built in the late 18th century by the famous English engineer, Thomas Telford, to channel water from the River Dee into the Llangollen canal. In Victorian times the falls and the famous Chain bridge (built in 1817 to transport coal across the Afon Dyfrdwy) became tourist attractions and that tradition has endured.

On this warm, late summer day, the place was packed with visitors making the most of their holidays after being locked down for so many months. Some families were having picnics on the grass lawns near the river. Others queued at a café for ice cream. My feet were aching after so much walking so I sat down by the bank of the river next to the weir. An old weary oak tree stood nearby, its boughs bent so low that the leaves almost touched the water. I removed my boots and socks and dipped my feet into the cool water as it ran down from the weir. It was the most pleasurable experience I'd had in days.

Even as I relaxed by the water it was a shock to be surrounded by so many people after having spent so much time alone in the woods and hills. The canal path was busy with walkers and, when I arrived in Llangollen, the main street and bridge over the river was heaving. Normally, the town is a magnet for retirees – a sort of Liverpudlian Ft. Lauderdale complete with early bird specials. Today though, tourists of all ages milled around.

I sat outside a café, ordered a beer and indulged in a dose of people watching. As I observed this mass throng, I thought about the challenges we'll face in trying to get the nature tourism balance right. On the one hand, we want more people to experience nature: surely that way they'll value it more. Yet at the same time, the summer of 2020 had shown how fragile the nature tourism infrastructure is when inundated by the volume of tourists Wales was currently hosting. Part of the problem was that the visitors tended to gravitate towards the best-known beauty spots like Yr Wyddfa (Snowdon), Wales's highest peak. That summer (2020) Eyri (Snowdonia) received an estimated 50 per cent more visitors than the year before. On one particularly busy day, there had been a queue 300 metres long to reach the summit; at one point a fight broke out when a 'summiteer' attempted to jump the queue.

Helping people reconnect with nature was going to take more than a day trip to marvel at the mountains. A new form of immersive and accessible nature tourism was needed and the idea for the National Forest was a good start. I had started out on my journey looking to sketch out one imaginary route for the forest but I could already see that a far more ambitious vision was needed – one that put people in walking and touching distance of nature wherever they were in Wales.

The Ladies of Llangollen and a New Built Environment

In 1780, two members of the Irish gentry arrived in Llangollen. They were Lady Eleanor Butler and Miss Sarah Ponsonby. They eloped together from their homes in Ireland two years before – causing quite a scandal among the local gentry. In Llangollen, they settled in a stone house and scenic gardens known as Plas Newydd (New Hall) which they would transform into a Gothic fantasy and where they would live for the next 50 years.

In 1796, the Romantic poet, Anna Seward, a close friend of the ladies, described their home and way of life in this way:

Certainly this interesting retreat of Lady Eleanor Butler, and Miss Ponsonby, might have been placed where it would have had sublimer scenic accompaniments – but its site is sufficiently lovely, sufficiently romantic. Situated in an opener part of the valley, they breathe a purer air, while their vicinity of the town of Langollen affords the comforts of convenience, and the confidence of safety.

She dedicated a poem, 'Llangollen Vale', to the ladies as did Wordsworth after visiting in 1824, the last lines of which read:

> In ours the Vale of Friendship, let this spot
> Be nam'd, where faithful to a low roof'd Cot
> On Deva's banks, ye have abode so long,
> Sisters in love, a love allowed to climb
> Ev'n on this earth, above the reach of time.

Percy Shelley, Lord Byron, Robert Southey, J. M. W. Turner and Sir Walter Scott also visited Plas Newydd, drawn it appears both by the Romantic appeal of Butler and Ponsonby's companionship and by their interest in the mansion's location, which allowed the ladies seemingly to have one foot in nature and one foot in the town of Llangollen.

Back in the early 19th century, striking the right balance between urbanisation and nature was just starting to become an issue. The new wave of industrialisation and the rush to the cities was disconcerting to parts of society that still cherished the ideal of a simpler, rural way of life. Today, our desire to balance urban and rural sensibilities has become even more pressing. In fact, it will be one of the most important challenges we face as we try and reconnect our society with nature. Already 56 per cent of the human race lives in an urban environment.[*] By 2050 that will increase to 68 per cent.[†]

From a sustainability point of view, city living is often viewed as preferable to the suburban sprawl that dominated urban planning for much

---

[*] https://www.weforum.org/agenda/2020/11/global-continent-urban-population-urbanisation-percent/

[†] https://www.un.org/development/desa/en/news/population/2018-revision-of-world-urbanization-prospects.html

of the later 20th century. Large, dense urban environments can be more energy efficient and cleaner than smaller cities or even small towns. One reason is that urban households emit less carbon dioxide than suburban and rural homes. Also, mass transportation is better for the environment than commuting by car. And housing people in cities can also help reduce human encroachment on natural habitats.

Yet cities still have to be liveable and breathable. And if the majority of us are going to live our lives in a planned urban space, creating a lasting connection to nature in cities will be even more important than it is today – as all of us who found sanctuary walking our local parks during lockdown can attest.

Preserving and expanding those parks so that they offer a true experience of nature and even wilderness is one part of the puzzle. My hometown is blessed with many parks but only a few offer the ability to really immerse and lose yourself in nature. When I was wandering Cardiff's parks and woodlands during the early days of lockdown I constantly found myself gravitating towards the furthest, wildest and most isolated tracts of the city. Escaping the city while still being in the city was part of the fun and finding new pieces of nature was like stumbling on a piece of treasure. I compared notes with other friends who had also started walking to help get them through lockdown, almost turning our accidental discoveries into a game.

This sense of well-being in wilderness has been validated by at least one scientific study. In 2019 researchers from the University of Washington invited 320 people to wander around Seattle's Discovery Park, a mammoth 500-acre expanse on the city's western edge, and report back on how being in the park affected their mood. Ninety-six per cent of those who encountered wilderness on their walks said the experience contributed to a positive state of mind.

Not every city has a large wilderness to lose yourself in but having some connection to nature on a daily basis is still important. Take the trees that line many residential streets in the UK. Many of those were planted in the 19th century by Victorian urban planners and horticulturists eager to instil their new cities with an air of sophistication and balance that they had seen and admired in Europe's great cities. As Mark Johnston writes in his account of urban horticulture *Street Trees in Britain: A History*, they embraced the idea that 'If trees could adorn major thoroughfares in Paris, Brussels and Berlin, this could also happen in London, Edinburgh and Cardiff.'

A century and a half later those trees that line the streets of so many of the UK's major towns and cities play an invaluable role in the health of society (even if prominent voices like Peter Wohlleben lament their lonely way of life distanced from other trees). We know they help in trapping carbon and their roots and crowns help slow and distribute rainfall, mitigating urban flooding. Their process of transpiration and the shade they provide reduce temperatures in the summer and studies have shown that having trees on streets also reduces crime rates and improves mental health. These positive attributes start to add up in real money terms. One mature street tree can have a net ecosystem service value of thousands of pounds: Cardiff's tree footprint is valued at more than £3 million each year.

All too often though, urban planning fails to account for the positive impact trees have on a city's inhabitants. Concrete deserts are commonplace in all major cities – no more so than in Cardiff where, in recent years, a main gateway to the city – the plaza in front of the railway station – has been redeveloped. It is, to be perfectly blunt, a monstrosity of characterless concrete surrounded by a fence of tall office buildings. If you like antiseptic and antisocial wind tunnels then the originally named Central Square is the place for you. As a calling card for visiting Cardiff – a city resplendent with parks – it couldn't get much worse.

When it was first built the developers planted a few trees in a line in front of one of the office blocks – the urban planning equivalent of wearing a buttonhole with a dull grey suit. They quickly succumbed to a fungus, however. Every time I returned by train from one of my walking trips I got steadily more annoyed at the wasteland in the heart of town. Surely there was a way of planting trees in a small space that was pleasing for people walking through, could help cool concrete jungles and be more productive in helping address our climate and nature emergency than the old model of single street trees?

That's how I discovered Tiny Forests – mini woodlands no larger than the size of a tennis court that can be planted and nurtured in urban centres. The concept was pioneered by an Indian engineer-turned-tree evangelist named Shubhendu Sharma and who, in turn, was inspired by the Japanese tree guru, Akira Miyawaki.

As a graduate student in the 1950s, Miyawaki visited ancient Shinto temple sites to learn about sacred shrine forests. He soon realised that they provided insight into the history of Japanese indigenous woodlands – one that had become clouded through centuries of planting non-native larch and other plantation trees (sound familiar?).

He deduced that the old growth forests grew out of four categories of native plantings: main tree species, sub-species, shrubs and ground-covering herbs. This would form the basis of a new supercharged system – the Miyawaki method – for planting forests in areas that had become denuded.

His method involved preparing the soil with enough natural, local and sustainable nutrients that it would support intensive planting of many different saplings – up to 100 local species planted randomly and very densely. Using this method, trees grow about 10 times faster than in commercial forestry plantations. Furthermore, the forest is left to flourish without human interference.

Over the past few decades Miyawaki has planted over 40 million trees in 15 countries. When Sharma learned about his method, he set about working out how to scale it down and make it work in smaller spaces. Sharma devised a formula and created a set of assembly line instructions (based on automobile industry best practice) to make mini multi-layered forests that can thrive in urban environments. Since 2010 Sharma's Tiny Forests have been sprouting up in cities across Asia and Africa and more recently Europe. Now the concept had arrived in Wales – the National Forest plan called for Tiny Forests to help urban areas boost their biodiversity and one was already planned for Cardiff Bay. Perhaps another could transform the city's concrete centre.

Towards the Oak at the Gate of the Dead

Because it was the final day of walking, and because I really didn't fancy any more climbs, I chose to follow the canal as it led eastwards with the predictable lack of elevation that I needed. I'd meander at my own pace, enjoying watching the occasional narrowboat putter along.

At first the canal seemed tranquil. Oak and birch hugged the stone cliffs that overhung this first section, fish popped up their heads out of the canal and amused themselves making air bubbles while a family convoy of ducks headed down the canal, single file, at an impressive pace.

I shared the towpath with a steady procession of dog walkers, runners and bikers. High on the mountain to my left I could just make out the ruined crag of Castell Dinas Bran, which was built in the 13th century as a stronghold for one of the local princes. Its name either means castle of the crow, castle of the stream called Bran or castle of some ancient Celtic leader called Bran. No one really knows, but ever since English tourists started visiting in the 18th century it has become known as Crow Castle.

The canal itself resembled a traffic jam of narrowboats as holidaymakers cooled their heels waiting to pass through the many locks. I must have walked past 20 boats that morning. Talk about slow travel.

At Trevor Uchaf I decided to leave the canal and take a shortcut through the woods. I joined the Offa's Dyke Trail – easily the best known and most travelled of all the long-distance walking paths in Wales. It roughly follows the ancient earthen barrier constructed by the Mercian king, Offa, in the 8th century to keep out the Celts, and for much of its route it hugs the modern-day border between England and Wales. The path through Trevor Hall wood was wide, well-kept and secure underfoot. After days of picking my way through faded and dilapidated public footpaths, this section of Offa's Dyke felt like I was strolling down a Parisian boulevard.

It led directly to one of Wales's most impressive feats of

engineering – the 18-arched stone and cast iron Pontcysyllte aqueduct that spans the Vale of Llangollen and the River Dee. The aqueduct, which opened in 1805, was the brainchild of Thomas Telford and William Jessop. At 305 metres in length it is the longest canal aqueduct in the UK and, sitting nearly 40 metres above the ground, the world's highest canal. Frighteningly, it is only 3.7 metres wide which means there is barely enough room to accommodate both the narrowboats and the towpath. The boats float across the aqueduct single file and, while an iron fence prevents pedestrians on the footpath side from plummeting down, passengers in the narrowboats have no such protection. Luckily I was on foot so I inched my way across the bridge along with a line of other tourists. I'm not normally scared of heights but this crossing was making me feel otherwise.

The Offa's Dyke path performed a switchback just outside the village of Pentre, departing from the canal and cutting across fields towards Chirk Castle. I wandered through what had to be at least my 100th field of sheep during this journey and headed towards a stile near the brow of a hill. Two middle-aged men were sitting at the top having lunch. I stopped for a minute to catch my breath and have a chat.

They were brothers, the elder one said. They had lost their parents earlier in the year and had been going on walks every couple of months to support each other and keep in touch. I told them about my project and how Wales was planning a National Forest to encourage people like them to explore the country more.

It made perfect sense they both agreed. 'I've travelled all around the world but if I never went anywhere again I wouldn't mind,' said the elder brother. 'There is just so much in this country to discover.'

His words really hit home. I too had spent nearly all my adult life travelling the world in pursuit of new experiences and thrills. I'd make mental notes of all the countries I had visited and the ones I still had to see. Thinking back on it now, I was probably more obsessed with saying I'd been somewhere rather than appreciating what it meant to be there. I also realised how little time and appreciation I'd given to my own homeland. I knew Wales was beautiful and I'd always been proud and outspoken of its virtues when I lived abroad (as so many expats do) but I hadn't ever explored it to the extent I was now. And I'd never thought about its natural beauty and its identity in the way this journey had made me do so.

All through my walks, I'd been thinking about how society could not only make peace with nature but come to accept and embrace it on equal terms – rebuilding a connection that had been lost over many centuries of so-called human progress. My imagining of one National Forest walking route had highlighted how we needed to completely recalibrate the complex systems that currently dictate how human society operates. For that to happen though, we would need to embrace nature as part of our own identity just as the ancient Celts – our ancestors – once did and indigenous communities throughout the world still do.

We can improve our legal systems, we can put an economic value on nature, we can plant new forests and we can protect old ones. But unless we start to see trees and nature as our equal rather than something we are superior to then we are still doomed. Because those lawsuits, smart accounting and feel-good policies are really all about protecting nature to protect us.

The National Forest promised to connect everyone in and visiting Wales with nature so we could learn to appreciate, value and fully respect it. If achieved, surely that could help make our new pact with nature an integral part of a national identity – much as the people of Costa Rica embrace *Pura Vida* (pure life) as a governing daily philosophy.

Creating a national identity that is underpinned by treating nature as equals would also help fulfil the promises and ideals of Wales's Future Generations Act and help establish the framework now for being 'a good ancestor' – the term coined by the philosopher Roman Krznaric to describe all of our responsibilities to act now to protect our world for our children and their children and their children.

The End of the Road
The end of my journey was in sight. Ahead of me, in the distance on a hill, I could see the white stone facade of Chirk Castle. It looked like a wedding

cake surrounded by green trimming in the form of its ornate gardens and grounds. Sitting at the head of the Ceiriog Valley, the castle had been built to be a fortress but over the centuries it had found its way into the hands of the Myddelton family who made it their home. Its reputation really took hold in the 17th century when Sir Thomas Myddelton, inspired by John Evelyn's book, *Sylva*, began to experiment with planting exotic trees on his grand estate while also creating new oak woodlands.

It was one of these oak woods that I found myself in now – acorns peppered my head as they were blown off the trees in the wind. On a path at the far end of the Chirk Estate I came across the stout, moss-covered trunk of an ancient tree. It was the famed Oak at the Gates of the Dead and was estimated to be more than 1,000 years old – from the same era as the Curley Oak in Wentwood where I'd started my journey a couple of months before.

This grand old tree had got its name because of the bloodshed it had witnessed through the centuries – most notably the 1165 Battle of Crogen when a guerrilla group of Welsh archers ambushed the invading army of Henry II, raining arrows down on them and turning the Afon Ceiriog River red with English blood. Legend has it that many of the bodies were buried in grounds around the tree, the river and nearby Offa's Dyke.

As I paused to admire the old oak and contemplate what 1,000 years might mean for the life of a tree, two families came walking down the path – exploring this hidden part of the woods away from the main tourist trail around Chirk Castle grounds.

They stopped to read about the old oak and the kids, three young boys and girl no more than 10 years old, showed their amazement at how old this one tree could be before finding other more exciting makeshift trails to follow in the wood. Their parents let them wander and explore – content to read more while hearing the kids enjoy themselves off in the distance.

As I watched their excitement at being in the woods I thought back to an interview I'd heard with the musician Brian Eno where he said: 'The only way to save the world is to fall in love with it again.'

Over the past 300 miles of walking and immersing myself in 100 woodlands of Wales I could say wholeheartedly that I had fallen back in love with nature. And by doing so I had starting learning to be happy with myself once again. The physical exercise had helped calm the feelings of anxiety I had been struggling with and, mentally, I had been buoyed on a daily basis by the places I visited and the things I learned along the way – the history of Wales, the ways of nature and the possibilities of moving beyond our liminal state so we can shape a better future for all of us.

I had returned to my trees.

A Note on Sourcing

I wanted to write a book that was intellectually stimulating yet easy and, yes, fun to read. That way I hoped that the important issues I explore along my walking journey through Wales would resonate with a readership who wouldn't necessarily be drawn to a book about sustainability.

When the Welsh government announced a plan to create a National Forest for Wales, I saw the opportunity to write a travel walking book that weaved together Welsh history, legend, folklore and culture with the globally-pressing topics of climate change, biodiversity loss, deforestation and even the future of food.

To do so, I undertook not just a 300-mile walk but also months and months of research, amassing scores of books, news articles, historical accounts and academic texts. I've included a number of key citations in the manuscript but, for the most part, I've let the narrative flow without including footnotes or endnotes. The reason being that I want the story to flow and be as easily digestible as possible.

Below, you'll find the full list of books that I drew upon to shape my narrative and present the arguments for how we as society move through our liminal state and build a truly sustainable future.

Reading List

Trees and Nature

Welsh Woods and Forests – A History by William Linnard. Gomer Press 2000

The Heritage Trees of Wales by Archie Miles. Graffeg 2012

Woodlands by Oliver Rackham. William Collins 2015

The History of the Countryside by Oliver Rackham. Weidenfeld & Nicolson 2000

Around the World in 80 Trees by Jonathan Drori. Laurence King 2018

The Wisdom Of Trees: A Miscellany by Max Adams. Head of Zeus 2018

American Canopy: Trees, Forests, and the Making of a Nation by Eric Rutkow. Scribner 2013

The Hidden Life of Trees: What They Feel, How They Communicate – Discoveries from a Secret World by Peter Wohlleben. HarperCollins 2015

The Glorious Life of the Oak by John Lewis-Stempel. Doubleday 2018

The Man Who Made Things from Trees by Robert Penn. Penguin 2016

The Secret Network of Nature by Peter Wohlleben. Vintage 2019

Into the Forest: How Trees Can Help You Find Health and Happiness by Dr Qing Li. Penguin Life 2019

The Spell of the Sensuous – Perception and language in a more-than-human world by David Abram. Vintage 1996

The Nature Fix: Why nature makes us happier, healthier, and more creative by Florence Williams. W. W. Norton 2017

The Overstory by Richard Powers. William Heinemann 2019

Travel Writing, Adventure and Walking

Wild Wales by George Borrow. Bridge Books 2009

Underland by Robert Macfarlane. W. W. Norton 2019

On Writing: A Memoir of the Craft by Stephen King. Scribner 2010

In Praise of Walking: The New Science of How We Walk and Why It's Good for Us by Shane O'Mara. Bodley Head 2019

The Gentle Art of Tramping by Stephen Graham. Bloomsbury Reader 2019

The Book of Trespass: Crossing the Lines that Divide Us by Nick Hayes. Bloomsbury Circus 2020

The book of South Wales, the Bristol channel, Monmouthshire and the Wye by Charles Frederick Cliffe. Palala Press 2015

Wild Guide Wales and the Marches by Daniel Start and Tania Pascoe. Wild Things Publishing 2018

A Walk in the Woods by Bill Bryson. Doubleday 1997

The Old Ways: A journey on foot by Robert Macfarlane. Viking 2012

Cambrian Way – The Mountain Connoisseur's Walk by A. J. Drake. Cambrian Way Trust 2016

Borth to Strata Florida by Des Marshall. Kittiwake 2016

One River by Wade Davis. Touchstone 1996

In Trouble Again by Redmond O'Hanlon. Vintage Departures 1988

Savages by Joe Kane. Vintage 1995

Wales and its History

The Making of Wales by John Davies. The History Press 2009

When Was Wales? by Gwyn A. Williams. Penguin 1991

A History of Wales by John Davies. Penguin 2007

The Druids by Peter Berresford Ellis. Little Brown 2022

The Druids by Stuart Piggott. Thames and Hudson 1968

The Welsh Academy Encyclopaedia of Wales by John Davies, Nigel Jenkins, Menna Baines and Peredur I. Lynch. University of Wales Press 2008

The Place-Names of Wales by Hywel Wyn Owen. University of Wales Press 2015

Welsh Place Names and their meanings by Dewi Davies. Y Lolfa 2016

The Tempus History of Wales by Prys Morgan (editor). Tempus 2001

Hando's Gwent – Volume II edited by Chris Barber. Blorenge Books 1989

American Interior by Gruff Rhys. Hamish Hamilton 2014

The Celtic Saints by Nigel Pennick. Godsfield Press 1997

The Celtic Year by Shirley Toulson. Element 2002

Llandaf – Past and present by John B. Hilling. Stewart Williams Publisher 1978

Stories from Welsh History by Howell T. Evans. The Educational Publishing Company 2021

History of the Kings of Britain by Geoffrey of Monmouth (translated by Aaron Thompson) 2012

Rhondda Coal, Cardiff Gold by Richard Watson. Merton Priory Press 1997

A Cardiff Anthology by Meic Stephens. Seren 1987

The Cardiff Story by Dennis Morgan. D. Brown & Sons 1991

Tiger Bay and the Docks – The story of a remarkable corner of the world by Dan O'Neill. Breedon Books 2001

The Mabinogion translated by Gwyn Jones and Thomas Jones. Everyman 1949

The Mabinogi – Legend and landscape of Wales by John K. Bollard. Gomer Press 2006

A Rattleskull Genius by Geraint H. Jenkins (editor). University of Wales Press 2005

The Physicians of Myddfai by Terry Breverton. Cambria Books 2012

Chwedlau Gwerin Cymru/Welsh Folk Tales. National Museum of Wales 1996

Mysterious Wales by Chris Barber. Amberly Publishing 2016

Welsh Ghosts and Phantoms – A collection of ghost stories from Wales by Jane Pugh. Emeralda 1979

The Liminal Lakes of South Wales by V. A. Grant. A. C. Paddison Associates 2017

Sustainability Themes

CADW – Heritage in Wales publications 1984 to 1999

Jungle – How tropical forests shaped the world and us by Patrick Roberts. Viking 2021

Sustainability – A History by Jeremy Caradonna. Oxford University
   Press 2014

#Futuregen – Lessons from a small country by Jane Davidson. Chelsea
   Green Publishing 2020

Client Earth by James Thornton and Martin Goodman. Scribe UK 2017

Doughnut Economics: Seven Ways to Think Like a 21st-Century
   Economist by Kate Raworth. Random House Business 2017

Land: How the Hunger for Ownership Shaped the Modern World by
   Simon Winchester. William Collins 2021

The Uninhabitable Earth: A Story of the Future by David
   Wallace-Wells. Tim Duggan Books 2020

The Good Ancestor: How to Think Long Term in a Short-Term World
   by Roman Krznaric. W. H. Allen 2021

Trust Inc. How business wins respect in a social media age by Matthew
   Yeomans. Taylor & Francis 2018

Acknowledgements

Firstly, I'd like to give my heartfelt thanks to my agent Sharon Bowers. She believed in this book from the very start and offered the encouragement I needed to keep going with it when I had the crisis of confidence many other writers will no doubt identify with.

Next, I owe a deep debt of gratitude to my editor Amy Feldman, global sales manager Maria Vassilopoulos and all the team at Calon who have expertly shaped and shepherded this book through editing and production. I'm also especially indebted to Neil Gower who created the wonderful front cover illustration. I'd also like to thank the crack publicity team of Ruth Killick and Amy Stewart who have worked hard to bring this book to the attention of an audience larger than the friends and family who I cajoled into buying a copy.

A number of friends helped and supported me through my journey either through walking parts of the route or offering various forms of encouragement. Andy Bethell, Jeff Jones, Tim Powell and Richard Winterbottom all laced up their walking boots to explore South Wales (often with blind and misplaced faith in my map reading abilities). Rob Leek, Neil Simmonds, Dale Hammond and Ross Dixon walked with me in North Wales and provided encouragement and a sounding board on our weekly Zoom calls during lockdown.

Mark Pigou was a rock when I needed one most and I am incredibly grateful for his many years of friendship. Mark Vose was also there for me during some of the more challenging times. Phil Vidler thought I was mad when I told him of my idea but backed me when I needed his help. Tim Holmes, a friend and former colleague from Cardiff University School of Journalism, introduced me to the work of George Borrow and provided great initial feedback and encouragement as I developed the idea. Then there is Martin McCabe, a kindred creative spirit who encouraged me to think about the ways I could tell this story in ways beyond the written word. He has spent hours filming and editing video footage of my walk through Wales – and all he wanted was a few pints in return.

As I walked through Wales I met experts who provided great insight. Dr. Madeleine Gray helped me make sense of the early Welsh saints and the importance of the Cistercian order in Wales. Dafydd Wyn Morgan is an expert not just on Twm Sion Cati but the whole Cambrian Mountains region and he kindly gave up his time to educate me. A special word of thanks to Dr. David Morfitt who introduced me to the expertise of Oliver Rackham and gently disavowed me of the clichés and stereotypes so many neophyte writers about trees and nature like myself often fall into.

Finally, as always, I want to thank my family. My parents supplied me with numerous books on Welsh and Cardiff history which helped my research. And my wife Jowa and my kids, Dylan and Zelda, were encouraging and also very patient as I disappeared down yet another research and writing rabbit hole. I couldn't do it without them.

Matthew Yeomans
July 2022